5 Longman Academic Reading Series

READING SKILLS FOR COLLEGE

Lorraine C. Smith

Dedication

To Donna, whose patience and wisdom have always been an inspiration to me.

Pearson Education, 221 River Street, Hoboken, NJ 07030

Staff Credits: The people who made up the **Longman Academic Reading Series 5** team, representing editorial, production, design, and manufacturing, are Pietro Alongi, Margaret Antonini, Stephanie Bullard, Iris Candelaria, Rosa Chapinal, Aerin Csigay, Ann France, Françoise Leffler, Amy McCormick, Liza Pleva, Mary Perrotta Rich, Massimo Rubini, and Robert Ruvo.

Cover image: The Loupe Project/Shutterstock
Text Composition: TSI Graphics

Library of Congress Cataloging-in-Publication Data
   Böttcher, Elizabeth.
    Longman Academic Reading Series / Elizabeth Bottcher.
        volumes cm
    Includes index.
    ISBN 978-0-13-278664-5 (Level 1)—ISBN 978-0-13-278582-2 (Level 2)—
    ISBN 978-0-13-276059-1 (Level 3)—ISBN 978-0-13-276061-4 (Level 4)—
    ISBN 978-0-13-276067-6 (Level 5)
    1. English language—Textbooks for foreign speakers. 2. Reading
    comprehension—Problems, exercises, etc. 3. College readers. I. Title.
     PE1128.B637 2013
     428.6'4—dc23
                                                   2013007701

ISBN 10: 0-13-477315-2
ISBN 13: 978-0-13-477315-5

Printed in the United States of America
1 17

CONTENTS

To the Teacher v

Chapter Overview viii

Scope and Sequence xviii

Acknowledgments xxvi

CHAPTER 1 **SOCIOLOGY: How We Become Who We Are** 1

Reading One Becoming a Person 2

Reading Two The Birth of Personality 8

Reading Three Agents of Socialization 19

CHAPTER 2 **ART HISTORY: Origins of Modern Art** 30

Reading One Breaking with Tradition: The Beginnings of Impressionism 31

Reading Two Post-Impressionism 39

Reading Three Abstract Expressionism 47

CHAPTER 3 **ANTHROPOLOGY:
The Study of Human Cultures** 60

Reading One The Challenge of Defining Culture 61

Reading Two The Nature of Foraging and Horticultural Societies 69

Reading Three Night Flying Woman: An Ojibway Narrative 78

CHAPTER 4 **SCIENCE: Human Achievements over Time** 88

Reading One A Great Human Endeavor: Building the Gothic Cathedrals 89

Reading Two From Stone to Satellite: Finding Our Way 98

Reading Three Reaching for the Stars: The 100-Year Starship Project 106

CHAPTER 5 **POLITICAL SCIENCE: Managing Hard Times** ... 119

Reading One The Great Depression: A Nation in Crisis 120

Reading Two The Works Progress Administration and the
Federal Arts Project 131

Reading Three An Artist's Perspective on the Federal Arts Project 139

■ **CHAPTER 6** **HEALTH SCIENCES:**
Medical Mysteries Solved..................................148

Reading One Solving a Deadly Puzzle.................................149

Reading Two Imprisoned without a Trial: The Story of Typhoid Mary.............158

Reading Three The Discovery of a Miracle Drug................................168

■ **CHAPTER 7** **LITERATURE: Storytelling through Poetry**..........176

Reading One Themes and Characters in *The Rime of the Ancient Mariner*....177

Reading Two *The Rime of the Ancient Mariner* 184

Reading Three *The Rime of the Ancient Mariner* (continued) 195

■ **CHAPTER 8** **HISTORY: Encountering New Worlds**..................208

Reading One Europe on the Eve of Conquest................................209

Reading Two Native American Histories before the Conquest 218

Reading Three West Africa at the Time of European Exploration 229

■ **CHAPTER 9** **BUSINESS: Ethical Issues**................................239

Reading One Promoting Ethics in the Workplace 240

Reading Two Ethical Reasoning................................249

Reading Three Should Mary Buy Her Bonus? 257

■ **CHAPTER 10** **MIGRATION STUDIES:**
In Search of a New Life..................................267

Reading One Human Migration................................268

Reading Two The Westward Journey: A Personal Perspective...................276

Reading Three Wooden Trunk from Buchenwald 287

Vocabulary Index 299

Credits 302

Welcome to the *Longman Academic Reading Series*, a five-level series that prepares English language learners for academic work. The aim of the series is to make students more effective and confident readers by providing **high-interest readings on academic subjects** and teaching them **skills and strategies** for

- effective reading
- vocabulary building
- note-taking
- critical thinking

Last but not least, the series encourages students to **discuss and write** about the ideas they have discovered in the readings, making them better speakers and writers of English as well.

High-Interest Readings On Academic Subjects

Research shows that if students are not motivated to read, if reading is not in some sense enjoyable, the reading process becomes mechanical drudgery and the potential for improvement is minimal. That is why high-interest readings are the main feature in the *Longman Academic Reading Series*.

Varied High-Interest Texts

Each chapter of each book in the series focuses on an engaging theme from a wide range of academic subjects such as art history, sociology, political science, and business. The reading selections in each chapter (two readings in Level 1 and three in Levels 2–5) are chosen to provide different and intriguing perspectives on the theme. These readings come from a variety of sources or genres—books, textbooks, academic journals, newspapers, magazines, online articles—and are written by a variety of authors from widely different fields. The Level 5 book, for instance, offers a narrative from the Ojibway people of North America, a memoir describing a 19th century wagon trip across the Great Plains, an article on the birth of personality, a description of how the Gothic cathedrals were built, an oral history from a Depression-era artist, and the classic poem *The Rime of the Ancient Mariner*—all challenging reading selections that spark students' interest and motivate them to read and discuss what they read.

Academic Work

The work done in response to these selections provides students with a reading and discussion experience that mirrors the in-depth treatment of texts in academic coursework. Although the readings may be adapted for the lower levels and excerpted for the upper levels, the authentic reading experience has been preserved. The series sustains students' interest and gives a sample of the types of content and reasoning that are the hallmark of academic work.

Skills and Strategies

To help students read and understand its challenging readings, the *Longman Academic Reading Series* provides a battery of skills and strategies for effective reading, vocabulary building, note-taking, and critical thinking.

Effective Reading

The series provides students with strategies that will help them learn to skim, scan, predict, preview, map, and formulate questions before they begin to read. After they read, students are routinely asked to identify main ideas as well as supporting details, progressing through the chapter from the "literal" to the "inferential." Students using this series learn to uncover what is beneath the surface of a reading passage and are led to interpret the many layers of meaning in a text. Each text is an invitation to dig deeper.

Vocabulary Building

In all chapters students are given the opportunity to see and use vocabulary in many ways: guessing words in context (an essential skill, without which fluent reading is impossible), identifying synonyms, recognizing idioms, practicing word forms as well as using new words in their own spoken and written sentences. At the same time, students learn the best strategies for using the dictionary effectively, and have ample practice in identifying roots and parts of words, recognizing collocations, understanding connotations, and communicating in the discourse specific to certain disciplines. The intentional "recycling" of vocabulary in both speaking and writing activities provides students with an opportunity to use the vocabulary they have acquired.

Note-Taking

As students learn ways to increase their reading comprehension and retention, they are encouraged to practice and master a variety of note-taking skills, such as highlighting, annotating, paraphrasing, summarizing, and outlining. The skills that form the focus of each chapter have been systematically aligned with the skills practiced in other chapters, so that scaffolding improves overall reading competence within each level.

Critical Thinking

At all levels of proficiency, students become more skilled in the process of analysis as they learn to read between the lines, make inferences, draw conclusions, make connections, evaluate, and synthesize information from various sources. The aim of this reflective journey is the development of students' critical thinking ability, which is achieved in different ways in each chapter.

> In addition to these skills and strategies, **Level 4** and **Level 5** of the series include a **Grammar for Reading** activity in each chapter. Grammar for Reading presents a short review and practice of a grammar structure often encountered in academic texts, such as the passive or parallel forms. This activity helps students realize how their understanding of a particular grammar point will enhance their general reading comprehension ability.

Speaking and Writing

The speaking activities that frame and contribute to the development of each chapter tap students' strengths, allow them to synthesize information from several sources, and give them a sense of community in the reading experience. In addition, because good readers make good writers, students are given the opportunity to express themselves in a writing activity in each chapter.

The aim of the *Longman Academic Reading Series* is to provide "teachable" books that allow instructors to recognize the flow of ideas in each lesson and to choose from many types of exercises to get the students interested and to maintain their active participation throughout. By showing students how to appreciate the ideas that make the readings memorable, the series encourages students to become more effective, confident, and independent readers.

The Online Teacher's Manual

The Teacher's Manual is available at www.pearsonelt.com/tmkeys. It includes general teaching notes, chapter teaching notes, answer keys, and reproducible chapter quizzes.

CHAPTER OVERVIEW

All chapters in the *Longman Academic Reading Series, Level 5* have the same basic structure.

Objectives

BEFORE YOU READ
A. Consider These Questions/Facts/etc.
B. Your Opinion *[varies; sometimes only Consider activity]*

READING ONE: [+ *reading title*]
A. Warm-Up
B. Reading Strategy
[Reading One]

COMPREHENSION
A. Main Ideas
B. Close Reading

VOCABULARY *[not necessarily in this order; other activities possible]*
A. Guessing from Context
B. Synonyms
C. Using the Dictionary

NOTE-TAKING *[in two reading sections per chapter]*

CRITICAL THINKING

READING TWO: [+ *reading title*]
A. Warm-Up
B. Reading Strategy
[Reading Two]

COMPREHENSION
A. Main Ideas
B. Close Reading

VOCABULARY *[not necessarily in this order; other activities possible]*
A. Word Usage
B. Antonyms
C. Collocations

CRITICAL THINKING

LINKING READINGS ONE AND TWO

READING THREE: [+ *reading title*]
A. Warm-Up
B. Reading Strategy
[Reading Three]

COMPREHENSION
A. Main Ideas
B. Close Reading

VOCABULARY *[not necessarily in this order; other activities possible]*
A. Categorizing Words
B. Idioms
C. Roots
D. Word Forms

GRAMMAR FOR READING *[in one reading section per chapter]*

NOTE-TAKING *[in two reading sections per chapter]*

CRITICAL THINKING

AFTER YOU READ

BRINGING IT ALL TOGETHER

WRITING ACTIVITY

DISCUSSION AND WRITING TOPICS

Vocabulary
Self-Assessment

Each chapter starts with a definition of the chapter's academic subject matter, objectives, and a Before You Read section.

A short **definition of the academic subject** mentioned in the chapter title describes the general area of knowledge explored in the chapter.

CHAPTER 1

SOCIOLOGY: How We Become Who We Are

SOCIOLOGY: the scientific study of human society and human group behavior. The focus of sociology is the individual in interaction with others or as he or she moves in the social environment.

OBJECTIVES

To read academic texts, you need to master certain skills.

In this chapter, you will:

- Preview a text and activate background knowledge
- Use headings to create an outline and fill in the outline with details from the text
- Create questions from the title and headings of a text to increase understanding
- Guess the meaning of words from the context
- Use dictionary entries to learn different meanings of words
- Use *one* as an impersonal pronoun
- Understand and use synonyms, antonyms, font styles, collocations, roots, and different word forms
- Create a chart and write notes to summarize information from a text

1

Chapter objectives provide clear goals for students by listing the skills they will practice in the chapter.

The **Before You Read** activities introduce the subject matter of the chapter, using a mix of information and questions to stimulate students' interest.

BEFORE YOU READ

Consider These Questions

Discuss the questions in a small group. Share your answers with the class.

1. How do you describe people's personalities? Write descriptions in the word web.

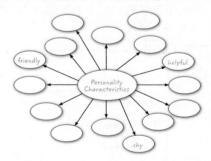

2. Work alone. In your journal or on a piece of paper, write a description of your personality. Some questions to think about: Are you shy? outgoing? cautious? reckless? Do you tend to be solitary? Are you group-oriented? Were you born this way, or did your personality develop as you grew up? Share your description with your group.

3. As we grow up, we learn what is normal (that is, acceptable) behavior in our society. We develop specific values, too. Who teaches us these behaviors and values?

READING ONE: Becoming a Person

A Warm-Up

Discuss the questions with a partner.

1. What does it mean to become a person?
2. In what ways do humans change as they grow from babies to adults?
3. Do babies have personalities?

Each of the three reading sections in a chapter starts with a Warm-Up activity and a Reading Strategy presentation and practice, followed by the reading itself.

The **Warm-Up** activity presents discussion questions that activate students' prior knowledge and help them develop a personal connection with the topic of the reading.

Reading One sets the theme and presents the basic ideas that will be explored in the chapter. Like all the readings in the series, it is an example of a genre of writing (here, an online article).

BEFORE YOU READ

Consider These Questions

Discuss the questions in a small group. Share your answers with the class.

1. What is your concept of *art*? Write a definition of *art*.
2. Consider this definition of *art history*: "the academic study of the historical development of the visual arts." Why is it important to understand styles of art from previous centuries, for example, 19th-century art?
3. When a new style of art is developed, people sometimes find it difficult to accept. Why do you think people might react this way?

READING ONE: Breaking with Tradition: The Beginnings of Impressionism

A Warm-Up

Discuss the questions in a small group.

1. Why would artists reject a traditional, accepted style of painting and choose to paint in a totally different way, knowing that their work might not be accepted and that they might not be able to sell their paintings?
2. What do you know about Impressionist art and artists? Do you like Impressionist art? Why or why not?

B Reading Strategy

Using Visuals to Enhance Understanding

Many texts include **illustrations, maps, photographs, charts, graphs,** and **art images.** These visuals help you to **understand information** in all types of texts. When you read art history texts, visuals are essential because they will help you understand artists, art movements, and how art changes over time.

Look at the art images in the reading. Then choose the correct answers.

1. What phrases best describe Jacques-Louis David's painting on page 32? Check (✓) all that apply.
   - ☐ a. a historical scene
   - ☐ b. an everyday scene
   - ☐ c. a painting that shows the artist's skills
   - ☐ d. a painting that shows the artist's feelings
   - ☐ e. accurate in its details
   - ☐ f. not accurate in its details
   - ☐ g. a painting of a famous person
   - ☐ h. a painting of a person who is not famous

(continued on next page)

Art History: Origins of Modern Art **31**

The **Reading Strategy** box gives a general description of a reading strategy, such as predicting content from first paragraph, and the reasons for using it. The **activity** below the box shows students how to apply that strategy to the reading.

---

2. What phrases best describe Claude Monet's painting on page 33? Check (✓) all that apply.
   - ☐ a. a historical scene
   - ☐ b. an everyday scene
   - ☐ c. a painting that shows the artist's skills in painting details
   - ☐ d. a painting that shows the artist's feelings
   - ☐ e. accurate in its details
   - ☐ f. not accurate in its details
   - ☐ g. a painting of a famous person
   - ☐ h. a painting of a person who is not famous

Now read the text and refer to the images of David's and Monet's paintings to help you understand what you are reading.

Breaking with Tradition: The Beginnings of Impressionism

1   As you saw with David's painting *Napoléon Crossing the Alps*, art was very representational. That is, it was very true to life. Traditional art also usually depicted scenes from history or mythology.[1] Artists had the opportunity to demonstrate their skills, but they were not expected to paint how they felt. This tradition is what the Impressionists challenged with their new style of art.

2   "If one wants to characterize them with a single word that explains their efforts, one would have to create the term of Impressionists. They are Impressionists in the sense that they render not a landscape but the impression produced by a landscape." Jules Castagnary, in *Le Siècle*, April 29, 1874

3   In 1874, a group of artists got together and dared to risk it all. Frustrated by the strict rules of composition and subject matter imposed by academic institutions, these artists decided to free themselves to pursue their own ideas and mount their own exhibition. This was the first independent group show of Impressionist art. Calling themselves *Société anonyme*, these artists' impressionist art was considered shocking, unfinished, and insulting. With their daring color and quick brushstrokes, these revolutionary paintings were a radical departure from tradition.

Napoléon Crossing the Alps,
Jacques-Louis David, 1801

[1] *Mythology:* a body of ancient stories, especially those invented to explain natural or historical events

32 CHAPTER 2

Post-Impressionism

By H. W. Janson and Anthony F. Janson

The Mont Sainte-Victoire, Paul Cézanne, 1904–1906

1   The Impressionist art movement effectively began in France in the early 1860s. Edouard Manet is considered the "Father of Impressionism," and Impressionist artists included Edgar Degas, Claude Monet, Pierre Auguste Renoir, Frédéric Bazille, among others. Their work is characterized by quick brushstrokes and less detail than the work of previous painters. By the later part of the 19th century, painting had developed further, into what has become known as Post-Impressionist painting.

2   By 1882, Impressionism had gained wide acceptance among artists and the public—but, by the same token, it was no longer a pioneering movement. When the Impressionists held their last group show (in 1886), the future already belonged to the "Post-Impressionists." This colorless label designates a group of artists who passed through an Impressionist phase in the 1880s but became dissatisfied with the style and pursued a variety of directions. Because they did not have a common goal, it is difficult to find a more descriptive term for them than Post-Impressionists. They certainly were not "anti-Impressionists." Far from trying to undo the effects of the "Manet

revolution," they wanted to carry it further. Thus Post-Impressionism is in essence just a later stage, though a very important one, of the development that had begun in the 1860s.

3   Paul Cézanne (1839–1906) was the oldest of the Post-Impressionists . . . . . A man of intensely emotional temperament, Cézanne went to Paris in 1861 imbued with enthusiasm for the Romantics.[1] Delacroix was his first love among painters, and he never lost his admiration for him. Cézanne quickly grasped the nature of the Manet revolution as well, but he did not share his fellow Impressionists' interest in "slice-of-life" subjects, in movement, and in change. Instead, his goal was "to make of Impressionism something solid and durable, like the art of the museums." This quest, or search, for the "solid and durable" can be seen in Cézanne's still lifes,[2] such as *Still Life with Apples*. The ornamental backdrop is integrated with the three-dimensional[3] shapes, and the brushstrokes have a rhythmic pattern that gives the canvas its shimmering texture.

4   *[Joachim Gasquet had been a friend of Cézanne's for a time. Gasquet published conversations he said he had had with Cézanne. Although later critics say Gasquet added to these conversations, they do give an idea of what Cézanne thought about art. Below is an excerpt from Gasquet's book in which he quotes from interviews with Cézanne.]*

(continued on next page)

[1] *Romantics:* artists of the Romantic period. This artistic and literary movement lasted from approximately 1800 to 1840. Delacroix was a Romantic painter.

[2] *Still life:* a painting or photograph of an arrangement of objects, especially flowers and fruit

[3] *three-dimensional:* having or seeming to have length, depth, and height

Art History: Origins of Modern Art   **41**

Reading Two addresses the same theme as Reading One, but from a completely different perspective. In most cases, it is also an example of a different genre of writing (here, a textbook excerpt).

Reading Three addresses the same theme as Readings One and Two, but again from a different perspective from the first two. And in most cases, it is also an example of a different genre of writing (here, a textbook excerpt).

Most readings have **glosses** and **footnotes** to help students understand difficult words and names.

All readings have **numbered paragraphs** (with the exception of literary readings that have numbered lines) for easy reference. The **target vocabulary** that students need to know in order to read academic texts is set in boldface blue for easy recognition. Target vocabulary is recycled through the chapter and the level.

Abstract Expressionism

By Wayne Craven

1   The most dynamic movement of the postwar period[1] was Abstract Expressionism, sometimes also called action painting. It is called Abstract Expressionism because the imagery is abstract or even nonobjective,[2] and the way in which the paint is put on to the canvas expresses the action with which the work was made. Naturalistic representation of objects is of less importance than the artist's feelings about them or the aesthetic[3] experience of the act of painting itself. In Abstract Expressionism, explosive energy is a part of the method of creating—an emotional drama builds through the technique itself. Accidents inevitably occur in the frenetic execution of a work and are often retained as evidence of spontaneity. The scale of such paintings soon increased to heroic dimensions, mainly because broad areas were required for the free-swinging movements of the artist's arm and hand.

One of the most famous Abstract Expressionists, or action painters, was Jackson Pollock (1912–1956), who created one of the most original forms of expression in the history of American painting.

2   Abstract Expressionist work is a thing unto itself, and it should not be judged by how well or how badly it represents something else. It does not have to be a still life, a portrait, or a landscape. It is aesthetically sufficient for it to be simple pigment,[4] color, canvas, and brushwork—the result of spontaneous, energetic creation.

3   One of the best ways to understand Abstract Expressionism—or any art form—is through the words of an artist, while considering one of his paintings.

4   In Pollock's work *Autumn Rhythm: No. 30*, the paint is dribbled and flung upon the canvas, which, as Pollock worked on it, was placed flat on the floor rather than upright on an easel. The end result is unpremeditated, and the "happy accident" is an integral part of the imagery and a reference to its spontaneity. On an off-white ground, the primary color is black, with a secondary color of rust-orange and touches of numerous other hues.

5   The painting exists as an exciting aesthetic experience—an experience the viewer can share because the painting itself explains in an instant the process of its making. Typically of Pollock's work, the overall effect is without depth of

[1] *postwar period:* refers to the time after World War II, which ended in 1945

[2] *nonobjective:* not representing any real person, object, or scene

[3] *aesthetic:* relates to beauty and the study of beauty

[4] *pigment:* dry, colored powder made from natural or chemical sources, which is mixed with oil, water, etc. to make paint

48 CHAPTER 2

Each reading in the chapter is followed by Comprehension and Vocabulary activities.

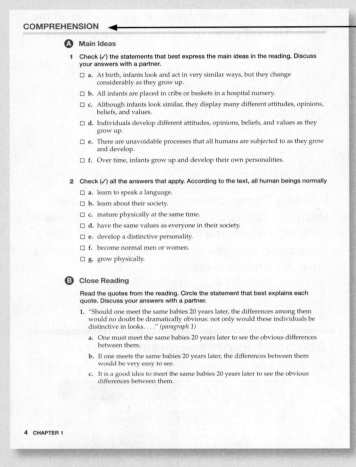

COMPREHENSION

A Main Ideas

1 Check (✓) the statements that best express the main ideas in the reading. Discuss your answers with a partner.

☐ **a.** At birth, infants look and act in very similar ways, but they change considerably as they grow up.

☐ **b.** All infants are placed in cribs or baskets in a hospital nursery.

☐ **c.** Although infants look similar, they display many different attitudes, opinions, beliefs, and values.

☐ **d.** Individuals develop different attitudes, opinions, beliefs, and values as they grow up.

☐ **e.** There are unavoidable processes that all humans are subjected to as they grow and develop.

☐ **f.** Over time, infants grow up and develop their own personalities.

2 Check (✓) all the answers that apply. According to the text, all human beings normally

☐ **a.** learn to speak a language.

☐ **b.** learn about their society.

☐ **c.** mature physically at the same time.

☐ **d.** have the same values as everyone in their society.

☐ **e.** develop a distinctive personality.

☐ **f.** become normal men or women.

☐ **g.** grow physically.

B Close Reading

Read the quotes from the reading. Circle the statement that best explains each quote. Discuss your answers with a partner.

1. "Should one meet the same babies 20 years later, the differences among them would no doubt be dramatically obvious: not only would these individuals be distinctive in looks. . . ." *(paragraph 1)*

   a. One must meet the same babies 20 years later to see the obvious differences between them.

   b. If one meets the same babies 20 years later, the differences between them would be very easy to see.

   c. It is a good idea to meet the same babies 20 years later to see the obvious differences between them.

4 CHAPTER 1

The **Comprehension** activities help students identify and understand the main ideas of the reading and their supporting details.

The **Vocabulary** activities focus on the target vocabulary in the reading, presenting and practicing skills such as guessing meaning from context or from synonyms, understanding word forms, and using a dictionary.

Guessing from Context helps students guess the meaning of the target vocabulary by encouraging them to go back to the reading to find clues in the context and base their guesses on these clues.

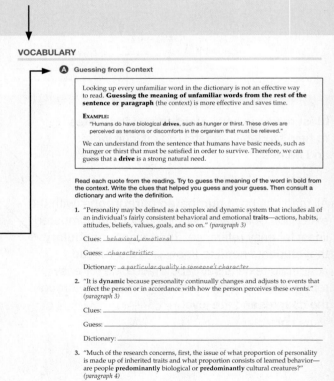

VOCABULARY

A Guessing from Context

Looking up every unfamiliar word in the dictionary is not an effective way to read. **Guessing the meaning of unfamiliar words from the rest of the sentence or paragraph** (the context) is more effective and saves time.

EXAMPLE:
"Humans do have biological **drives**, such as hunger or thirst. These drives are perceived as tensions or discomforts in the organism that must be relieved."

We can understand from the sentence that humans have basic needs, such as hunger or thirst that must be satisfied in order to survive. Therefore, we can guess that a **drive** is a strong natural need.

Read each quote from the reading. Try to guess the meaning of the word in bold from the context. Write the clues that helped you guess and your guess. Then consult a dictionary and write the definition.

1. "Personality may be defined as a complex and dynamic system that includes all of an individual's fairly consistent behavioral and emotional **traits**—actions, habits, attitudes, beliefs, values, goals, and so on." *(paragraph 3)*

   Clues: _behavioral, emotional_

   Guess: _characteristics_

   Dictionary: _a particular quality in someone's character_

2. "It is **dynamic** because personality continually changes and adjusts to events that affect the person or in accordance with how the person perceives these events." *(paragraph 3)*

   Clues: _____

   Guess: _____

   Dictionary: _____

3. "Much of the research concerns, first, the issue of what proportion of personality is made up of inherited traits and what proportion consists of learned behavior—are people **predominantly** biological or **predominantly** cultural creatures?" *(paragraph 4)*

   Clues: _____

   Guess: _____

   Dictionary: _____

(continued on next page)

Sociology: How We Become Who We Are **13**

VOCABULARY

A Synonyms

Complete each sentence with a word from the box. Use the synonym or phrase in parentheses to help you select the correct word. Be sure to use the correct tense of the verbs. Compare answers with a partner.

collective	efficacy	feat	span
counteract	entail	magnitude	rudimentary
devise	evoke	meager	undertaking
edifice			

1. Although architects are aware of physical limitations, they are constantly trying to

   _____ new ways of creating taller buildings.
   (come up with)

2. Building a structure as large and complex as a cathedral _____
   (necessitated)
   a lot of planning. There were many details to consider.

3. In many cases, the people involved in building the cathedrals were poor farmers

   with _____ resources.
   (insufficient)

4. Some of the tallest cathedrals have collapsed over time. This has caused modern-

   day architects to question the _____ of methods used by
   (effectiveness)
   medieval builders.

5. The city is planning to build a new church in my neighborhood. Unlike the

   building of the cathedrals in medieval times, this construction project will

   _____ only five years.
   (take place over)

6. The Cologne Cathedral in Germany is an impressive _____.
   (structure)
   Its towers are over 500 feet tall, and it is 284 feet wide and 474 feet long.

7. Even with the most up-to-date technology and equipment, lifting massive pieces

   of stone off the ground is a difficult and dangerous _____.
   (endeavor)
   Historians are still amazed at how medieval builders were able to accomplish

   such a(n) _____.
   (achievement)

8. The architects responsible for planning the Gothic cathedrals had a _____
   (shared)
   vision for creating a dramatic new architectural design.

94 CHAPTER 4

Synonyms also helps students understand the meaning of the target vocabulary in the reading, but here for each target word students are given synonyms to match or choose from.

Word Forms helps students expand their vocabulary by encouraging them to guess or find out the different forms some of the target words can have. Then students are challenged to use the forms correctly.

C Word Forms

Fill in the chart with the correct word forms. Use a dictionary if necessary. An *X* indicates there is no form in that category.

	NOUN	VERB	ADJECTIVE	ADVERB
1.			acquainted	X
2.	conformity			X
3.	controversy	X		
4.		X	emotional	
5.	ethnicity	X		
6.		X	receptive	

Complete the sentences with the correct form of one of the words above. Be sure to use the correct tense of the verbs and the singular or plural form of the nouns. Compare answers with a partner.

1. The students in the beginning-level English class represent a variety of

   _____ethnic_____ backgrounds.

2. Depending on their experiences, humans may feel a variety of different

   _____ throughout the day.

3. The university psychology professor has been caught up in a major

   _____ over the results of his recent research. His findings

   have angered many people.

4. Most colleges hold an orientation for new students. College personnel

   _____ the students with the school and its facilities.

5. When people enter the armed forces, they _____ to very

   strict rules.

6. The speaker was pleased by the crowd's _____. They were

   very interested in listening to what he had to say.

26 CHAPTER 1

Chapter Overview **xiii**

B Using the Dictionary

B Using the Dictionary

Read the dictionary entries and the sentences that follow. Then match the number of the definition with the appropriate sentence. Compare answers with a partner.

> **harmony** *n.* **1** notes of music combined together in a pleasant way   **2** a situation in which people live or work together without fighting or disagreeing with each other   **3** agreement with another idea, feeling, etc.   **4** the pleasant effect made by different things that form an attractive whole

1.

_____ **a.** General harmony, such as we find in color, is located all around us.

_____ **b.** Monet valued the quality of light and believed that he painted light rather than objects. His artwork was in harmony with his philosophy.

_____ **c.** The musicians created a wonderful harmony at the concert last night.

_____ **d.** Cézanne was a difficult man to get along with. He did not paint with other artists because he could not work in harmony with others.

> **resolve** *v.* **1** to find a satisfactory way of dealing with a problem   **2** to make a definite decision to do something   **3** to make a formal decision, especially by voting   **4** to gradually change into something else, especially by becoming clearer

2.

_____ **a.** Monet's paintings were rejected so often by the official salon that he resolved never to submit a painting there again.

_____ **b.** Nature's stirrings are resolved, deep down in one's brain, into a movement sensed equally by our eyes, our ears, our mouth, and our nose, each with its special kind of poetry.

_____ **c.** In a vote of nine to one, the members of the Art Committee resolved to open committee membership to all who apply.

_____ **d.** The Impressionists decided to resolve their problem of not having their work exhibited by renting space and putting on an exhibit of their own.

Using the Dictionary shows students how to understand a dictionary entry for one of the target words. Students choose the appropriate meaning of the word as it is used in the reading and in other contexts.

VOCABULARY

A Collocations

> **Collocations** refer to word partners or words that are often used together. These pairs of words appear in texts often and sound natural together.
>
> *Changing, emotional,* and *wider* appear in the reading. Each of these words has several collections.
>
> **Examples:**
>
> | | |
> |---|---|
> | changing attitudes | emotional impact |
> | changing circumstances | emotional intelligence |
> | changing needs | emotional reaction |
> | changing world | emotional support |
>
> | |
> |---|
> | wider audience |
> | wider context |
> | wider implications |
> | wider range |

Complete each sentence with the appropriate collocation from the box above. Compare answers with a partner.

1. Because the children were used to being in plays in their classroom, they were comfortable performing for a(n) _____wider audience_____ when they performed before the entire school population.

2. Most people know that sad experiences can deeply affect them. However, they often don't realize the _____ of positive experiences.

3. We live in a(n) _____. Technological advances, improvements in medical care, and societal changes are all happening at a faster and faster pace.

4. Even as adults, people mature, gain experience, and develop _____ about other people and the world around them.

5. The new law seems to be very clear and simple, but it has _____ for society as a whole.

6. When someone experiences a crisis in his or her life, such as the illness of a loved one, _____ becomes very important.

The **Collocation** activity helps students understand how words go together in English. Students are encouraged to go back to the reading to find the vocabulary words and the words they are regularly used with.

Each chapter has a Grammar for Reading activity and two Note-Taking activities. These can be in any of the three reading sections.

GRAMMAR FOR READING

Parallel Structure for Emphasis

Parallel structure refers to **repetition of specific grammatical forms**. Writers sometimes use parallel structure for emphasis. The repetition keeps the reader focused on the main points the author wishes to make.

EXAMPLES:

"How, we may wonder, did ordinary people manage these feats of tremendous physical and creative effort? Technology in the 12th to the 16th centuries was rudimentary, famine and disease were rampant, the climate was often harsh, and communal life was unstable and incessantly violent." *(Reading One, paragraph 1)*

The author repeated the past form of "be" four times in one sentence to emphasize the number of challenges facing the builders of the Gothic cathedrals. Essentially, the author wants the four "facts" to form a list in a single sentence in order to heighten our interest in the answer to the question.

Work with a partner. Examine the sentences from Readings One and Three. Underline the repeated forms in each. What does the repeated element emphasize in each passage?

1. "Before work could begin, an overall plan was needed. Next, a site had to be found and cleared. Building materials had to be located, delivered to the site, and assembled there. To do all of this, a workforce with the necessary skills had to be found and hired. This workforce had to be instructed, supervised, and paid, and the work checked for quality." *(Reading One, paragraph 3)*

What does the repeated element emphasize? _____

_____

2. "Building a cathedral entailed an ongoing, difficult, yet energizing form of collective enterprise in which people could take enormous pride and around which they could rally a community." *(Reading One, paragraph 6)*

What does the repeated element emphasize? _____

_____

3. "No one knows who discovered the magnetic property of the lodestone. Nor does anyone know who discovered that the stone's attractive power could be imparted to steel or hardened iron, or that the magnet could be used in determining geographic directions." *(Reading Two, paragraph 1)*

What does the repeated element emphasize? _____

_____

The **Grammar for Reading** activity leads students through a short review and practice of a grammar structure often encountered in academic texts, such as the passive, parallel forms, and adjective clauses. Understanding this type of grammar point enhances students' general reading comprehension ability.

The **Note-Taking** activity teaches students to use skills such as circling, underlining, writing margin notes, categorizing, completing an outline, and summarizing information to increase their reading comprehension.

NOTE-TAKING: Filling in an Outline

Go back to the reading and read it again. Take notes as you read and fill in the outline you created.

The Birth of Personality

I. _Introduction_

   A. _need to learn from others to become human_

   B. _____

   C. _____

II. Personality

   A. _____

   B. _____

   C. _____

   D. _____

   E. _____

III. A Social Product on a Biological Basis

   A. _____

   B. _____

   C. _____

IV. Universal Human Needs

   _____

   _____

   _____

Sociology: How We Become Who We Are **17**

All three reading sections end with a Critical Thinking activity. The Linking Readings One and Two activity comes at the very end of the Reading Two section.

The **Critical Thinking** activity encourages students to analyze and evaluate the information in the reading. This activity develops students' critical thinking skills and their ability to express their opinions coherently.

CRITICAL THINKING

Fact or Opinion?

Recognizing the **difference between a fact and an opinion** is an important reading skill because it helps you decide which statements are factual, and which statements are someone's views or personal perspective. A **fact** is something that can be **proven with evidence**. An **opinion** is **something that a person believes**. It may or may not be true, but it has not been proven.

EXAMPLES:
Gothic cathedrals were constructed in the first half of the twelfth century.

This is a fact because it can be confirmed using historical records.

One imagines that those who built Gothic cathedrals would be pleased to know that we admire them today.

This is an opinion because we do not know for sure whether people hundreds of years ago would have thought this way.

Read these statements. Decide if each one expresses a fact or an opinion. Check (✓) the appropriate box. Compare answers with a partner.

	FACT	OPINION
1. Before work could begin, a site had to be found and cleared.	☐	☐
2. During the period of cathedral building, the population of England was about six million.	☐	☐
3. Everyone in the community that built a cathedral was united in their pride for the achievement.	☐	☐
4. Gothic cathedrals evoke awe, humility, and inspiration.	☐	☐
5. It could take 100 years or more to build a cathedral.	☐	☐

Science: *Human Achievements over Time* **97**

The **Linking Readings One and Two** activity leads students to compare and contrast the ideas expressed in the first two readings. It helps students make connections and find correlations between the two texts.

LINKING READINGS ONE AND TWO

Discuss the questions in a small group. Be prepared to share your answers with the class.

1. Reading One discusses several components of culture: cognitive processes such as learning, knowing and perceiving, and behaviors, including traditions and social interactions. Describe some examples of components of culture from Reading Two.

2. What artifacts might a nomadic, foraging society create? What might they do without?

3. Foraging societies are often described as sharing and egalitarian (that is, believing that everyone is equal and has equal rights). Why might these particular characteristics be common among these particular societies? Use concepts from Reading One to explain your answer.

READING THREE: Night Flying Woman: An Ojibway Narrative

Ⓐ Warm-Up

Discuss the questions in a small group. Share your answers with the class.

1. Consider the title of the reading. What do you think the narrative might be about?

2. Do you think it is important to pass cultural traditions on to younger generations? If so, why? If not, why not?

Ⓑ Reading Strategy

Recognizing Point of View

The **point of view** of a reading can be **objective or subjective**. A reading that has an objective point of view focuses on **factual** information. An objective reading presents the information in a neutral way. A reading that has a subjective point of view focuses on **feelings, beliefs, and opinions**. You can tell if a reading has a subjective point of view because the words used suggest strong emotions.

Recognizing the point of view of a reading can help you to better understand the author's message, which aids in overall comprehension of the text.

EXAMPLE:
It is well that they are asking, for the Ojibway young must learn their cycle. These children are again honoring the Old People by asking them to speak.

The sentence above is subjective because the underlined words indicate the opinion of the speaker.

The two girls poked holes in the ground in the many open spaces in the forest. Then Aunt On-da-g dropped in the seed. She had saved much seed from the last harvest, so there would be a big crop of pumpkins, squash, beans, and ma-da-min, the corn.

The sentence above is objective because the speaker is presenting the factual events of the story without expressing emotions or opinions.

78 CHAPTER 3

Each chapter ends with an After You Read section, a Vocabulary chart, and a Self-Assessment checklist.

The **After You Read** activities go back to the theme of the chapter, encouraging students to discuss and write about related topics using the target vocabulary of the chapter.

AFTER YOU READ

BRINGING IT ALL TOGETHER

Discuss the questions in a small group. Then share your group's answers with the class. Use the vocabulary you studied in the chapter (for a complete list, go to page 29).

1. Reading One defines *socialization* as the process of learning the norms and values of society as an individual grows up. Work in a small group. Select a specific value, such as honesty, respect for others, or punctuality. Discuss how each of you learned this value. Describe when you exhibit this value. Are your experiences in learning this value and the way you exhibit this value the same for everyone in the group? Why or why not?

2. According to Reading Two, "Research to date seems to indicate that personality development occurs as a consequence of the interplay of biological inheritance, physical environment, culture, group experience, and personal experience." How might the interaction of these factors have affected an aspect of your personality?

3. Reading Two points out the human need for social and physical contact, and that it may be interpreted as a need to receive and give love. Review the agents of socialization you read about in Reading Three. Do all these agents help fulfill this need to receive and give love? If so, in what ways? If not, why not?

WRITING ACTIVITY

Write a short composition in which you describe what it means to become human. In the first paragraph, write what human beings experience as they become human. In the second paragraph, describe what influences human beings in their process of becoming human. In the third paragraph, tell a brief anecdote (story) about one of your own experiences in becoming human.

DISCUSSION AND WRITING TOPICS

Discuss these topics in a small group. Choose one of them and write a paragraph or two about it. Use the vocabulary from the chapter.

1. The media are a very powerful source of socialization today. Think of recent or past events in the news where the media have had a powerful influence on people's actions. Select one event and write about how the media influenced people to act in a certain way.

2. According to Reading Three, "Socialization, in fact, is reciprocal. The way infants look and act has a bearing on how parents feel and act toward them." Write about specific ways that infants behave that influence how their parents feel and respond to them. Provide examples from your own experiences and observations.

3. We all develop unique personalities as we grow up. Even identical twins who grow up together develop distinctive personalities. How does this happen?

The **Vocabulary chart**, which lists all the target vocabulary words of the chapter under the appropriate parts of speech, provides students with a convenient reference.

VOCABULARY

Nouns	Verbs	Adjectives	Adverbs
anthropologist	engage in	acquainted	dramatically*
appearance	incite	(with)	predominantly*
changing nature	hinder	distinctive*	unintentionally
conformity*	inhibit*	dynamic*	
controversy*	initiate*	functioning*	
drive	neglect	indeterminate	
emotional ties	predispose	receptive	
ethnicity*	proceed*	surrogate	
manner	relieve		
maturation*			
norms*			
socialization			
trait			
wider range			
wider society			

* = AWL (Academic Word List) item

The **Self-Assessment** checklist encourages students to evaluate their own progress. Have they mastered the skills listed in the chapter objectives?

SELF-ASSESSMENT

In this chapter you learned to:

○ Preview a text and activate background knowledge

○ Use headings to create an outline and fill in the outline with details from the text

○ Create questions from the title and headings of a text to increase understanding

○ Guess the meaning of words from the context

○ Use dictionary entries to learn different meanings of words

○ Use *one* as an impersonal pronoun

○ Understand and use synonyms, antonyms, font styles, collocations, roots, and different word forms

○ Create a chart and write notes to summarize information from a text

What can you do well? ☉

What do you need to practice more? ☉

SCOPE AND SEQUENCE

CHAPTER	READING	VOCABULARY
1 SOCIOLOGY: **How We Become Who We Are** **Theme:** Is all or part of our personality set at birth? What factors influence our personality as we grow from infants to adults? **Reading One:** *Becoming a Person* (a textbook excerpt) **Reading Two:** *The Birth of Personality* (a textbook excerpt) **Reading Three:** *Agents of Socialization* (a textbook excerpt)	• Understand and practice different reading strategies • Preview the content of a text by looking at the titles and images • Use the headings to create an outline of important points • Create questions to prepare for the reading • Identify the main ideas of a text • Understand the details that support the main ideas	• Guess the meaning of words from the context • Use dictionary entries to choose the correct meaning of words for the context • Recognize how font styles can aid in understanding new words • Understand and use synonyms, antonyms, word roots, and word forms • Recognize and use collocations • Use the vocabulary list at the end of the chapter to review the words, phrases, and idioms learned in the chapter • Use this vocabulary in the After You Read speaking and writing activities
2 ART HISTORY: **Origins of Modern Art** **Theme:** Art movements in the 19th and 20th centuries: Impressionism, Post-Impressionism, and Abstract Expressionism **Reading One:** *Breaking with Tradition: the Beginnings of Impressionism* (an online article) **Reading Two:** *Post-Impressionism* (a textbook excerpt) **Reading Three:** *Abstract Expressionism* (a textbook excerpt)	• Understand and practice different reading strategies • Use visuals to enhance understanding • Paraphrase to aid comprehension • Highlight important information • Identify the main ideas of a text • Understand the details that support the main ideas	• Guess the meaning of words from the context • Categorize words by their usage • Use dictionary entries to choose the correct meaning of words for the context • Understand and learn the different meanings of words • Understand and use synonyms, antonyms, and word forms • Recognize and use collocations • Use the vocabulary list at the end of the chapter to review the words, phrases, and idioms learned in the chapter • Use this vocabulary in the After You Read speaking and writing activities
3 ANTHROPOLOGY: **The Study of Human Cultures** **Theme:** Universal components of human societies; foraging vs. horticultural societies; the personal perspective of a Native American **Reading One:** *The Challenge of Defining Culture* (a textbook excerpt) **Reading Two:** *The Nature of Foraging and Horticultural Societies* (a textbook excerpt) **Reading Three:** *Night Flying Woman: An Ojibway Narrative* (an oral history narrated in a book)	• Understand and practice different reading strategies • Create a concept map to organize what you read • Use textual clues to aid comprehension • Recognize point of view to better understand the message of a text • Identify the main ideas of a text • Understand the details that support the main ideas	• Guess the meaning of words from the context • Use dictionary entries to choose the correct meaning of words for the context • Understand and use synonyms, idioms, and word forms • Understand and learn content-specific vocabulary • Use the vocabulary list at the end of the chapter to review the words, phrases, and idioms learned in the chapter • Use this vocabulary in the After You Read speaking and writing activities

NOTE-TAKING/GRAMMAR	CRITICAL THINKING	SPEAKING/WRITING
• Fill in an outline • Create a chart to summarize information from a text • GRAMMAR: *One* as an impersonal pronoun	• Express your opinions and support them with examples from the text or from your own experience and culture • Analyze and evaluate information • Infer information not explicit in a text • Draw conclusions • Make connections between ideas • Synthesize information and ideas	• In a small group, discuss the ways that people's personalities are continuously changing and adjusting to events • Discuss the factors that contribute to the development of each person's distinctive personality • In a small group discuss what might happen at a job when a person fails to successfully socialize • Choose one of the topics and write a paragraph or two about it • Write a short composition describing what it means to become human
• Chart the differences between two ideas in a reading • Consolidate information from several readings • GRAMMAR: Recognize referents	• Express your opinions and support them with examples from the text or from your own experience and culture • Analyze and evaluate information • Infer information not explicit in a text • Draw conclusions • Hypothesize about someone else's point of view • Make connections between ideas • Synthesize information and ideas	• In a small group, discuss quotations from various artists and interpret the artists' meaning • Choose one of the topics and write two or three paragraphs about it • Write a composition describing what art appreciation means to you personally • Paraphrase text to restate the general idea of a reading
• Write notes from headings and subheadings • Create a chart to compare different ideas in a text • GRAMMAR: Understand and use gerunds	• Express your opinions and support them with examples from the text or from your own experience and culture • Analyze and evaluate information • Infer information not explicit in a text • Draw conclusions • Hypothesize about the reasons why rules of reciprocity differ between foraging and horticultural societies • Make connections between information in the text and your own culture • Synthesize information and ideas • Identify the writer's point of view • Find relevance in the 19th century culture of the Ojibway in today's world	• In a small group, consider the nature of foraging and horticultural societies, and discuss Ojibway values and the behaviors that reflect those values in light of these two types of societies • Choose one of the topics and write a paragraph or two about it • Write a three-paragraph essay in which you use personal experience to explain the expression *Culture is what makes us strangers when we are away from home.*

CHAPTER	READING	VOCABULARY
4 SCIENCE: Human Achievements over Time **Theme:** What technological innovations have been created over the past 1,000 years? What effect have these innovations had on our everyday lives? **Reading One:** *A Great Human Endeavor: Building the Gothic Cathedrals* (a book excerpt) **Reading Two:** *From Stone to Satellite: Finding Our Way* (an online article) **Reading Three:** *Reaching for the Stars: The 100-Year Starship Project* (an online article)	• Understand and practice different reading strategies • Use the information in a text box to understand a difficult concept • Skim for the main idea by reading topic sentences • Use visuals to understand terms and concepts • Identify the main ideas of a text • Understand the details that support the main ideas	• Guess the meaning of words from the context • Use dictionary entries to choose the correct meaning of words for the context • Understand and use word forms, synonyms, idioms, and roots • Understand and learn the different meanings of words • Recognize and use collocations • Use the vocabulary list at the end of the chapter to review the words, phrases, and idioms learned in the chapter • Use this vocabulary in the After You Read speaking and writing activities
5 POLITICAL SCIENCE: Managing Hard Times **Theme:** How does a government respond to an economic crisis? What government policies best help a country and its people recover from economic depression? **Reading One:** *The Great Depression: A Nation in Crisis* (a book excerpt) **Reading Two:** *The Works Progress Administration and the Federal Arts Project* (a book excerpt) **Reading Three:** *An Artist's Perspective on the Federal Arts Project* (a book excerpt)	• Understand and practice different reading strategies • Analyze graphs to understand statistics • Predict content from the first paragraph • Paraphrase to clarify the main ideas • Identify the main ideas of a text • Understand the details that support the main ideas	• Guess the meaning of words from the context • Use dictionary entries to choose the correct meaning of words for the context • Understand and use synonyms, word forms, prefixes, and idioms • Recognize and learn collocations • Use the vocabulary list at the end of the chapter to review the words, phrases, and idioms learned in the chapter • Use this vocabulary in the After You Read speaking and writing activities
6 HEALTH SCIENCES: Medical Mysteries Solved **Theme:** Medical research and discoveries that have improved the health of people around the world **Reading One:** *Solving a Deadly Puzzle* (a magazine article) **Reading Two:** *Imprisoned without a Trial: The Story of Typhoid Mary* (an online article) **Reading Three:** *The Discovery of a Miracle Drug* (an online article)	• Understand and practice different reading strategies • Read the last paragraph first to get an overview • Identify tone and point of view • Draw inferences • Identify the main ideas of a text • Understand the details that support the main ideas	• Guess the meaning of words from the context • Understand and use prefixes, suffixes, phrasal verbs, idioms, word forms, and synonyms • Categorize words • Understand and learn content-specific vocabulary • Use the vocabulary list at the end of the chapter to review the words, phrases, and idioms learned in the chapter • Use this vocabulary in the After You Read speaking and writing activities

NOTE-TAKING/GRAMMAR	CRITICAL THINKING	SPEAKING/WRITING
• Organize information chronologically • List problems and solutions identified in the text • GRAMMAR: How to use parallel structure for emphasis	• Express your opinions and support them with examples from the text or from your own experience and culture • Analyze and evaluate information • Infer information not explicit in a text • Draw conclusions • Hypothesize about someone else's point of view • Make connections between ideas • Synthesize information and ideas • Distinguish fact from opinion • Decide the advantages and disadvantages to using a compass and to using a GPS system	• Debate the question, "Do you think the endeavors of building Gothic cathedrals, developing navigational technology, and pursuing the 100-year starship project are worthwhile pursuits?" • Discuss in a small group the meaning of the statement, *Necessity is the mother of invention.* Consider its relevance to the innovations described • In a small group, discuss what you consider the greatest human achievement ever attempted • Choose one of the topics and write a paragraph or two about it • Write a three-paragraph essay in which you describe a major scientific break-through from the distant or recent past
• Create a timeline • Make lists • GRAMMAR: Use adverb clauses to show time relationships	• Express your opinions and support them with examples from the text or from your own experience and culture • Analyze and evaluate information • Infer information not explicit in a text • Draw conclusions • Hypothesize about someone else's point of view • Make connections between ideas • Synthesize information and ideas • Find similarities and differences between the policies of two presidents in response to the Great Depression • Make connections between a president's policies and the perspective of an artist	• Write a narrative in which you imagine you are a young person who is out of work during the Great Depression, and your efforts to find work and to live • In a small group, discuss whether artists who were paid by the Federal Arts Project should have been able to keep or to sell their work • Choose one of the topics and write three paragraphs about it
• Create a flowchart • Create a chain of events • GRAMMAR: Understand the use of the passive voice	• Express your opinions and support them with examples from the text or from your own experience and culture • Analyze and evaluate information • Infer information not explicit in a text • Draw conclusions • Hypothesize about someone else's point of view • Make connections between ideas • Synthesize information and ideas	• Set up a panel discussion to debate the two sides of the issue of Mary Mallon's forced seclusion • In a small group, discuss what major changes in medical practices resulted from the work of Dr. Snow and Dr. Fleming • Choose one of the topics and write three paragraphs about it • Write a three-paragraph paper on a health threat that exists today

CHAPTER	READING	VOCABULARY
7 LITERATURE: **Storytelling through Poetry** **Theme:** A story through poetry of a thoughtless act that has lifelong consequences and that teaches a moral for all time **Reading One:** Themes and Characters in *The Rime of the Ancient Mariner* (an online article) **Reading Two:** *The Rime of the Ancient Mariner* (a poem) **Reading Three:** *The Rime of the Ancient Mariner* (continued) (a poem)	• Understand and practice different reading strategies • Understand literary terms • Identify allegorical references to understand symbolism • Paraphrase poetry to ease comprehension • Identify the main ideas of a text • Understand the details that support the main ideas	• Guess the meaning of words from the context • Understand and use prefixes, word forms, and synonyms • Understand and learn the unfamiliar meanings of familiar words • Understand literary meanings of words • Categorize words within themes • Use the vocabulary list at the end of the chapter to review the words, phrases, and idioms learned in the chapter • Use this vocabulary in the After You Read speaking and writing activities
8 HISTORY: **Encountering New Worlds** **Theme:** The causes and effects of exploration and conquest on peoples over the course of history. **Reading One:** *Europe on the Eve of Conquest* (a textbook excerpt) **Reading Two:** *Native American Histories before the Conquest* (a textbook excerpt) **Reading Three:** *West Africa at the Time of European Exploration* (a textbook excerpt)	• Understand and practice different reading strategies • Make connections between sentences • Draw inferences • Summarize to remember the main points of a text • Identify the main ideas of a text • Understand the details that support the main ideas	• Guess the meaning of words from the context • Use dictionary entries to choose the correct meaning of words for the context • Understand and use synonyms and word forms • Understand and learn the different meanings of words • Understand and learn content-specific vocabulary • Recognize and use collocations • Use the vocabulary list at the end of the chapter to review the words, phrases, and idioms learned in the chapter • Use this vocabulary in the After You Read speaking and writing activities

NOTE-TAKING/GRAMMAR	CRITICAL THINKING	SPEAKING/WRITING
• Create a literary semantic web • Make double entry notes • GRAMMAR: Identifying verb forms and word order that are no longer in use	• Express your opinions and support them with examples from the text or from your own experience and culture • Analyze and evaluate information • Infer information not explicit in a text • Draw conclusions • Hypothesize about someone else's point of view • Make connections between ideas • Synthesize information and ideas • Analyze a poem using literary terms • Find connections between the mariner's rash act and the historical context of the poem's author • Consider the moral of the poem and whether the mariner's penance was just	• Discuss in a small group the symbolism of the expression *having an albatross around one's neck* • In a small group, discuss the deeper meaning of sections of the poem • Choose one of the topics and write a short essay about it • Write a three-paragraph paper in which you focus on one of the themes in the poem
• Create an outline • Create a semantic map • GRAMMAR: How to use the adverb "even"	• Express your opinions and support them with examples from the text or from your own experience and culture • Analyze and evaluate information • Infer information not explicit in a text • Draw conclusions • Hypothesize about factors that might have facilitated Europe's ability to engage in exploration prior to the 15th century • Make connections between ideas	• Discuss in a small group the similarities and differences between the European's experiences with Native Americans and West Africans • In a small group discuss how the experiences of the Europeans might have been different if the Europeans' diseases had had the same effect in Africa that they did in North America • Choose one of the topics and write three or four paragraphs about it • Write a three-paragraph paper to summarize the readings and to give your opinion

CHAPTER	READING	VOCABULARY
9 BUSINESS: **Ethical Issues** **Theme:** The importance of ethical behavior in the business world; how companies can foster ethical behavior at all levels of a firm **Reading One:** *Promoting Ethics in the Workplace* (a textbook excerpt) **Reading Two:** *Ethical Reasoning* (a textbook excerpt) **Reading Three:** *Should Mary Buy Her Bonus?* (an online article)	• Understand and practice different reading strategies • Prepare for a test by anticipating questions • Predict answers to questions • Scan a text for specific information • Identify the main ideas of a text • Understand the details that support the main ideas	• Guess the meaning of words from the context • Use advanced vocabulary to accurately convey meaning and vary style • Use dictionary entries to choose the correct meaning of words for the context • Recognize and learn collocations • Understand and learn the different meanings of words • Understand and use synonyms, word forms, and idioms • Understand and learn preposition combinations with adjectives • Use the vocabulary list at the end of the chapter to review the words, phrases, and idioms learned in the chapter • Use this vocabulary in the After You Read speaking and writing activities
10 MIGRATION STUDIES: **In Search of a New Life** **Theme:** What factors influence or force people to permanently relocate from one area or country to another? What stories do people have to tell about their personal experiences moving to a new, unknown land? **Reading One:** *Human Migration* (a textbook excerpt) **Reading Two:** *The Westward Journey:* *A Personal Perspective* (a book excerpt) **Reading Three:** *Wooden Trunk from Buchenwald* (a book excerpt)	• Understand and practice different reading strategies • Skim for the main idea by reading topic sentences • Draw inferences • Respond to a text • Identify the main ideas of a text • Understand the details that support the main ideas	• Guess the meaning of words from the context • Understand and learn the different meanings of words • Use dictionary entries to choose the correct meaning of words for the context • Understand and use suffixes, word forms, synonyms, and phrasal verbs • Sort words by category • Recognize and learn collocations • Use the vocabulary list at the end of the chapter to review the words, phrases, and idioms learned in the chapter • Use this vocabulary in the After You Read speaking and writing activities

NOTE-TAKING/GRAMMAR	CRITICAL THINKING	SPEAKING/WRITING
• Write a summary for studying • Summarize the argument • GRAMMAR: Recognize transition words	• Express your opinions and support them with examples from the text or from your own experience and culture • Analyze and evaluate information • Infer information not explicit in a text • Draw conclusions • Make connections between ideas • Synthesize information and ideas • Find correlations between the ideas of two thinkers through the lens of another thinker	• Form a panel to create a code of ethics for a hypothetical new company • Discuss in a small group alternate ethical choices Mary might have made • In a small group, compare and contrast information between readings • Choose one of the topics and write a short essay about it • Write a four-paragraph paper to summarize the reading
• Create a timeline • Fill out an organizer • GRAMMAR: Recognize the words that indicate contrast	• Express your opinions and support them with examples from the text or from your own experience and culture • Analyze and evaluate information • Infer information not explicit in a text • Draw conclusions • Hypothesize about someone else's point of view • Make connections between ideas • Synthesize information and ideas • Find reasons to account for apparent contradictions in a person's descriptions of his or her experiences • Identify similarities between the experiences of the people in the readings and people today	• Discuss in a small group what factors might account for the frequency with which Americans relocate • In a small group discuss what push and pull factors influenced the people in the readings to relocate • Write personal responses to quotes you select from a journal • Choose one of the topics and write a paragraph or two about it • Write a four-paragraph essay about migration

I thank Massimo Rubini for inviting me to write Book 5 of this series. Massimo was always cheerful and optimistic, and most of all, dedicated to the success of the series.

I especially thank Amy McCormick, whose professionalism, patience, and insight helped me through some of the more challenging phases of the book. Amy always kept the project on track.

Many people were involved in Book 5 at various stages in the project. I thank Jaime Lieber, who assisted me with technical issues, as well as those who edited, obtained reprint permissions, researched artwork, proofread, and performed a myriad of essential tasks, particularly Mary Rich, who worked with me on the final phase of the book.

My gratitude goes to my fellow authors, Elizabeth Böttcher, Robert Cohen, Judy Miller, and particularly Kim Sanabria, who gave me moral support at the times I needed it most. All of you were creative, persevering, and committed to the quality of the series—and it shows so clearly in the books you have written.

To my colleagues and the students at the English Language Institute at Queens College CUNY, I offer my sincere appreciation. You are always with me in spirit.

I am indebted to my husband Joseph, who has stood by me throughout my writing career. His unwavering support, encouragement, and willingness to listen are priceless to me.

Lorraine C. Smith

Reviewers

The publisher would like to thank the following reviewers for their many helpful comments.

Jeff Bette, Naugatuck Valley Community College, Waterbury, Connecticut; **Kevin Knight**, Japan; **Melissa Parisi**, Westchester Community College, Valhalla, New York; **Jason Tannenbaum**, Pace University, Bronx, New York; **Christine Tierney**, Houston Community College, Stafford, Texas; **Kerry Vrabel**, GateWay Community College, Phoenix, Arizona.

CHAPTER 1

SOCIOLOGY: How We Become Who We Are

SOCIOLOGY: the scientific study of human society and human group behavior. The focus of sociology is the individual in interaction with others or as he or she moves in the social environment.

OBJECTIVES

To read academic texts, you need to master certain skills.

In this chapter, you will:

- Preview a text and activate background knowledge

- Use headings to create an outline and fill in the outline with details from the text

- Create questions from the title and headings of a text to increase understanding

- Guess the meaning of words from the context

- Use dictionary entries to learn different meanings of words

- Use *one* as an impersonal pronoun

- Understand and use synonyms, antonyms, font styles, collocations, roots, and different word forms

- Create a chart and write notes to summarize information from a text

Consider These Questions

Discuss the questions in a small group. Share your answers with the class.

1. How do you describe people's personalities? Write descriptions in the word web.

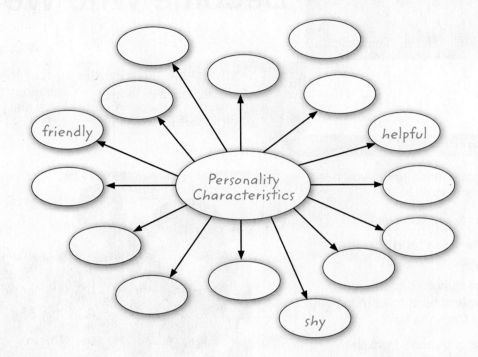

2. Work alone. In your journal or on a piece of paper, write a description of your personality. Some questions to think about: Are you shy? outgoing? cautious? reckless? Do you tend to be solitary? Are you group-oriented? Were you born this way, or did your personality develop as you grew up? Share your description with your group.

3. As we grow up, we learn what is normal (that is, acceptable) behavior in our society. We develop specific values, too. Who teaches us these behaviors and values?

READING ONE: Becoming a Person

A Warm-Up

Discuss the questions with a partner.

1. What does it mean to become a person?

2. In what ways do humans change as they grow from babies to adults?

3. Do babies have personalities?

Previewing

Previewing refers to **preparing for the content of a reading**. You can do so by considering the title of the chapter or reading, looking at the photographs in the chapter, thinking about what you may already know about the topic, and asking yourself questions to activate your background knowledge. For example, when you read the title, you may ask, *How does an infant become a person?*

Work with a partner. Discuss the answers to the questions.

1. Consider the title of the reading.

    a. How does an infant become a person?

    b. What factors influence our personality as we grow up?

2. Look at the photograph below.

    a. Where are these babies? How old are they?

    b. Can you tell which ones are boys and which are girls?

    c. What else can you tell about babies at this age?

Now read the text and keep in mind the questions and answers you discussed.

Becoming a Person

By John A. Perry and Erna K. Perry

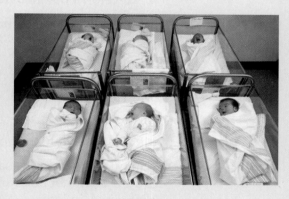

1   If one were to look into a hospital nursery almost anywhere in the world, the picture would be similar: rows of cribs or baskets containing infants of **indeterminate** gender, some of whom are squirming and crying while others are sleeping peacefully. A closer look will reveal differences in **appearance**, but at first glance, all the babies look very much alike. Should one meet the same babies 20 years later, the differences among them would no doubt be **dramatically** obvious: not only would these individuals be **distinctive** in looks, but also, if **engaged** in conversation, they would display a variety of attitudes, opinions, beliefs, and values. Moreover, they would differ in the **manner** in which they expressed them.

2   The infants we met in the hospital have been subjected to two unavoidable processes. One is *maturation*, or the physical development of the body, which **proceeds** at approximately the same rate for everyone. The other is *socialization*, or the process of becoming human, learning societal **norms** and values while developing a personality unique to each individual.

Work with a partner. Identify one or two facts in the reading that explain how humans change as they grow.

COMPREHENSION

Ⓐ Main Ideas

1 Check (✓) the statements that best express the main ideas in the reading. Discuss your answers with a partner.

☑ **a.** At birth, infants look and act in very similar ways, but they change considerably as they grow up.

☐ **b.** All infants are placed in cribs or baskets in a hospital nursery.

☐ **c.** Although infants look similar, they display many different attitudes, opinions, beliefs, and values.

☑ **d.** Individuals develop different attitudes, opinions, beliefs, and values as they grow up.

☐ **e.** There are unavoidable processes that all humans are subjected to as they grow and develop.

☑ **f.** Over time, infants grow up and develop their own personalities.

2 Check (✓) all the answers that apply. According to the text, all human beings normally

☑ **a.** learn to speak a language.

☑ **b.** learn about their society.

☑ **c.** mature physically at the same time.

☐ **d.** have the same values as everyone in their society.

☑ **e.** develop a distinctive personality.

☐ **f.** become normal men or women.

☑ **g.** grow physically.

Ⓑ Close Reading

Read the quotes from the reading. Circle the statement that best explains each quote. Discuss your answers with a partner.

1. "Should one meet the same babies 20 years later, the differences among them would no doubt be dramatically obvious: not only would these individuals be distinctive in looks. . . ." *(paragraph 1)*

   a. One must meet the same babies 20 years later to see the obvious differences between them.

   b. If one meets the same babies 20 years later, the differences between them would be very easy to see.

   c. It is a good idea to meet the same babies 20 years later to see the obvious differences between them.

2. "If engaged in conversation, they would display a variety of attitudes, opinions, beliefs, and values. Moreover, they would differ in the manner in which they expressed them." *(paragraph 1)*

By the time they are 20 years old, these individuals would

   a. argue about their attitudes, opinions, beliefs, and values in the same way.

   b. learn attitudes, opinions, beliefs, and values in different ways.

   c. have different attitudes, opinions, beliefs, and values and express these in different ways.

3. "The other [unavoidable process] is socialization, or the process of becoming human, learning societal norms and values while developing a personality unique to each individual." *(paragraph 2)*

   a. Each individual develops a personality unlike anyone else's.

   b. Each individual avoids becoming an individual through socialization.

   c. Each individual learns societal norms unlike anyone else's.

VOCABULARY

 Synonyms

> We can build our vocabulary by learning the meanings of unfamiliar words and connecting them with their **synonyms**.
>
> **EXAMPLE:**
>   If one were to look into a hospital nursery almost anywhere in the world, the picture would be similar: rows of cribs or baskets containing infants of **indeterminate** gender.
>
> Given a choice of words—*unknown, uncertain, obscure, clear*—by comparing the words we can figure out that *unknown, uncertain,* and *obscure* are synonyms of *indeterminate,* but that *clear* is not.

Cross out the word or phrase that is not a synonym for the word in bold. Compare answers with a partner.

1. **distinctive**	unlike	dissimilar	different	~~identical~~
2. **manner**	~~situation~~	way	style	form
3. **norms**	standards	models	patterns	~~ceremonies~~
4. **proceed**	advance	~~delay~~	progress	go along
5. **appearance**	semblance	look	~~attitude~~	aspect

B Using the Dictionary

Words can have many different meanings. We need to consider the context in order to understand vocabulary words. Even simple or familiar words can have several very different meanings, depending on the context.

Read the dictionary entries and the sentences that follow. Then match the number of the definition with the appropriate sentence. Compare answers with a partner.

engage *v.* **1** to do or take part in an activity   **2** to arrange to employ someone   **3** to make one part fit into another part of a machine   **4** to begin to fight with an enemy

1.

_2_ **a.** The Sociology Department is changing its computer systems and programs. The department chair is engaging a computer expert to help with the new equipment and software.

_4_ **b.** During the war, the generals engaged the opposing army in a fight for control of an important bridge.

_1_ **c.** If engaged in conversation, they would display a variety of attitudes, opinions, beliefs, and values.

_3_ **d.** The old equipment in the laboratory needs repair. The gears are not engaging the motor in a special apparatus.

dramatic *adj.* **1** exciting and impressive   **2** connected with drama or the theater   **3** showing a lot of emotion in a way that makes other people notice

2.

_2_ **a.** The boy felt he was a member of the school community when he was given a dramatic role in the school play.

_1_ **b.** Sometimes children become very dramatic when they don't get something they want.

_3_ **c.** Children sometimes make a dramatic entrance when they come home from school, to get attention from a family member.

> **Font styles** such as *italics* **call attention to important vocabulary**. These words are often defined or explained or have synonyms in the same sentence or a sentence nearby. When you see italicized words, look in the nearby text for help in understanding them.

Read the sentences from the reading that contain the words below. Then write the definition of each word. Compare answers with a partner.

1. maturation: _____

2. socialization: _____

GRAMMAR FOR READING

One as an Impersonal Pronoun

One can be used in different ways within a text. As a **pronoun**, *one* is used in formal English **in place of the informal *you***. *One* refers to anyone or to people in general. The more common use of *one* is as a **number to refer to the first thing in a list** of two or more. When used in this way, sometimes it is followed by the phrase "the other," referring to the second thing in the list.

Read the sentences from the reading. Decide how *one* is being used in each sentence. Then circle the correct answer. Discuss your answers with a partner.

1. If **one** were to look into a hospital nursery almost anywhere in the world, the picture would be similar: rows of cribs or baskets containing infants of indeterminate gender, some of whom are squirming and crying while others are sleeping peacefully.

   a. impersonal pronoun

   b. number

2. Should **one** meet the same babies 20 years later, the differences among them would no doubt be dramatically obvious.

   a. impersonal pronoun

   b. number

3. **One** is maturation, or the physical development of the body, which proceeds at approximately the same rate for everyone.

   a. impersonal pronoun

   b. number

CRITICAL THINKING

Discuss the questions in a small group. Be prepared to share your answers with the class.

1. First, work alone and write in your journal. Think about how you became the way you are. Where did your attitudes, opinions, beliefs, and values come from? How did you learn the norms and values of society? Then discuss your responses with your group.

2. The writer states that all human beings are subjected to the same two processes: maturation and socialization. Do you think these two processes are independent of each other or interdependent? In other words, does one influence the other as we grow up? Discuss your answers.

READING TWO: The Birth of Personality

A Warm-Up

Discuss the questions in a small group. Share your answers with the class.

1. Write a definition of the term *personality*.

2. Do you think that personality develops after we are born, or are we born with a personality?

B Reading Strategy

Using Headings to Create an Outline

Creating an **outline** of a reading using the **headings** helps you focus on the **most important points** in each section. Keep in mind that the first paragraph of a text usually does not have a heading because it serves as the introduction.

Look at the reading and use the headings to create an outline of it.

The Birth of Personality

I. _Introduction_

II. _____

III. _____

IV. _____

The Birth of Personality

By John A. Perry and Erna K. Perry

1   The question may be asked whether it is necessary to become human, whether in fact people are not born human. The answer seems to be that one must learn from others to become human. That is, the infant is basically a creature capable of a few bodily functions but little more. Infants who have been left alone without any human companionship, even if their biological needs are attended to, either die or fail to develop normally. It is only in the process of relating to others of our species and learning from them that we become unique individuals with **distinctive** personalities who fit into a particular social structure.

Personality

2   It is frequently said of a person that he or she either has a nice personality or no personality at all. The first description is only partial and vague, and the second one is impossible, for every person has a personality. People tend to use the term *personality* imprecisely.

3   **Personality** may be defined as a complex and **dynamic** system that includes all of an individual's fairly consistent behavioral and emotional **traits**—actions, habits, attitudes, beliefs, values, goals, and so on. It is, of course, an abstract term. It is dynamic because personality continually changes and adjusts to events that affect the person or in accordance with how the person perceives these events. Personality may also be seen as a circular system: while the roles people fill in society affect their personalities, personalities also influence the way roles are seen and accomplished. Finally, personalities are distinctive because each individual is born with a specific set of inherited traits and potentials and then has experiences that are exclusively his or her own. Even identical twins, with the same biological heredity, may display personality differences based on different life experiences.

A Social Product on a Biological Basis

4   The study of personality has involved a number of scientists—psychologists, sociologists, **anthropologists**, and ethologists (scientists who study animal behavior in natural surroundings). Much of the research concerns, first, the issue of what proportion of personality is made up of inherited traits and what proportion consists of learned behavior—are people **predominantly** biological or predominantly cultural creatures?

(continued on next page)

Unfortunately, no easy answer can be given. Research to date seems to indicate that personality development occurs as a consequence of the interplay of biological inheritance, physical environment, culture, group experience, and personal experience.

5   The biological inheritance that all humans share is one that, in some respects, **predisposes** them toward accepting learning from others, in the process of which they acquire a personality. Humans lack strong instincts; thus, to a great extent they must learn how to act to their best advantage. (While they lack instincts, humans do have biological **drives**, such as hunger or thirst. These drives are perceived as tensions or discomforts in the organism that must be **relieved**. How best to relieve the discomfort is the function of culture, which represents the accumulated learning of countless preceding generations of people.)

Universal Human Needs

6   Biology is also responsible for the universal human need for social and physical contact, which humans share with a number of animals and which may be interpreted as a need to receive and give love. It has been shown repeatedly that infants deprived of loving human contact— for example, those badly **neglected**—do not develop normally, either physically or mentally. Some fail to thrive and die in infancy. Others grow up to be mentally or otherwise damaged. Although the reasons are not clearly understood, it seems that absence of body contact and stimulation in infancy **inhibits** the development of higher learning functions. In this need, humans are not alone: our close biological cousins, members of the ape family, show a need for similar closeness and body contact. In a well-known experiment involving rhesus monkeys, researchers found that rhesus infants separated from their biological mothers preferred a soft and cuddly "mother" made of terrycloth, even though she did not feed them, to a **surrogate**, or substitute, mother made of wire from which they did receive food. The infants ran to the soft "mother" in times of stress and preferred to spend most of their time near "her."

Work with a partner. Compare the sentences you underlined and discuss how the sentences help explain each heading.

COMPREHENSION

A **Main Ideas**

Read each question. Circle the correct answer. Compare answers with a partner.

1. What is the main idea of the reading?

   a. Every human is born with a unique personality, but we lose it if we do not have contact with others.

   b. Infants who have little or no human contact never develop normally, either physically or mentally.

   c. ✓ All humans have a need for contact with others, and personality development depends on learning from other humans.

2. At what point in a human's life does an individual's personality change?

   a. An individual's personality never changes after the person becomes an adult.

   b. ✓ An individual's personality changes throughout the person's life.

   c. An individual's personality changes only if the person has a role in society.

3. What is the focus of the research mentioned in paragraph 4?

   a. ✓ whether people's personalities are formed mainly by biology or by external factors

   b. whether people, who are mainly biological, are affected by culture

   c. whether it is better to be affected by biology or by our physical environment

B **Close Reading**

Read the quotes from the reading. Circle the statement that best explains each quote. Discuss your answers with a partner.

1. "It is only in the process of relating to others of our species and learning from them that we become unique individuals with distinctive personalities who fit into a particular social structure." *(paragraph 1)*

   a. Humans need to be with other species to understand their own uniqueness.

   b. ✓ Humans need to be with other humans in order to learn how to be human and become unique.

   c. Only when humans develop distinct personalities, can they can fit into society.

2. "Personality may be defined as a complex and dynamic system that includes all of an individual's fairly consistent behavioral and emotional traits—actions, habits, attitudes, beliefs, values, goals, and so on." *(paragraph 3)*

   a. An individual's personality is a very complex system and is difficult to define.

   b. ✓ An individual's personality encompasses all the thoughts and behaviors of that person.

   c. An individual's personality can be judged by how consistently he or she behaves.

(continued on next page)

3. "The study of personality has involved a number of scientists—psychologists, sociologists, anthropologists, and ethologists (scientists who study animal behavior in natural surroundings)." *(paragraph 4)*

    a. Personality is so complex that few scientists are able to understand it.

    b. The study of personality is relevant to animal scientists.

    ✓ c. There are many scientific approaches to studying personality.

4. "The biological inheritance that all humans share is one that, in some respects, predisposes them toward accepting learning from others, in the process of which they acquire a personality. Humans lack strong instincts; thus, to a great extent they must learn how to act to their best advantage." *(paragraph 5)*

    a. Human biology predisposes us to developing a personality.

    b. Human instinct allows us to act to our best advantage.

    ✓ c. Humans are predisposed to learn from others because they lack instinct.

5. "Biology is also responsible for the universal human need for social and physical contact, which humans share with a number of animals and which may be interpreted as a need to receive and give love." *(paragraph 6)*

    a. Unlike other animals, all humans need social and physical contact.

    ✓ b. Like some other animals, humans need social and physical contact.

    c. Humans and animals learn to need social and physical contact.

6. "In a well-known experiment involving rhesus monkeys, researchers found that rhesus infants, separated from their biological mothers, preferred a soft and cuddly 'mother' made of terrycloth, even though she did not feed them, to a surrogate, or substitute, mother made of wire from which they did receive food. The infants ran to the soft 'mother' in times of stress and preferred to spend most of their time near 'her.'" *(paragraph 6)*

    ✓ a. The baby rhesus monkeys needed comfortable physical contact when stressed.

    b. The baby rhesus monkeys needed food when stressed.

    c. The baby rhesus monkeys were stressed by the wire objects.

VOCABULARY

A **Guessing from Context**

> Looking up every unfamiliar word in the dictionary is not an effective way to read. **Guessing the meaning of unfamiliar words from the rest of the sentence or paragraph** (the context) is more effective and saves time.
>
> **EXAMPLE:**
>
> "Humans do have biological **drives**, such as hunger or thirst. These drives are perceived as tensions or discomforts in the organism that must be relieved."
>
> We can understand from the sentence that humans have basic needs, such as hunger or thirst that must be satisfied in order to survive. Therefore, we can guess that a **drive** is a strong natural need.

Read each quote from the reading. Try to guess the meaning of the word in bold from the context. Write the clues that helped you guess and your guess. Then consult a dictionary and write the definition.

1. "Personality may be defined as a complex and dynamic system that includes all of an individual's fairly consistent behavioral and emotional **traits**—actions, habits, attitudes, beliefs, values, goals, and so on." (*paragraph 3*)

   Clues: _behavioral, emotional_

   Guess: _characteristics_

   Dictionary: _a particular quality in someone's character_

2. "It is **dynamic** because personality continually changes and adjusts to events that affect the person or in accordance with how the person perceives these events." (*paragraph 3*)

   Clues: _____

   Guess: _____

   Dictionary: _____

3. "Much of the research concerns, first, the issue of what proportion of personality is made up of inherited traits and what proportion consists of learned behavior— are people **predominantly** biological or **predominantly** cultural creatures?" (*paragraph 4*)

   Clues: _____

   Guess: _____

   Dictionary: _____

(continued on next page)

4. "[Biological drives] drives are perceived as tensions or discomforts in the organism that must be **relieved**. How best to **relieve** the discomfort is the function of culture." *(paragraph 5)*

   Clues: _____

   Guess: _____

   Dictionary: _____

5. "It has been shown repeatedly that infants deprived of loving human contact—for example, those badly **neglected**—do not develop normally, either physically or mentally." *(paragraph 6)*

   Clues: _____

   Guess: _____

   Dictionary: _____

6. "Although the reasons are not clearly understood, it seems that absence of body contact and stimulation in infancy **inhibits** the development of higher learning functions." *(paragraph 6)*

   Clues: _____

   Guess: _____

   Dictionary: _____

7. "Rhesus infants separated from their biological mothers, preferred a soft and cuddly 'mother' made of terrycloth, even though she did not feed them, to a **surrogate**, or substitute, mother made of wire from which they did receive food." *(paragraph 6)*

   Clues: _____

   Guess: _____

   Dictionary: _____

B Antonyms

> Learning words and their **antonyms** helps you build your vocabulary.
>
> For example, if you learn *hot/cold* or *young/old* together, you are more likely to remember them.

Match each word with its antonym. Compare answers with a partner.

_b_ 1. **predispose**   a. aggravate

_e_ 2. **dynamic**   b. averse

_c_ 3. **inhibit**   c. help

_d_ 4. **predominantly**   d. minimally

_a_ 5. **relieve**   e. unchanging

Complete each sentence with the correct vocabulary word or its antonym. Compare answers with a partner.

1. The administration is trying to attract more female students to the college, which

   currently has a _____predominantly_____ male population.

2. Doctors recommend that injured patients get plenty of rest because physical

   activity could _____aggravate_____ an injury.

3. It is a good idea to start reading to children at an early age. It can really

   _____help_____ the development of their vocabulary.

4. Being overweight can _____predispose_____ an individual to serious

   health problems such as diabetes and high blood pressure.

5. Big cities are usually _____dynamic_____ and exciting; however, they

   are stressful for people who have a hard time with change and growth.

In the **sciences and social sciences**, people often create terms using **Greek and Latin roots**. In this way, the terms can be easily understood by scientists who speak different languages.

anthropo- means "man, human"
bacteria- refers to tiny living organisms with a single cell
bio- relates to living things
immuno- relates to the body's ability to fight disease
psycho- refers to the mind
socio- relates to society

-ology means "the study of"
-ologist indicates a person who studies a subject professionally

When you know the meanings of these roots, you can understand the names of certain subjects and professions.

Example: *Anthropologist* combines *anthropo-* and *-ologist*. Using what we know about the roots, we can determine that an anthropologist is someone who studies people.

Complete each sentence with the correct term from the box. Compare answers with a partner.

anthropology	biologist	immunology	sociologist
bacteriologist	biology	psychologist	sociology
bacteriology	immunologist	psychology	

1. A(n) _____immunologist_____ is someone who studies the prevention of disease and how the body reacts to disease.

2. _____psychology_____ is the study of the human mind.

3. _____sociology_____ is the scientific study of people, their societies, cultures, languages, and so on.

4. A(n) _____anthropology_____ studies the behavior of people in groups.

5. A(n) _____biologist_____ is a scientist who studies living things.

6. _____bacteriology_____ is the study of single-celled living organisms.

NOTE-TAKING: Filling in an Outline

Go back to the reading and read it again. Take notes as you read and fill in the outline you created.

The Birth of Personality

I. _Introduction_

    A. _need to learn from others to become human_

    B. _____

    C. _____

II. **Personality**

    A. _____

    B. _____

    C. _____

    D. _____

    E. _____

III. **A Social Product on a Biological Basis**

    A. _____

    B. _____

    C. _____

IV. **Universal Human Needs**

_____

_____

_____

CRITICAL THINKING

Discuss the questions in a small group. Be prepared to share your answers with the class.

1. The reading states that infants who have been left alone without any human companionship, even if their biological needs are attended to, either die or fail to develop normally. Why do you think this is so?

2. According to the reading, our personalities are dynamic, continuously changing and adjusting to events, depending on how the events affect us and how we perceive them. Can we also consciously change our personalities ourselves? Explain your answer.

3. Make a list of the roles you fill in society. For example, you are a student, a classmate, a son or a daughter. You may also be a wife or a husband, a coworker, and so on.

   _____   _____   _____

   _____   _____   _____

   _____   _____   _____

4. Select two of the roles you listed. How does each role affect how you respond to a particular situation? For example, if you are a student and a son/daughter, and you do not do well on an exam, how does your role as student and as a son/daughter affect the way you perceive your poor grade and the way you behave? If you are also a parent, how would your behavior change if your son/daughter reported a poor grade?

LINKING READINGS ONE AND TWO

Discuss the questions in a small group. Be prepared to share your answers with the class.

1. Reading One introduces the concept of socialization as "the process of becoming human, learning societal norms and values while developing a personality unique to each individual." In Reading Two, what factors contribute to the development of each person's distinctive personality?

2. In Reading Two, we learn that humans have a universal need for social and physical contact. What processes did you learn about in Reading One that might be affected by an infant's lack of human contact?

3. How is it that children raised in the same family, within the same society, grow up to "display a variety of attitudes, opinions, beliefs, and values"? Use information from Readings One and Two to support your response.

A Warm-Up

Consider the title of the reading. Work in a small group. Use the questions to guide your discussion. Share your answers with the class.

1. What agents, or causes, of socialization help transform human infants into human beings capable of functioning in society? In a small group, create a list of agents.

   _____parents_____ _____ _____ _____

   _____ _____ _____ _____

2. As a class, write all the agents you have listed on the board. Then arrange them in order of importance as agents of socialization. Which one do you think has the most influence? The second most influence?

   _____ _____ _____ _____

   _____ _____ _____ _____

B Reading Strategy

Creating Questions to Increase Understanding

Use **titles and headings** to help you prepare for reading a text by **changing them into questions**. For example, change the title "Agents of Socialization" into a question:

  What are some agents of socialization?

After you read the text, you will be asked to answer the questions you created.

Go through the reading and write questions for each heading. Write a new question for the title. Compare questions with a partner.

Title: _____

1. _____

2. _____

3. _____

4. _____

5. _____

Now read the text. As you read, underline the answers to the questions you wrote for the title and each heading.

Agents of Socialization

By John A. Perry and Erna K. Perry

1   Specific people, groups, and organizations are chiefly responsible for transforming a raw bundle of tissues and nerves into a **functioning** human being, knowledgeable in the ways of society, competent in enough skills to survive and sometimes to thrive and excel in the society, and with features and traits familiar to others yet still recognizably unique.

The Family

2   The foremost socializers are the people who raise the newborn. Barring unusual circumstances, in most societies these people are generally the infant's parents. Thus, most socialization occurs within the family. The role of the family in socialization is crucial. First, the family influences the child in its earliest stage of development, when the child is most **receptive**. It meets all of the child's needs, both physical and emotional. It is a constant influence because most people maintain family relationships from infancy into adulthood. The family is also a primary group, and the personal and **emotional ties** are conducive to effective socialization. The family, finally, provides the new individual with his or her first identity, as the infant is born into a particular racial group, religion, and social class.

3   Although parents try to teach, guide, influence, and control the behavior of their children, the latter are not merely clay in parental hands. Socialization, in fact, is reciprocal. The way infants look and act has a bearing on how parents feel and act toward them. And even the most helpless infant can **initiate** interaction simply by crying. Infants who obtain a positive response to the crying—who are picked up, cuddled, and comforted—receive a different view of the world and their position in it than infants whose crying is ignored.

4   Parental behavior varies in each family. It also has been shown to vary according to social class and even to race and **ethnicity**. For instance, in African-American families and among Afro-Caribbean immigrants, child rearing appears to be the responsibility of a **wider range** of relatives than among white families. In addition, because of the **changing nature** of the family, many children are being reared by single parents or in households that combine children from previous marriages or by same-sex parents. As a result, socialization experiences are varied.

The School

5   Second to the family, the school acts as a powerful agent of socialization. It is the first formal agency charged with the task of socializing children and represents the first link, or connection, to the **wider society**. In school, children must learn not only basic skills needed in the society but also the hidden curriculum of how to cope successfully in a competitive

environment. American schools have often been hotbeds of **controversy** (e.g., school prayer, the decline in standards), probably because they are recognized as being such important socializing agents.

6   Many children are becoming **acquainted** with a type of school much earlier than children did in the past. Day care centers have become necessities as increasing numbers of women have joined the workforce. Such centers are by no means sufficiently numerous to meet the demand, nor are they free from controversy. Many Americans are against them on the basis that a child's own mother is the best socializing agent for the child. This has not always been found to be true: many women are, in fact, better mothers when their lives are focused on things other than house and family exclusively. In addition, research has shown that when children from stable families attend high-quality day care centers (in which the ratio of staff to children is one to three for infants and no higher than one to six for toddlers), their intellectual development is neither helped nor **hindered** to any great extent, though their ability to interact with others is increased.

The Peer Group

7   Of increasing importance in American society, where school-age children spend more time with their friends than they do with their parents, is the peer group. Socialization within the peer group takes place informally and **unintentionally**. In addition, activities within the peer group tend to be strictly pleasurable, unlike those in school and in the family, which involve work as well as fun. Membership is voluntary, again unlike the situation in the family or school, and members treat each other as equals without having to answer to those higher in authority. All these factors explain the attraction of the peer group and its great influence on the individual. Finally, the peer group offers a source of identification: adolescents especially turn to their peers to learn what kinds of people they are.

The Media

8   One of the most powerful sources of socialization, equaling the socializing influence of the peer group and in many instances surpassing that of school and family, is the influence of the *mass media*. Newspapers, magazines, radio, the Internet, and most especially television have infiltrated every American home to the point where characters from the innumerable TV shows are much more familiar to people, especially to children, than any other heroes or villains past or present. The amount of time spent watching television and the quality of the entertainment presented (centering on sex and violence) have been blamed for **inciting** criminal and delinquent behavior as well as for the decreasing level of taste and general knowledge of the population. However, no simple cause-and-effect relationships have ever been unfailingly established, although there are definite factors pointing to the negative influence of television as a socializing agent.

Occupational Groups

9   The role of occupational groups or organizations as socializing agents cannot be ignored. The experience provided by such groups is termed

(continued on next page)

specialized or occupational socialization, and it consists, basically, of training to fit a particular occupational role: that of clergyman or labor-union public relations official or corporate executive. The successfully socialized individual eventually displays personality traits that reflect the needs of the occupational role: **conformity**, cooperation, team orientation, and so on.

With a partner, compare the answers you underlined. Discuss how writing questions and then identifying answers to the questions helped you understand the text.

COMPREHENSION

A **Main Ideas**

Match each socializing agent with the correct description. Compare answers with a partner.

c _____ 1. **the family**

d _____ 2. **the school**

a _____ 3. **the peer group**

e _____ 4. **the media**

b _____ 5. **occupational groups**

a. organizes informal activities, which tend to be strictly pleasurable, and members treat each other as equals

b. influences certain personality traits that reflect the needs of the job, for example, conformity, cooperation, and team orientation

c. influences the child in its earliest stage of development, meets all of the child's physical and emotional needs, and is a constant influence

d. teaches basic skills needed in the society as well as the hidden curriculum of how to cope successfully in a competitive environment

e. introduces characters and situations that some say incite criminal and delinquent behavior

B **Close Reading**

Read the quotes from the reading. Circle the statement that best explains each quote. Discuss your answers with a partner.

1. "[The family] meets all of the child's needs, both physical and emotional." *(paragraph 2)*

    a. When we are children, we are entirely dependent on our family.

    b. When we are children, we meet all the members of our family.

    c. When we are children, we have certain specific needs.

2. "Parental behavior varies in each family. It also has been shown to vary according to social class and even to race and ethnicity. In addition, many children are being reared by single parents or in households that combine children from previous marriages or by same-sex parents. As a result, socialization experiences are varied." *(paragraph 4)*

   a. Socialization among families is usually very similar.

   b. Socialization within families differs from family to family.

   c. Socialization is better among some families than among others.

3. "Second to the family, the school acts as a powerful agent of socialization. It is the first formal agency charged with the task of socializing children and represents the first link, or connection, to the wider society." *(paragraph 5)*

   a. The school is the most important agent of socialization.

   b. The school is the second most important agent of socialization.

   c. The school connects families and children.

4. "Day care centers have become necessities as increasing numbers of women have joined the workforce. Such centers are by no means sufficiently numerous to meet the demand." *(paragraph 6)*

   a. There are increasing numbers of women who work in day care centers, but not enough day care centers to meet the need.

   b. There are definitely sufficient day care centers to meet the demand as more and more women join the workforce.

   c. There are definitely not sufficient day care centers to meet the demand.

5. "One of the most powerful sources of socialization, equaling the socializing influence of the peer group and in many instances surpassing that of school and family, is the influence of the mass media." *(paragraph 8)*

   a. The socializing influence of mass media is equal to the socializing influence of the school.

   b. The socializing influence of mass media is equal to the socializing influence of the family.

   c. The socializing influence of mass media is equal to the socializing influence of the peer group.

6. "The role of occupational groups or organizations as socializing agents cannot be ignored. . . . The successfully socialized individual eventually displays personality traits that reflect the needs of the occupational role: conformity, cooperation, team orientation, and so on." *(paragraph 9)*

   When a person is socialized into a particular occupation, that individual

   a. develops the characteristics that the role requires

   b. displays the characteristics of conformity and cooperation

   c. becomes a team member in that particular occupation

Collocations

Collocations refer to word partners or words that are often used together. These pairs of words appear in texts often and sound natural together.

Changing, emotional, and *wider* appear in the reading. Each of these words has several collections.

EXAMPLES:

changing attitudes   emotional impact
changing circumstances   emotional intelligence
changing needs   emotional reaction
changing world   emotional support

wider audience
wider context
wider implications
wider range

Complete each sentence with the appropriate collocation from the box above. Compare answers with a partner.

1. Because the children were used to being in plays in their classroom, they were comfortable performing for a(n) _____wider audience_____ when they performed before the entire school population.

2. Most people know that sad experiences can deeply affect them. However, they often don't realize the _emotional impact_____ of positive experiences.

3. We live in a(n) _changing world_____. Technological advances, improvements in medical care, and societal changes are all happening at a faster and faster pace.

4. Even as adults, people mature, gain experience, and develop _changing attitudes_____ about other people and the world around them.

5. The new law seems to be very clear and simple, but it has _wider implications_____ for society as a whole.

6. When someone experiences a crisis in his or her life, such as the illness of a loved one, _emotional support_____ becomes very important.

7. As children grow up, parents respond to their _changing needs_.

   Older children can feed and dress themselves, but they still require assistance

   with their homework.

8. The _emotional reaction_ that children form with their parents and

   siblings are a critical part of their socialization.

9. After family and school, children move on to the _wider context_

   of peer groups and occupational groups.

B Synonyms

Read the sentences from the reading. Match each word or phrase in bold with its synonym in the box below. Compare answers with a partner.

_b_ 1. Even the most helpless infant can **initiate** interaction simply by crying.

_f_ 2. The amount of time spent watching television and the quality of the
entertainment presented (centering on sex and violence) have been blamed
for **inciting** criminal and delinquent behavior.

_e_ 3. Specific people, groups, and organizations are chiefly responsible for
transforming a raw bundle of tissues and nerves into a **functioning** human
being, knowledgeable in the ways of society.

_a_ 4. Socialization within the peer group takes place informally and
unintentionally.

_c_ 5. American schools have often been hotbeds of **controversy** (e.g., school
prayer, the decline in standards), probably because they are recognized as
being such important socializing agents.

_d_ 6. When children from stable families attend high-quality day care centers
(in which the ratio of staff to children is one to three for infants and no
higher than one to six for toddlers), their intellectual development is neither
helped nor **hindered** to any great extent.

a. accidentally	**d.** impeded
b. begin	**e.** operating
c. dispute	**f.** triggering

C Word Forms

Fill in the chart with the correct word forms. Use a dictionary if necessary. An *X* indicates there is no form in that category.

	NOUN	VERB	ADJECTIVE	ADVERB
1.	acquaintance	acquaint	acquainted	X
2.	conformity	conform	conformable	X
3.	controversy	X	controversial	
4.	emotion	X	emotional	emotionly
5.	ethnicity	X	ethnic	ethricly
6.	reception	X	receptive	receptively

Complete the sentences with the correct form of one of the words above. Be sure to use the correct tense of the verbs and the singular or plural form of the nouns. Compare answers with a partner.

1. The students in the beginning-level English class represent a variety of

   _____ethnic_____ backgrounds.

2. Depending on their experiences, humans may feel a variety of different

   _____ throughout the day.

3. The university psychology professor has been caught up in a major

   _____ over the results of his recent research. His findings

   have angered many people.

4. Most colleges hold an orientation for new students. College personnel

   _____ the students with the school and its facilities.

5. When people enter the armed forces, they _____ to very

   strict rules.

6. The speaker was pleased by the crowd's _____. They were

   very interested in listening to what he had to say.

NOTE-TAKING: Creating a Chart to Summarize Information from a Text

Complete the chart to organize the detailed information in the reading. Compare answers with a partner.

Agent	What This Agent Provides the Individual	How This Agent Influences the Individual
the family	It provides for all the child's physical and emotional needs.	It helps form the child's first identity, the child's view of the world, and the child's position in it.
school		
the peer group		
the media		
occupational group		

CRITICAL THINKING

Discuss the questions in a small group. Be prepared to share your answers with the class.

1. The reading presents a few examples of how school can help connect children to the wider society. What additional examples can you think of?

2. The reading states that the mass media may sometimes surpass the family as a socializing influence. How might this powerful source of socialization be used in a positive manner?

3. What might happen at a job when one person fails to successfully socialize? What kinds of problems might arise?

BRINGING IT ALL TOGETHER

Discuss the questions in a small group. Then share your group's answers with the class. Use the vocabulary you studied in the chapter (for a complete list, go to page 29).

1. Reading One defines *socialization* as the process of learning the norms and values of society as an individual grows up. Work in a small group. Select a specific value, such as honesty, respect for others, or punctuality. Discuss how each of you learned this value. Describe when you exhibit this value. Are your experiences in learning this value and the way you exhibit this value the same for everyone in the group? Why or why not?

2. According to Reading Two, "Research to date seems to indicate that personality development occurs as a consequence of the interplay of biological inheritance, physical environment, culture, group experience, and personal experience." How might the interaction of these factors have affected an aspect of your personality?

3. Reading Two points out the human need for social and physical contact, and that it may be interpreted as a need to receive and give love. Review the agents of socialization you read about in Reading Three. Do all these agents help fulfill this need to receive and give love? If so, in what ways? If not, why not?

WRITING ACTIVITY

Write a short composition in which you describe what it means to become human. In the first paragraph, write what human beings experience as they become human. In the second paragraph, describe what influences human beings in their process of becoming human. In the third paragraph, tell a brief anecdote (story) about one of your own experiences in becoming human.

DISCUSSION AND WRITING TOPICS

Discuss these topics in a small group. Choose one of them and write a paragraph or two about it. Use the vocabulary from the chapter.

1. The media are a very powerful source of socialization today. Think of recent or past events in the news where the media have had a powerful influence on people's actions. Select one event and write about how the media influenced people to act in a certain way.

2. According to Reading Three, "Socialization, in fact, is reciprocal. The way infants look and act has a bearing on how parents feel and act toward them." Write about specific ways that infants behave that influence how their parents feel and respond to them. Provide examples from your own experiences and observations.

3. We all develop unique personalities as we grow up. Even identical twins who grow up together develop distinctive personalities. How does this happen?

VOCABULARY

Nouns	Verbs	Adjectives	Adverbs
anthropologist	engage in	acquainted (with)	dramatically*
appearance	incite	distinctive*	predominantly*
changing nature	hinder	dynamic*	unintentionally
conformity*	inhibit*	functioning*	
controversy*	initiate*	indeterminate	
drive	neglect	receptive	
emotional ties	predispose	surrogate	
ethnicity*	proceed*		
manner	relieve		
maturation*			
norms*			
socialization			
trait			
wider range			
wider society			

* = AWL (Academic Word List) item

SELF-ASSESSMENT

In this chapter you learned to:

○ Preview a text and activate background knowledge

○ Use headings to create an outline and fill in the outline with details from the text

○ Create questions from the title and headings of a text to increase understanding

○ Guess the meaning of words from the context

○ Use dictionary entries to learn different meanings of words

○ Use *one* as an impersonal pronoun

○ Understand and use synonyms, antonyms, font styles, collocations, roots, and different word forms

○ Create a chart and write notes to summarize information from a text

What can you do well? ☑

What do you need to practice more? ☑

CHAPTER 2

ART HISTORY:
Origins of Modern Art

ART HISTORY: The academic study of the historical development of the visual arts

OBJECTIVES

To read academic texts, you need to master certain skills.

In this chapter, you will:

- Use visuals to enhance understanding

- Paraphrase sentences to increase comprehension

- Highlight important information in a reading

- Recognize referents

- Guess the meaning of words from the context, categorize words, and understand word usage

- Use dictionary entries to learn different meanings of words

- Understand and use synonyms, antonyms, collocations, and different word forms

- Use note-taking to chart differences and to consolidate information from readings

Vase on a Console, Eugène Delacroix, 1848–1849

Consider These Questions

Discuss the questions in a small group. Share your answers with the class.

1. What is your concept of *art*? Write a definition of *art*.

2. Consider this definition of *art history*: "the academic study of the historical development of the visual arts." Why is it important to understand styles of art from previous centuries, for example, 19th-century art?

3. When a new style of art is developed, people sometimes find it difficult to accept. Why do you think people might react this way?

READING ONE: Breaking with Tradition: The Beginnings of Impressionism

Ⓐ Warm-Up

Discuss the questions in a small group.

1. Why would artists reject a traditional, accepted style of painting and choose to paint in a totally different way, knowing that their work might not be accepted and that they might not be able to sell their paintings?

2. What do you know about Impressionist art and artists? Do you like Impressionist art? Why or why not?

Ⓑ Reading Strategy

Using Visuals to Enhance Understanding

Many texts include **illustrations, maps, photographs, charts, graphs,** and **art images.** These visuals help you to **understand information** in all types of texts. When you read art history texts, visuals are essential because they will help you understand artists, art movements, and how art changes over time.

Look at the art images in the reading. Then choose the correct answers.

1. What phrases best describe Jacques-Louis David's painting on page 32? Check (✓) all that apply.

   ☐ **a.** a historical scene

   ☐ **b.** an everyday scene

   ☐ **c.** a painting that shows the artist's skills

   ☐ **d.** a painting that shows the artist's feelings

   ☐ **e.** accurate in its details

   ☐ **f.** not accurate in its details

   ☐ **g.** a painting of a famous person

   ☐ **h.** a painting of a person who is not famous

(continued on next page)

2. What phrases best describe Claude Monet's painting on page 33? Check (✓) all that apply.

☐ **a.** a historical scene

☐ **b.** an everyday scene

☐ **c.** a painting that shows the artist's skills in painting details

☐ **d.** a painting that shows the artist's feelings

☐ **e.** accurate in its details

☐ **f.** not accurate in its details

☐ **g.** a painting of a famous person

☐ **h.** a painting of a person who is not famous

Now read the text and refer to the images of David's and Monet's paintings to help you understand what you are reading.

Breaking with Tradition: The Beginnings of Impressionism

Napoléon Crossing the Alps,
Jacques-Louis David, 1801

1   As you saw with David's painting *Napoléon Crossing the Alps*, art was very **representational**. That is, it was very true to life. Traditional art also usually **depicted** scenes from history or mythology.[1] Artists had the opportunity to demonstrate their skills, but they were not expected to paint how they felt. This tradition is what the Impressionists challenged with their new style of art.

2   "If one wants to **characterize** them with a single word that explains their efforts, one would have to create the term of Impressionists. They are Impressionists in the sense that they render not a landscape but the **impression** produced by a landscape." Jules Castagnary, in *Le Siècle*, April 29, 1874

3   In 1874, a group of artists got together and dared to risk it all. Frustrated by the strict rules of composition and subject matter imposed by academic institutions, these artists decided to free themselves to **pursue** their own ideas and mount their own exhibition. This was the first independent group show of Impressionist art. Calling themselves *Société anonyme*, these artists' impressionist art was considered shocking, unfinished, and insulting. With their daring color and quick brushstrokes, these **revolutionary** paintings were a **radical** departure from tradition.

---

[1] *Mythology:* a body of ancient stories, especially those invented to explain natural or historical events

4   The Impressionists painted everyday scenes from the world we know rather than following traditional religious, historical, or mythological subjects. They painted real life landscapes as they saw them and *without* **idealization**. They were not concerned with a **meticulous** finish and applied their paint with quick, **spontaneous** brushstrokes. In their attempts to capture the **fleeting** moment and the ways in which objects reflect or absorb light, Monet, Renoir, Manet, Pissarro, and others have created a new and brilliantly vivacious world on canvas; they have also influenced the work of their friends, most notably Cézanne, Degas, and Van Gogh.

5   Claude Monet (1840–1926) spoke often about Impressionist painting. He once said, "When you go out to paint, try to forget what object you have before you—a tree, a house, a field, or whatever. Merely think, here is a little square of blue, here an oblong of pink, here a streak of yellow, and paint it just as it looks to you, the exact color and shape, until it **emerges** as your own naive impression of the scene before you."

Woman with a Parasol, Turned to the Left,
Claude Monet, 1886

6   The Impressionists risked everything by breaking away from tradition. Against harsh criticism and negative reviews, they pursued a desire to create a fresh way of looking at things and a new kind of painting that reflected a modern way of life. They struggled against poverty and **hostility**, but their perseverance paid off, and they were rewarded with the recognition they deserved. This new, revolutionary movement changed the very nature of the way people think about art. Impressionism **liberated** other artists from the strict rules of composition, subject matter, and **technique** and set them free to paint what they wanted and follow their own ideas and talents. The masterworks of the Impressionists have become the most widely loved and admired paintings of the past hundred years.

Discuss how the images of artists' work help you understand traditional art, Impressionist art, and the differences between them.

COMPREHENSION

A Main Ideas

Read each statement. Decide if it is *True* or *False* according to the reading. Check (✓) the appropriate box. If it is false, change it to make it true. Discuss your answers with a partner.

	TRUE	FALSE
1. The first Impressionist artists did not want to be restricted to certain art subjects like history or mythology.	☐	☐
2. When people first saw Impressionist art, they strongly disliked it.	☐	☐
3. The first Impressionist artists painted with realistic detail.	☐	☐
4. The Impressionist artists painted historical or mythological subjects.	☐	☐
5. The Impressionist artists often painted colors and shapes without a finished look.	☐	☐
6. The Impressionists' art style was so different that it was never recognized or accepted.	☐	☐

B Close Reading

Read each statement. Circle the correct answer. Compare answers with a partner.

1. The Impressionists rejected painting in a traditional style because
    a. they didn't understanding history or mythology.
    b. they wanted to show their art in exhibits.
    c. they didn't want to follow established rules.

2. The Impressionists' work was considered shocking, unfinished, and insulting because
    a. it was so different from traditional art.
    b. it was painted too quickly.
    c. it involved using bright colors.

3. We can understand from Claude Monet's advice to painters that
    a. he liked to use only three colors.
    b. he was more interested in colors and shapes than details.
    c. he liked to paint only outdoor scenes.

4. By breaking away from tradition, the Impressionists took the chance that

    a. they would not be able to paint the way they wanted.

    b. they would never be successful artists.

    c. they would immediately be seen as heroes in the art world.

VOCABULARY

Ⓐ Guessing from Context

Read each quote from the reading. Try to guess the meaning of the word in bold from the context. Write the clues that helped you guess and your guess. Then consult a dictionary and write the definition. Compare answers with a partner.

1. "If one wants to **characterize** them with a single word that explains their efforts, one would have to create the term of Impressionists." *(paragraph 2)*

    Clues: _a single word that explains_

    Guess: _describe_

    Dictionary: _describe the qualities of someone or something in a particular way_

2. "They are Impressionists in the sense that they render not a landscape but the **impression** produced by a landscape." *(paragraph 2)*

    Clues: _____

    Guess: _____

    Dictionary: _____

3. "Calling themselves *Société anonyme*, these artists' impressionist art was considered shocking, unfinished, and insulting. With their daring color and quick brushstrokes, these revolutionary paintings were a **radical** departure from tradition." *(paragraph 3)*

    Clues: _____

    Guess: _____

    Dictionary: _____

4. "Against harsh criticism and negative reviews, they pursued a desire to create a fresh way of looking at things and a new kind of painting that reflected a modern way of life. They struggled against poverty and **hostility**, but their perseverance paid off, and they were rewarded with the recognition they deserved." *(paragraph 6)*

    Clues: _____

    Guess: _____

    Dictionary: _____

(continued on next page)

5. "Impressionism **liberated** other artists from the strict rules of composition, subject matter, and technique and set them free to paint what they wanted and follow their own ideas and talents." (*paragraph 6*)

Clues: _____

Guess: _____

Dictionary: _____

6. "Impressionism liberated other artists from the strict rules of composition, subject matter, and **technique** and set them free to paint what they wanted and follow their own ideas and talents." (*paragraph 6*)

Clues: _____

Guess: _____

Dictionary: _____

B Categorizing Words

Work with a partner. Put the words in the box into the appropriate category according to whether they relate to traditional or Impressionist art.

idealization	meticulous	representational	spontaneous
liberate	radical	revolutionary	

TRADITIONAL ART	IMPRESSIONIST ART

ⓒ Synonyms

Read the sentences. Match each word in bold with its synonym in the box below. Compare answers with a partner.

_____ 1. The Impressionists' paintings **depicted** ordinary people in real-life scenes.

_____ 2. Monet, Renoir, Manet, and other artists rejected the rules of traditional art and decided to **pursue** their own artistic ideas.

_____ 3. For Impressionists, a painting only appears unfinished. It invites the viewer to enter the painting and look at it until a scene **emerges** as a complete picture.

_____ 4. More than any of the other Impressionists, Claude Monet was very aware of the **fleeting** moment created by sunlight as it changes throughout the day.

_____ 5. The first Impressionist exhibition took place in 1874. The people who came to see the paintings displayed **hostility** against the artists and their work.

a. appears	**d.** showed
b. opposition	**e.** temporary
c. follow	

GRAMMAR FOR READING

Recognizing Referents

Referents are the **people, things, or ideas that pronouns and determiners represent.** When you recognize referents, you connect the meaning of one idea to another. Pronouns such as *we, it, they, their, them,* and *others* and determiners including *this* and *these* appear in the reading.

EXAMPLE:
As you saw with David's painting *Napoléon Crossing the Alps,* traditional art was very representational. That is, **it** was very true to life.

In this example, **it** refers to traditional art.

Read the sentences. Then write the correct referent on the line. Compare answers with a partner.

1. Artists had the opportunity to demonstrate their skills, but **they** were not expected to paint how they felt.

   they: _artists_

2. Frustrated by the strict rules of composition and subject matter imposed by academic institutions, these artists decided to free themselves to pursue their own ideas and mount their own exhibition. **This** was the first independent group show of Impressionist art.

   this: _____

(continued on next page)

3. With **their** daring color and quick brushstrokes, these revolutionary paintings were a radical departure from tradition.

   their: _____

4. In **their** attempts to capture the fleeting moment and the ways in which objects reflect or absorb light, Monet, Renoir, Manet, Pissarro, and others have created a new and brilliantly vivacious world on canvas; they have also influenced the work of their friends, most notably Cézanne, Degas, and Van Gogh.

   their: _____

5. "When you go out to paint, try to forget what object you have before you—a tree, a house, a field, or whatever. Merely think, here is a little square of blue, here an oblong of pink, here a streak of yellow, and paint it just as it looks to you, the exact color and shape, until **it** emerges as your own naive impression of the scene before you."

   it: _____

NOTE-TAKING: Charting Differences

Go back to the reading and read it again. List the differences between traditional art as it was practiced before the Impressionist movement, and Impressionist art.

DIFFERENCES BETWEEN TRADITIONAL ART AND IMPRESSIONIST ART	
TRADITIONAL ART	IMPRESSIONIST ART
• depicts famous people	• depicts ordinary people
•	•
•	•
•	•
•	•

CRITICAL THINKING

Discuss the questions in a small group. Be prepared to share your answers with the class.

1. Look at the images of Delacroix's, David's, and Monet's paintings on pages 30, 32, and 33. What would people who were used to meticulous, representational art have found shocking about Delacroix's and Monet's work? Why would people have felt insulted by an artist presenting such work to the public?

2. The Impressionists experienced poverty, hostility, and rejection. However, they continued to pursue their style. What do you think helped them continue in their efforts in spite of such difficult conditions?

READING TWO: Post-Impressionism

Ⓐ Warm-Up

Discuss the questions in a small group.

1. Examine the image below and the one on page 30. Although they are both paintings of flowers, they are very different. How do the artists' paintings differ? Why do you think their styles are so different?

2. How is Cézanne's style similar to that of the Impressionists'? How is it different?

The Blue Vase, Paul Cézanne, 1885–1887

Paraphrasing for Comprehension

A **paraphrase** is a **shorter restatement** of something someone has written. When we paraphrase, we use our own words to express the general idea of what we are reading, but are careful not to copy the original text.

In the reading, the artist Cézanne describes what he believes all artists must do and what he tries to do in his own work.

EXAMPLE:
Cézanne's words:
"Nature is always the same, and yet its appearance is always changing."

Paraphrase:
Nature doesn't change, but it never looks the same.

Read the first excerpt from the reading and write a paraphrase. Compare your paraphrase with a partner.

WHAT CÉZANNE SAID	WHAT YOU THINK HE MEANS
It is our business as artists to convey the thrill of nature's permanence along with the elements and the appearance of all its changes.	**1.**
Cézanne quickly grasped the nature of the Manet revolution as well, but he did not share his fellow Impressionists' interest in "slice-of-life" subjects, in movement, and in change. Instead, his goal was "to make of Impressionism something solid and durable, like the art of the museums."	**2.**
The pure blue smell of pine, which is sharp in the sun, ought to blend with the fresh green smell of meadows in the morning, and with the smell of stones and the distant marble smell of Sainte-Victoire. I have not achieved that effect. It must be achieved, and achieved through the colors, not by literary means.	**3.**
Nature's stirrings are resolved, deep down in one's brain, into a movement sensed equally by our eyes, our ears, our mouth, and our nose, each with its special kind of poetry.	**4.**

Now read the text. Then return to the chart and write paraphrases of the remainder of the excerpts from the reading.

Post-Impressionism

By H. W. Janson and Anthony F. Janson

The Mont Sainte-Victoire, Paul Cézanne, 1904–1906

1 The Impressionist art movement effectively began in France in the early 1860s. Edouard Manet is considered the "Father of Impressionism," and Impressionist artists included Edgar Degas, Claude Monet, Pierre Auguste Renoir, Frédéric Bazille, among others. Their work is **characterized** by quick brushstrokes and less detail than the work of previous painters. By the later part of the 19th century, painting had developed further, into what has become known as Post-Impressionist painting.

2 By 1882, Impressionism had gained wide acceptance among artists and the public—but, by the same token, it was no longer a **pioneering** movement. When the Impressionists held their last group show (in 1886), the future already belonged to the "Post-Impressionists." This colorless label **designates** a group of artists who passed through an Impressionist phase in the 1880s but became dissatisfied with the style and **pursued** a variety of directions. Because they did not have a common goal, it is difficult to find a more descriptive term for them than Post-Impressionists. They certainly were not "anti-Impressionists." Far from trying to undo the effects of the "Manet revolution," they wanted to carry it further. Thus Post-Impressionism is in essence just a later stage, though a very important one, of the development that had begun in the 1860s.

3 Paul Cézanne (1839–1906) was the oldest of the Post-Impressionists . . . . . A man of **intensely** emotional **temperament**, Cézanne went to Paris in 1861 imbued with enthusiasm for the Romantics.[1] Delacroix was his first love among painters, and he never lost his **admiration** for him. Cézanne quickly grasped the nature of the Manet revolution as well, but he did not share his fellow Impressionists' interest in "slice-of-life" subjects, in movement, and in change. Instead, his goal was "to make of Impressionism something solid and **durable**, like the art of the museums." This quest, or search, for the "solid and durable" can be seen in Cézanne's still lifes,[2] such as *Still Life with Apples.* The ornamental backdrop is **integrated** with the three-dimensional[3] shapes, and the brushstrokes have a rhythmic pattern that gives the canvas its shimmering texture.

4 [*Joachim Gasquet had been a friend of Cézanne's for a time. Gasquet published conversations he said he had had with Cézanne. Although later critics say Gasquet added to these conversations, they do give an idea of what Cézanne thought about art. Below is an excerpt from Gasquet's book in which he quotes from interviews with Cézanne.*]

(continued on next page)

---

[1] **Romantics:** artists of the Romantic period. This artistic and literary movement lasted from approximately 1800 to 1840. Delacroix was a Romantic painter.

[2] **Still life:** a painting or photograph of an arrangement of objects, especially flowers and fruit

[3] **three-dimensional:** having or seeming to have length, depth, and height

What He Told Me

By Joachim Gasquet

5   Nature is always the same, and yet its **appearance** is always changing. It is our business as artists to convey the thrill of nature's **permanence** along with the elements and the appearance of all its changes. Painting must give us the **flavor** of nature's eternity. Everything, you understand. So I join together nature's straying hands. From all sides, here there and everywhere. I select colors, tones, and shades; I set them down, I bring them together. They make lines. They become objects—rocks, trees—without my thinking about them. They take on **volume**, value. If, as I perceive them, these volumes and values **correspond** on my canvas to the planes and patches of color that lie before me, that appear to my eyes, well, then, my canvas "joins hands." It holds firm.

6   (Looking at Cézanne's painting of pine trees with Mont Sainte-Victoire in the distance:) The pure blue smell of pine, which is sharp in the sun, ought to blend with the fresh green smell of meadows in the morning, and with the smell of stones and the distant marble smell of Sainte-Victoire. I have not achieved that effect. It must be achieved, and achieved through the colors, not by literary means. Whenever sensation is at its fullest, it harmonizes with the whole of creation. Nature's stirrings are **resolved**, deep down in one's brain, into a movement sensed equally by our eyes, our ears, our mouth, and our nose, each with its special kind of poetry. And art puts us, I believe, in a state of grace in which we experience a universal emotion in an, as it were, religious but at the same time perfectly natural way. General **harmony**, such as we find in color, is located all around us.

Compare the paraphrases you wrote with those of a classmate. If a classmate wrote different paraphrases, discuss why you think there were differences.

COMPREHENSION

Ⓐ Main Ideas

Check (✓) the statements that best express the main ideas in the reading. Discuss your answers with a partner.

☐ 1. Cézanne hoped to create paintings that would be placed in museums.

☐ 2. The Post-Impressionists, including Paul Cézanne, were unhappy with the older Impressionist style of painting.

☐ 3. Post-Impressionism represents a clear break from Impressionism.

☐ 4. Cézanne did not care for Delacroix's work.

☐ 5. Post-Impressionism represents a later stage of Impressionism.

☐ 6. Post-Impressionists, including Paul Cézanne, tried to make viewers see nature as eternal.

☐ 7. Post-Impressionism tried to undo the effects of the "Manet revolution."

☐ 8. Cézanne hoped to express nature so viewers could experience it through their senses.

B Close Reading

Read each statement. Circle the correct answer. Compare answers with a partner.

1. What best characterizes the move from Impressionism to Post-Impressionism?

   a. a focus on the senses rather than on bright colors

   b. a radical shift involving rejection of Impressionism

   c. a developmental change from Impressionism to Post-Impressionism

2. How does Cézanne describe how he paints nature?

   a. He makes an outline of a scene in nature, then fills it in with colors.

   b. He paints without thinking about what he's doing.

   c. He chooses his colors, brings the colors together, and creates objects.

3. What is Cézanne most concerned with in his art?

   a. having the viewer of his art use his/her senses

   b. creating something solid and durable

   c. improving on Impressionism

VOCABULARY

A Synonyms

Work with a partner. Read the text again and discuss the meanings of the words in bold. Then cross out the word or phrase that is not a synonym for the word in bold.

1. **durable**	long-lasting	valuable	enduring	permanent
2. **flavor**	quality	mood	impression	food
3. **integrate**	cross	combine	join	incorporate
4. **temperament**	character	nature	anger	personality
5. **volume**	liquid	dimension	body	mass

B Using the Dictionary

Read the dictionary entries and the sentences that follow. Then match the number of the definition with the appropriate sentence. Compare answers with a partner.

> **harmony** *n.* **1** notes of music combined together in a pleasant way **2** a situation in which people live or work together without fighting or disagreeing with each other **3** agreement with another idea, feeling, etc. **4** the pleasant effect made by different things that form an attractive whole

1.

_____ **a.** General harmony, such as we find in color, is located all around us.

_____ **b.** Monet valued the quality of light and believed that he painted light rather than objects. His artwork was in harmony with his philosophy.

_____ **c.** The musicians created a wonderful harmony at the concert last night.

_____ **d.** Cézanne was a difficult man to get along with. He did not paint with other artists because he could not work in harmony with others.

> **resolve** *v.* **1** to find a satisfactory way of dealing with a problem **2** to make a definite decision to do something **3** to make a formal decision, especially by voting **4** to gradually change into something else, especially by becoming clearer

2.

_____ **a.** Monet's paintings were rejected so often by the official salon that he resolved never to submit a painting there again.

_____ **b.** Nature's stirrings are resolved, deep down in one's brain, into a movement sensed equally by our eyes, our ears, our mouth, and our nose, each with its special kind of poetry.

_____ **c.** In a vote of nine to one, the members of the Art Committee resolved to open committee membership to all who apply.

_____ **d.** The Impressionists decided to resolve their problem of not having their work exhibited by renting space and putting on an exhibit of their own.

C Word Forms

Fill in the chart with the correct word forms. Use a dictionary if necessary. An *X* indicates there is no form in that category.

	NOUN	VERB	ADJECTIVE	ADVERB
1.	admiration			
2.		correspond		
3.		designate		X
4.				intensely
5.	permanence	X		
6.			pioneering	X

Complete the sentences with the correct form of one of the words above. Be sure to use the correct tense of the verbs in the affirmative or negative and the singular or plural form of the nouns. Compare answers with a partner.

1. The _____ Post-Impressionist was not one Cézanne applied to his own work.

2. Although Monet is often given credit as the first Impressionist painter, other artists were true _____ in this movement as well.

3. The label on this painting does not _____ to the information in my art book. The label says "by Manet," but my book says "by Renoir."

4. The exhibit on the second floor of this museum is temporary, but the exhibit in this room is _____. It will always be here for people to see.

5. The _____ of Cézanne's emotions often made him difficult to deal with.

6. The art critic likes all the Impressionists' work, but the artist she _____ the most is Edgar Degas.

CRITICAL THINKING

Discuss the questions in a small group. Be prepared to share your answers with the class.

1. Cézanne described how he used colors and shapes to create a painting. Examine *The Blue Vase* on page 39 and the view of Mont Sainte-Victoire on page 41. Does Cézanne achieve his goal? Explain your reasons for your response. Do the colors and shapes serve to inform the viewer?

2. A 21st-century artist noted that in a composition different colors are used as words, and a painter's palette is similar to a vocabulary. Would Cézanne agree with this opinion? Why or why not?

3. When Cézanne talked about the painting on page 41, he observed, "The pure blue smell of pine, which is sharp in the sun, ought to blend with the fresh green smell of meadows in the morning, and with the smell of stones and the distant marble smell of Sainte-Victoire." What was he trying to communicate by describing a painting in terms of the sense of smell?

LINKING READINGS ONE AND TWO

Discuss the questions in a small group. Be prepared to share your answers with the class.

1. Read the quotes from Manet, Monet, Degas, and Cézanne. These Impressionist/ Post-Impressionist artists all describe art in terms of other senses besides sight. What are they trying to communicate to us?

   It is not enough to know your craft—you have to have feeling.
   —*Edouard Manet (1830–1883)*

   I would like to paint the way a bird sings.
   —*Claude Monet (1840–1926)*

   The air we breathe in the paintings of the Old Masters[1] is never the air we breathe.
   —*Edgar Degas (1834–1917)*

   For an Impressionist to paint from nature is not to paint the subject, but to realize sensations.
   —*Paul Cézanne (1839–1906)*

2. A major difference between traditional paintings and those of the Impressionists and Post-Impressionists is that the viewer is more involved in an Impressionist or Post-Impressionist work. Why might this be?

---

[1] The term Old Masters refers to famous European painters of the past.

A **Warm-Up**

Discuss the questions in a small group.

1. Examine Pollock's painting in the photograph on page 48. How would you describe this painting? How is it different from David's, Manet's, and Cézanne's works on pages 32, 33, 39, and 41?

2. Consider the title of the reading. What do the words *abstract* and *expressionism* mean to you?

B **Reading Strategy**

Highlighting Important Information

Highlighting important information as you read helps you **maintain your focus**, and makes it **easier to review** a passage. You will find it especially helpful to highlight the main ideas in each paragraph. Doing so will help you identify supporting details.

Read these paragraphs from the reading. Notice the sample highlighting.

The most dynamic movement of the postwar period was Abstract Expressionism, sometimes also called action painting. . . . It is called Abstract Expressionism because the imagery is abstract or even nonobjective, and the way in which the paint is put on to the canvas expresses the action with which the work was made. Naturalistic representation of objects is of less importance than the artist's feelings about them or the aesthetic experience of the act of painting itself. . . .

Abstract Expressionist work is a thing unto itself, and it should not be judged by how well or how badly it represents something else. It does not have to be a still life, a portrait, or a landscape. It is aesthetically sufficient for it to be simple pigment, color, canvas, and brushwork—the result of spontaneous, energetic creation.

Now read the text. Then reread and highlight important information as you read.

Abstract Expressionism

By Wayne Craven

1   The most **dynamic** movement of the postwar period[1] was Abstract Expressionism, sometimes also called action painting. It is called Abstract Expressionism because the imagery is **abstract** or even nonobjective,[2] and the way in which the paint is put on to the canvas expresses the action with which the work was made. Naturalistic representation of objects is of less importance than the artist's feelings about them or the aesthetic[3] experience of the act of painting itself. In Abstract Expressionism, **explosive** energy is a part of the method of creating—an emotional drama builds through the **technique** itself. Accidents inevitably occur in the frenetic **execution** of a work and are often retained as evidence of **spontaneity**. The **scale** of such paintings soon increased to heroic dimensions, mainly because broad areas were required for the free-swinging movements of the artist's arm and hand.

2   Abstract Expressionist work is a thing unto itself, and it should not be judged by how well or how badly it represents something else. It does not have to be a still life, a portrait, or a landscape. It is aesthetically **sufficient** for it to be simple pigment,[4] color, canvas, and brushwork—the result of spontaneous, energetic creation.

3   One of the best ways to understand Abstract Expressionism—or any art form—is through the words of an artist, while considering one of his paintings.

One of the most famous Abstract Expressionists, or action painters, was Jackson Pollock (1912–1956), who created one of the most original forms of expression in the history of American painting.

4   In Pollock's work *Autumn Rhythm: No. 30*, the paint is dribbled and flung upon the canvas, which, as Pollock worked on it, was placed flat on the floor rather than upright on an easel. The end result is **unpremeditated**, and the "happy accident" is an **integral** part of the imagery and a reference to its spontaneity. On an off-white ground, the primary color is black, with a secondary color of rust-orange and touches of numerous other hues.

5   The painting exists as an exciting aesthetic experience—an experience the viewer can share because the painting itself explains in an instant the process of its making. Typically of Pollock's work, the overall effect is without depth of

---

[1] *postwar period:* refers to the time after World War II, which ended in 1945

[2] *nonobjective:* not representing any real person, object, or scene

[3] *aesthetic:* relates to beauty and the study of beauty

[4] *pigment:* dry, colored powder made from natural or chemical sources, which is mixed with oil, water, etc. to make paint

space or focal center. While the action glides across the surface, a structure, a unity, and even an order eventually evolve in the multitude of **complexities**.

6   It was noted in interviews that Pollock and other Abstract Expressionists "are not concerned with representing a **preconceived** idea, but rather with being involved with an experience of paint and canvas, without **interference** from the suggested forms and colors of existing objects. Pollock does not know beforehand how a particular work of his will end. He is **impelled** to work by the urge, the strong need, to create, and this urge and what it produces are forever unknowable. We can experience the unknowable but not understand it intellectually."

7   Pollack has explained, "My painting does not come from the easel. I prefer to tack the unstretched canvas to the hard wall or the floor. I need the resistance of a hard surface. On the floor I am more at ease. I feel nearer, more part of the painting, since this way I can walk around it, work from the four sides and literally be *in* the painting. When I am in my painting, I'm not aware of what I'm doing. It is only after a sort of 'get **acquainted**' period that I see what I have been about. I have no fear of making changes, destroying the image, etc., because the painting has a life of its own. I try to let it come through. It is only when I lose contact with the painting that the result is a mess. Otherwise there is pure **harmony**, an easy give and take, and the painting comes out well."

Review your highlighting with a partner. You will refer back to the information you highlighted when you complete the chart on page 56.

COMPREHENSION

A Main Ideas

Read each statement. Decide if it is *True* or *False* according to the reading. Check (✓) the appropriate box. If it is false, change it to make it true. Discuss your answers with a partner.

	TRUE	FALSE
1. Abstract Expressionism is sometimes a depiction of something specific.	☐	☐
2. Abstract Expressionism is nonrepresentational art created in a very active manner.	☐	☐
3. Jackson Pollock was not successful during his lifetime.	☐	☐
4. Paintings by Abstract Expressionists clearly demonstrate the actions the artist used to apply paint to the canvas.	☐	☐
5. Jackson Pollock never planned his paintings.	☐	☐
6. Abstract Expressionism is also called action painting because this style of painting is a very active process.	☐	☐
7. Abstract Expressionism expresses the beauty of nature through action.	☐	☐

Read the quotes from the reading. Circle the statement that best explains each quote. Discuss your answers with a partner.

1. "The most dynamic movement of the postwar period was Abstract Expressionism, sometimes also called action painting. It is called Abstract Expressionism because the imagery is abstract or even nonobjective, and the way in which the paint is put on to the canvas expresses the action with which the work was made." *(paragraph 1)*

   a. The Abstract Expressionist movement represented a major change in the way paintings were created because the imagery was very different and the method involved considerable action.

   b. The Abstract Expressionist movement was a further development of the Post-Impressionist movement that came before it because this new movement was a type of representational art.

   c. The Abstract Expressionist movement was new because paint was put on to the canvas by the action of the artist.

2. "Abstract Expressionist work is a thing unto itself, and it should not be judged by how well or how badly it represents something else. It does not have to be a still life, a portrait, or a landscape. It is aesthetically sufficient for it to be simple pigment, color, canvas, and brushwork." *(paragraph 2)*

   a. Abstract Expressionist work never represents anything in real life such as a portrait, and the painting may not be done very well, just very simply.

   b. In Abstract Expressionist work, the artist's goal is to paint something that is not a still life, a portrait, or a landscape.

   c. In Abstract Expressionist work, the canvas, the colors used, and the brushwork are what is important, not the actual picture, which may not represent anything in real life.

3. "The painting exists as an exciting aesthetic experience—an experience the viewer can share because the painting itself explains in an instant the process of its making." *(paragraph 5)*

   a. An Abstract Expressionist painting is never a bad painting, because it is not representational.

   b. An Abstract Expressionist painting gives the viewer the opportunity to share the artist's experience of the process of painting.

   c. An Abstract Expressionist painting is painted so the viewer can understand it in an instant.

4. "When I am *in* my painting, I'm not aware of what I'm doing. It is only after a sort of 'get acquainted' period that I see what I have been about. I have no fear of making changes, destroying the image, etc., because the painting has a life of its own." *(paragraph 7)*

   a. For Jackson Pollock, painting meant experiencing the process more than painting an idea.

   b. For Jackson Pollock, painting meant simply flinging paint on a large canvas placed on the floor.

   c. For Jackson Pollock, painting meant knowing ahead of time how a work would look when it was finished.

VOCABULARY

A **Word Usage**

Read the group of sentences using *scale*, *explosion*, and *execution*. The words are used with a different meaning in each sentence. Match the word as used in each sentence with the appropriate meaning. Compare answers with a partner.

1. **scale**

   _b_ 1. The scale of such paintings soon increased to heroic dimensions, mainly because broad areas were required for the free-swinging movements of the artist's arm and hand.

   ____ 2. The architect is planning a new office building. His plans are on a scale of 1:15 with 1 inch equaling 15 feet.

   ____ 3. The reviewers indicated how much they liked each painting on a scale of 1 to 10, where 1 indicates a strong dislike and 10 means the reviewers liked an artwork very much.

a. a system for measuring something
b. the size of something in relation to something else
c. the relationship between the size of a map, drawing, or model and the actual size of the place or thing it represents

(continued on next page)

2. **explosive**

_____ 1. In Abstract Expressionism, explosive energy is a part of the method of creating—an emotional drama builds through the technique itself.

_____ 2. In the 19th century, photographers used an explosive chemical to create a flash of light.

_____ 3. The controversy over Impressionist art was an explosive issue in the 19th century.

_____ 4. The first major exhibit of the Impressionists' work created an explosive situation where people actually tried to destroy the paintings.

> a. able to make people argue and become angry
> b. likely to become suddenly violent
> c. likely to increase quickly in amount or degree
> d. able or likely to burst into small pieces and cause damage

3. **execution**

_____ 1. Accidents inevitably occur in the frenetic execution of a work and are often retained as evidence of spontaneity.

_____ 2. The artist hired a lawyer to help him with the execution of a contract with a new art gallery.

_____ 3. The execution of King Louis XVI of France in 1793 shocked much of the world.

_____ 4. Renoir's execution of a very large painting took him six months.

> a. the process of making sure that the instructions in a legal document are followed
> b. the act of producing a painting, a movie, etc.
> c. the performance of something, especially a difficult action or movement
> d. the act of killing someone, especially as legal punishment for a serious crime

B Collocations

As you learned in Chapter 1, **collocations** refer to word partners or words that are often used together. These pairs of words appear in texts often and sound natural together.

The words *dynamic, preconceived,* and *complexities* appear in the reading. Each of these words has several collocations:

EXAMPLES:

dynamic nature	preconceived ideas	complex interaction
dynamic process	preconceived image	complex pattern
dynamic system	preconceived notions	complex process
		complex relationship

Complete each sentence with the appropriate collocation from the box above. Compare answers with a partner.

1. Pollack's painting displays a _____ *complex pattern* _____ of curved lines and colors that appear to be random.

2. Planning and executing a traditional, representational painting is often a _____ because of all the details that need to be thought through. Some paintings take years to complete.

3. There is often a _____ between an artist, his or her work, and the viewer that many people do not understand.

4. Creating an Abstract Expressionist painting is a very _____. The artist is very physically active, walking around a huge canvas, and throwing paint across the surface.

5. The feeling of action, of movement, one senses when viewing an Abstract Expressionist painting makes one understand the _____ of the creative process.

6. When looking at a painting, the viewer needs to keep an open mind, and not come to the painting with any _____ of what is "good" or "bad" art.

7. Impressionist, Post-Impressionist, and Abstract Expressionist artists invite the viewer to enter into a _____ with their work. The viewer must construct meaning from the painting, and so interacts with it.

(continued on next page)

8. People should not visit a museum of modern art with a _____

   of what a portrait, a landscape, or any other subject might look like.

9. People who have never studied another culture's art should try to avoid any

   _____ of what the sculptures or paintings will be like.

C Synonyms and Antonyms

We often find it easier to remember words when we connect them with an **antonym (a word with the opposite meaning)** or a **synonym (a word with a similar meaning).** For example, we might learn *difficult/hard* or *result/outcome* as pairs of synonyms and *easy/difficult* or *good/bad* as pairs of antonyms.

Review the words from the reading in the chart below the box. Fill in the chart with the synonym and antonym of each word from the box. Compare answers with a partner.

adequate	deficient	help	irrelevant	opposition
conceptual	drive	inhibit	moderate	planned
concrete	essential	intense	nonrepresentational	spontaneous

WORD	SYNONYM	ANTONYM
abstract	nonrepresentational	concrete
explosive		
impel		
integral		
interference		
sufficient		
unpremeditated		

Complete each sentence with a word from the box on page 54. Use the synonym or the antonym of the word in parentheses to help you select the correct word. Compare answers with a partner.

1. For the artist creating abstract art, movement is a(n) _____
   (integral)
   part of the artistic process.

2. Abstract art is unique in that the final outcome of the process was

   _____. Artists simply allowed the painting to take shape
   (unpremeditated)
   in a spontaneous way.

3. Placing a canvas on the floor was a(n) _____ to the
   (interference)
   abstract artist because it allowed for more freedom to move about during the

   process of painting.

4. Bright colors and interesting patterns make the _____
   (abstract)
   style of art very interesting.

5. Modern dance is similar to abstract art in that the artists and dancers use

   _____ movements to express themselves.
   (explosive)

6. The need for self-expression and the urge to move freely are what

   _____ the abstract artist to create a painting.
   (impel)

7. Abstract Expressionists needed canvases that allowed _____
   (sufficient)
   space for the free-swinging movements of their arms and hands.

NOTE-TAKING: Consolidating Information from Several Readings

Go back to Readings One, Two, and Three. Fill in the chart with information from all three readings. You will refer to this information when you do the Bringing It All Together activity.

TYPE OF ART	STYLE AND TECHNIQUES	SUBJECT MATTER	FEELINGS EXPRESSED	ARTISTS REPRESENTING THIS TYPE OF ART
Traditional	very detailed; representational			
Impressionist				
Post-Impressionist				
Abstract Expressionist				

CRITICAL THINKING

Discuss the questions in a small group. Be prepared to share your answers with the class.

1. The author states that "Abstract Expressionist work is a thing unto itself, and it should not be judged by how well or how badly it represents something else." Do you agree or disagree with this statement? Explain your reasons.

2. In Abstract Expressionism, paint is often flung or dripped upon the canvas. The result is considered a "happy accident," and is considered an integral part of the image that is created. Does a work of art always have to be planned, or is this unpremeditated method a legitimate art form? Explain your answer.

3. What do you think Pollock was trying to express in his paintings?

BRINGING IT ALL TOGETHER

Discuss the questions in a small group. Then share your group's answers with the class. Use the vocabulary you studied in the chapter (for a complete list, go to page 59). Refer to the charts you completed on pages 36, 38, and 40 for any information you might need.

1. Read and discuss the quotes from various artists. What do these artists think about art? What ideas and beliefs do they all have in common? Who do you agree with? Who do you disagree with?

    Science is all very well, but for us imagination is worth far more.

    —*Edouard Manet (1830–1883)*

    Art is not what you see, but what you make others see.

    —*Edgar Degas (1834–1917)*

    Painting from nature is not copying the object, it is realizing one's sensations.

    —*Paul Cézanne (1839–1906)*

    The painter, being concerned only with giving his impression, simply seeks to be himself and no one else.

    —*Claude Monet (1840–1926)*

    The modern artist is working with space and time, and expressing his feelings rather than illustrating.

    —*Jackson Pollock (1912–1956)*

2. When we critique a work of art we analyze it and comment on its good and bad qualities. Use the chart to analyze three of the paintings in this chapter, plus another work of art that you personally like. Then compare your critiques with your classmates'. What do your critiques have in common? Is there a particular artwork, artist, and/or period that all or most of you like?

	ARTWORK #1	ARTWORK #2	ARTWORK #3	ARTWORK #4 (YOUR CHOICE)
Artist's Name				
Title of the Work / Date Created				
Art Period / Art Form				
What is represented?				
What do you think / how do you feel when you look at it?				
Why do you like or not like this artwork?				

WRITING ACTIVITY

Do you have to like a painting in order to appreciate it? Why or why not? Write a composition. In the composition, describe what art appreciation means to you. Include your answers to the questions above. Explain the reasons for your opinion.

DISCUSSION AND WRITING TOPICS

Discuss these topics in a small group. Choose one of them and write two or three paragraphs about it. Use the vocabulary from the chapter.

1. "Abstract Expressionist work is a thing unto itself, and it should not be judged by how well or how badly it represents something else. It does not have to be a still life, a portrait, or a landscape. It is aesthetically sufficient for it to be simple pigment, color, canvas, and brushwork—the result of spontaneous, energetic creation." What is the writer saying here? Do you agree or disagree with this statement? Explain the reasons for your answer.

2. The Impressionists, Post-Impressionists, and Abstract Expressionists were all concerned with expressing their feelings in their work. Is this type of expression important to you as the viewer? Why or why not?

3. In talking about his work, Pollock said, "When I am *in* my painting, I'm not aware of what I'm doing. It is only after a sort of 'get acquainted' period that I see what I have been about." Is this art? Explain the reasons for your answer.

4. Read the paragraph below by Nigel Spivey.

   Once there was an artist who was also a teacher of art. He held classes at an art school, and many students signed up to follow them. So many students applied to take this artist's lessons that the directors of the art school became alarmed. There was not enough space, they said, to accommodate such a crowd of apprentices. They summoned the artist and ordered him to cut down the number of people taking his lessons. "You mean I must reject some people who apply?" he asked. "Of course!" replied his superiors. "Not possible," said the artist. "Why not?" they asked. "Because everyone is an artist," declared the artist. He refused to alter that faith: in the classroom he would write on the board, EVERYONE IS AN ARTIST. Eventually the directors of the art school had him dismissed.

   Do you agree with the artist's statement? Why or why not? Explain the reasons for your answer.

VOCABULARY

Nouns	Verbs	Adjectives	Adverb
admiration	characterize	abstract*	intensely*
complexities*	correspond*	durable	
execution	depict	dynamic*	
flavor	designate	explosive	
harmony	emerge*	fleeting	
hostility	impel	integral*	
idealization	integrate*	meticulous	
impression	liberate*	pioneering	
interference	pursue*	preconceived	
permanence	resolve*	radical*	
scale		representational	
technique*		revolutionary*	
temperament		spontaneous	
volume*		sufficient*	
		unpremeditated	

* = AWL (Academic Word List) item

SELF-ASSESSMENT

In this chapter you learned to:

○ Use visuals to enhance understanding

○ Paraphrase sentences to increase comprehension

○ Highlight important information in a reading

○ Recognize referents

○ Guess the meaning of words from the context, categorize words, and understand word usage

○ Use dictionary entries to learn different meanings of words

○ Understand and use synonyms, antonyms, collocations, and different word forms

○ Use note-taking to chart differences and to consolidate information from readings

What can you do well? ☑

What do you need to practice more? ☑

CHAPTER 3

ANTHROPOLOGY: The Study of Human Cultures

CULTURAL ANTHROPOLOGY: the scientific study of human cultures and societies

OBJECTIVES

To read academic texts, you need to master certain skills.

In this chapter, you will:

- Create concept maps and use textual clues to aid comprehension

- Identify point of view as objective or subjective

- Identify gerunds

- Guess the meaning of words from the context and understand word usage

- Use dictionary entries to learn different meanings of words

- Understand and use synonyms, idioms, content-specific vocabulary, and different word forms

- Use headings and subheadings to write notes

- Create a comparison chart

Native American Indian family at a tribal celebration.

Consider These Questions

Discuss the questions in a small group. Share your answers with the class.

1. Look at the photographs on pages 63, 70, and 71. How did the people learn to do what they are doing? In what ways are these activities important to the people engaged in performing them?

2. How would you describe your cultural group to someone from another country? What activities, traditions, and objects would you describe to help the person understand your culture?

READING ONE: The Challenge of Defining Culture

A Warm-Up

1 **Discuss the questions in a small group. Share your answers with the class.**

1. What does culture mean to you? Write a definition of *culture*.

_____

_____

2. Now as a class, discuss your definitions and write a single definition of *culture*.

_____

_____

Creating a Concept Map

Concept maps are useful **tools for organizing information**. Making a concept map can help you create a visual representation of the most important information in the text. Organizing the information visually will also help increase your understanding of the concepts.

Skim the text for headings and subheadings. Fill in the concept map for the components of culture. Include a definition of each subheading. Discuss your answers with a partner.

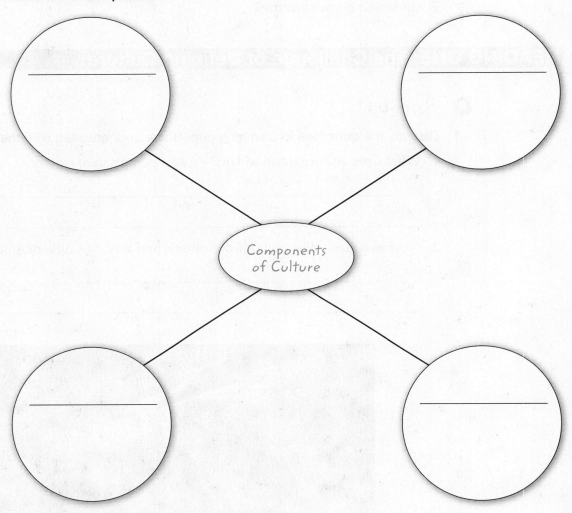

Now read the text and underline information that provides details and examples of the concepts you included in your concept map.

THE CHALLENGE OF DEFINING CULTURE

By Roberta Edwards Lenkeit

1   What exactly is culture? **Abstract** concepts such as culture are difficult to define. Other abstract concepts that are well known are love, justice, and equality. Not everyone, including experts in these areas, will agree on the precise definition of any of these concepts. If you were listening today to a group of anthropologists discussing culture, various specific **components** of culture would be mentioned. These components may be arranged in several categories: (1) **cognitive** (processes of learning, knowing, and perceiving): ideas, knowledge, symbols, standards, values; (2) behavior (how we act or conduct ourselves): gestures, manners of eating, marriage **ceremonies**, dancing, social interactions; and (3) artifacts (human material creations): tools, pottery, clothing, architectural features, machines. In other words, within this group of definitions, culture consists of what people process cognitively and how the cognitive processes are reflected in human behaviors and in the artifacts, or objects, that humans create.

Components of Culture

2   The various components of culture that are described in more detail below are universal. That is, they exist in every culture. They may differ in the details, but the components are always the same.

Cognitive Processes

3   What people think, how they think, what they believe, and what they value are a part of culture. Cognitive processes are not themselves directly observable, but they provide the **framework** of people's choices. All of the knowledge and **perspective** an individual acquires while growing up within a particular social group, including both formal and informal learning, is included in this component of culture. We cannot view the cognitive processes that create a value system within an individual's mind, but we can view the outcome of those processes. If honesty is a value held by a culture, we should be able to observe members of this culture carrying out behaviors that reflect this value.

Behaviors

4   Human behavior can be observed and described and includes all of the things we do—ways we use our bodies, all social interactions, and all creative expressions, such as playing a musical instrument or dancing. Cultural anthropologists spend much of their time in the field observing, describing, and recording behavior. Such descriptions include daily activities as well as ceremonial events that may occur only once a year or at

(continued on next page)

periodic intervals. Descriptions of behavior in a natural **setting** include similar execution of behaviors as well as the many individual variations that occur. Ethnographers[1] are trained to collect and record these data using a variety of techniques.

Material Creations

5   What people create, from artifacts to features, are products of human cultural activities. Ethnographers record and describe the artifacts and features of living cultural groups, whereas archaeologists describe artifacts and features made by peoples of past cultures. Artifacts and features provide a window into the minds and cultures of the people who make them. The objects we make reflect what and how we think.

Cultural Processes

6   Most definitions of culture include something about enculturation, the process of how culture is acquired, shared, and transmitted. Culture is learned, shared, and transmitted to future generations **primarily** by **symbolic** systems. The most obvious symbolic system humans use is language—both spoken and written. It is primarily through language that we humans learn the cultural **complexity** that allows us to survive. Other ways of learning include observation and **imitation** of others and **trial and error**.

---

[1] *ethnographer:* a person trained to do fieldwork to study cultures

Create a new concept map for this reading. Use the information in paragraph 1 to draw the concept map for the components of culture in a different way. Compare answers with a partner.

COMPREHENSION

Ⓐ Main Ideas

Read each statement. Decide if it is *True* or *False* according to the reading. Check (✓) the appropriate box. If it is false, change it to make it true. Discuss your answers with a partner.

	TRUE	FALSE
1. *Culture* is an abstract term that cannot be defined.	☐	☐
2. Although we cannot see how people think, how they think affects what they do.	☐	☐
3. Human behavior involves only movement and social interaction.	☐	☐
4. The objects that people make are a result of human cultural activities.	☐	☐
5. The objects that people make can tell a lot about their culture.	☐	☐
6. Humans learn culture through language and the use of artifacts.	☐	☐

B Close Reading

Read the quotes from the reading. Write a paraphrase for each quote. Discuss your answers with a partner.

1. "Not everyone, including experts in these areas, will agree on the precise definition of any of these concepts. If you were listening today to a group of anthropologists discussing culture, various specific components of culture would be mentioned." *(paragraph 1)*

   Paraphrase: _No one in the area will agree on the_
   _____ definition of any of these concepts_

2. "Culture consists of what people process cognitively and how the cognitive processes are reflected in human behaviors and in the artifacts, or objects, that humans create." *(paragraph 1)*

   Paraphrase: _____
   _____

3. "We cannot view the cognitive processes that create a value system within an individual's mind, but we can view the outcome of those processes. If honesty is a value held by a culture, we should be able to observe members of this culture carrying out behaviors that reflect this value." *(paragraph 3)*

   Paraphrase: _We can observe the outcome_
   individual mind that create value system

4. "Descriptions of behavior in a natural setting include similar execution of behaviors as well as the many individual variations that occur." *(paragraph 4)*

   Paraphrase: _____
   _____

5. "Artifacts and features provide a window into the minds and cultures of the people who make them." *(paragraph 5)*

   Paraphrase: _____
   _____

Vocabulary

A Guessing from Context

Read each quote from the reading. Try to guess the meaning of the word in bold from the context. Write your guess. Then consult a dictionary and write the definition. Compare answers with a partner.

1. "These components may be arranged in several categories: (1) **cognitive** (processes of learning, knowing, and perceiving): ideas, knowledge, symbols, standards, values." (*paragraph 1*)

   Guess: _intellectual_

   Dictionary: _related to the process of knowing, understanding, and learning something_

2. "All of the knowledge and **perspective** an individual acquires while growing up within a particular social group, including both formal and informal learning, is included in this component of culture." (*paragraph 3*)

   Guess: _____

   Dictionary: _____

3. "Descriptions of behavior in a natural **setting** include similar execution of behaviors as well as the many individual variations that occur." (*paragraph 4*)

   Guess: _____

   Dictionary: _____

4. "Other ways of learning include observation and **imitation** of others and trial and error." (*paragraph 6*)

   Guess: _____

   Dictionary: _____

5. "Culture is learned, shared, and transmitted to future generations primarily by **symbolic** systems. The most obvious symbolic system humans use is language—both spoken and written." (*paragraph 6*)

   Guess: _____

   Dictionary: _____

B Idioms

Read the sentences. Each one uses an idiom with *trial*. Match the idiom used in each sentence with one of the meanings from the box below. Use a dictionary if necessary. Compare answers with a partner.

__b__ 1. The **trials and tribulations** of adapting to a new culture made Maria reconsider whether moving to the United States was the right decision.

_____ 2. The new families felt that they faced a **trial by fire** when they moved into a neighborhood where the people did not understand them.

_____ 3. Children learn to speak a language through a process of **trial and error**. They experiment with sounds and words until they are successful.

_____ 4. Before committing to changing their customs completely, the immigrant family decided to do a **trial run** by only changing how they cooked and ate dinner.

---

a. a test of how well someone deals with a difficult situation

b. situations that are difficult to deal with, and that are worrying or annoying

c. an occasion when you test a new method or system to see if it works well

d. the testing of many different methods of doing something in order to find the best

---

C Synonyms

Read the sentences. Match each word in bold with its synonym in the box below. Compare answers with a partner.

_____ 1. In the past, certain Native American cultures in the Northwest held feasts where they gave away all they owned. These **periodic** events were demonstrations of their generosity in their community.

_____ 2. Honesty, respect for others, and generosity are **components** of my family's value system.

_____ 3. Cognitive processes, behavior, and the creation of artifacts provide a **framework** for exploring the concepts of culture.

_____ 4. Every year on December 21, the local community holds a **ceremony** to celebrate the arrival of winter.

_____ 5. Some cultures have celebrations to mark the changing of the seasons. These celebrations usually happen at three-month **intervals**.

_____ 6. Children learn to behave **primarily** by observing and imitating others.

---

a. mainly	d. lapses of time
b. occasional	e. ritual
c. elements	f. structure

NOTE-TAKING: Writing Notes Using Headings and Subheadings

Go back to the reading and use the headings and subheadings to focus on important details in each section. Then write notes about each concept. Compare your notes with a partner.

Heading / Subheading	Notes
Components of Culture	Cognitive processes, behavior, material creations; exist in every culture
Cognitive Processes	
Behaviors	
Material Creations	
Cultural Processes	

CRITICAL THINKING

Discuss the questions in a small group. Be prepared to share your answers with the class.

1. In a particular culture, how might the way people think (their cognitive processes) affect the types of objects they create? Give some examples from your own culture or from a culture you are familiar with.

2. Cultural anthropologists observe, describe, and record the behaviors of various cultures. How might their own culture influence how they perceive a culture different from their own?

3. What are some of the specific behaviors that children learn by observation and imitation? How might these behaviors differ across cultures?

A **Warm-Up**

Discuss the questions in a small group. Share your answers with the class.

1. How many different ways do human societies have to obtain food? Make a list.

2. What cultures do you know of that do not value land or property ownership? What are they? What do they value?

B **Reading Strategy**

Using Textual Clues to Aid Comprehension

Texts often contain **clues** that can help you understand a reading because they **introduce a definition, an explanation, additional information, or an example for an unfamiliar word or concept**. Examples of these textual clues include punctuation (dashes, commas, parentheses, colons), phrases (*for instance, such as*) and words (*include*).

EXAMPLE:
*Foraging represents a spectrum, or range, of food-getting activities. Foods gathered **include** berries, nuts, seeds, flowers, herbs, fungus, fruit, greens, eggs, shellfish, insects, and so forth.*

The commas set off a synonym of the word *spectrum*. The word **include** introduces examples of the foods that are gathered.

Read each statement and complete it using the information presented in the Reading Strategy box. Compare answers with a partner.

1. Most foragers are nomadic: they must continually move with the availability of food and water.

   The information after the colon explains ———————————————.

2. One type of foraging group is a family band, which consists of a number of nuclear families (parents and their offspring) living within an area.

   The information in parentheses is ———————————————.

3. Sharing, giving, receiving, and no one keeping track of what is given or received is the custom—a custom that is enculturated from infancy.

   The information that follows the dash is ———————————————.

4. Unlike foragers, horticulturalists own property. Property ownership is by kin groups, and these groups—lineages and clans, for instance—work the land and reap the benefits of their labors.

   The information between the two dashes ———————————————.

Now read the text and underline additional textual clues that help you understand unfamiliar words or concepts.

THE NATURE OF FORAGING AND HORTICULTURAL SOCIETIES

By Roberta Edwards Lenkeit

1   Food is important in all societies because it is essential for survival. We will examine how foraging and horticultural societies acquire and use their resources to obtain or produce food and how food and resources are **distributed**.

Foraging as a Subsistence Strategy

2   Foraging is food **procurement** that involves collecting wild plant and animal foods and was the earliest adaptive strategy used by humans. Foraging represents a spectrum, or range, of food-getting activities. Foods gathered include berries, nuts, seeds, flowers, herbs, fungus, fruit, greens, eggs, shellfish, insects, and so forth.

3   Most foragers are nomadic: they must continually move with the availability of food and water. As an adaptive strategy, foraging must be fine-tuned[1] to a particular environment. The frequency of movement is **orchestrated** to **coincide** with the availability of specific plants, animals, and water.

Social Groups

4   Foragers are organized into groups that anthropologists label bands. One type is a family band, which consists of a number of nuclear families (parents and their offspring) living within an area. These individual families come together to form a larger group when resources are **abundant** and split up again when resources are **scarce** or widely **dispersed**.

Property and Ownership

5   Foragers have few material possessions. While the land and its resources are generally considered to belong to the whole group, particular resources may belong to a family and a tool might be personal property. Sharing, giving, receiving, and no one keeping track of what is given or received is the custom—a custom that is enculturated from infancy. Most access to tools occurs by sharing and borrowing rather than everyone having one of his or her own.

Distribution of Resources

6   Foraging societies are marked by the economic distribution system known as reciprocity. Reciprocity is the enculturated pattern in which people give and receive items of value in predictable ways. The giving of food, a tool, or an item of personal **adornment** are examples of such value items. The giving of one's time in the form of helping to build a hut or watching someone's child also illustrates something of value. This giving of items of value is part of the fabric of band societies.

---

[1] *fine tune:* to make very small changes to something so that it works as well as possible

Horticulture as a Subsistence Strategy

7   Horticulture is a food-procurement strategy that is based on a simple level of crop production. Seeds or cuttings are planted without benefit of **cultivation** or preparation of the soil. Several features are associated with horticultural lifeways.

Production Based on Extensive Technology

8   Horticulturalists have **extensive** technology. The technology—knowledge, skills, and tools—used in simple cultivation is complex and requires understanding of plant cycles, seasonal weather conditions, soils, when and how to harvest,[2] and how to select and store seeds for the next season's planting. Horticulturalists need the knowledge and skills to **manipulate** nature. Knowledge builds through time as new discoveries are made and passed on to each generation.

Larger Groups and Kinship Structures

9   Horticulture results in larger populations and kinship[3] systems with more segments than those encountered among foragers. Horticultural societies are kin-based, meaning that kinship ties and the responsibilities

that accompany them are what weave the fabric of such societies. Kin groups based on descent[4] and residence are a consistent **correlate** to horticulturally-based societies.

Property and Ownership

10   Unlike foragers, horticulturalists own property. Property ownership is by kin groups, and these groups—lineages[5] and clans, for instance—work the land and reap the benefits of their labors. Common patterns among horticulturalists include small settlements of several related kin groups that are surrounded by gardens and fields. Horticulturalists have more possessions than foragers. Extended living in one place, plus the need for tools to produce, harvest, store, and process the crops, results in more artifacts.

Distribution of Goods

11   The systems of distribution found among horticulturalists are similar to those among foragers, but the emphasis is shifted. Generalized reciprocity still dominates within the nuclear family and extends to some other close kin, such as lineage members, but outside of these groups balanced reciprocity is the norm. Gifts of food, possessions, time, and energy are calculated, and the expectation is that items of equal value will be reciprocated within a reasonable period of time. Thus, alliances and **interdependencies** are formed outside of one's own lineage, and clan and status or reputation may be enhanced by participating in reciprocal exchanges.

---

[2] **harvest:** gather crops from the field

[3] **kinship:** refers to family relationships

---

[4] **descent:** refers to one's family origins—parents, grandparents, great grandparents, and so on

[5] **lineage:** the way in which members of a family are descended from other members

Work with a partner. Compare the textual clues you found in the text. Which clues did your partner find that you can add to your list?

COMPREHENSION

A Main Ideas

1 Check (✓) the statements that best express the main ideas in the reading. Discuss your answers with a partner.

☐ **a.** Horticultural societies have extensive technology, form larger groups, and own property.

☐ **b.** Foragers collect plant and animal foods.

☐ **c.** Societies that have large social groups that own land, such as horticultural societies, are more sophisticated than societies in which individuals do not own land.

☐ **d.** All foragers are organized into nuclear family bands.

☐ **e.** Reciprocity is a main characteristic of foraging societies.

☐ **f.** Foraging and horticultural societies are described by various characteristics including how they form social groups, view property and ownership, and distribute resources.

☐ **g.** Horticultural societies need and use technology for their cultivation processes.

2 According to the reading, foraging and horticultural societies share certain features, or characteristics. Check (✓) the characteristics that are common to these societies.

☐ **a.** food-procurement strategies

☐ **b.** gathering wild plant and animal foods

☐ **c.** planting seeds and growing food

☐ **d.** forming social groups

☐ **e.** basing social groups on family ties

☐ **f.** having many material possessions

☐ **g.** owning property

☐ **h.** passing knowledge on to the next generation

B Close Reading

Read each question. Write your answer in a complete sentence. Compare answers with a partner.

1. What do foragers usually do?

   _____

2. Why do foragers have few material possessions?

   _____

3. What is a main characteristic of foraging cultures?

   _____

4. What is a main characteristic of horticultural societies that differs from characteristics of foraging societies?

   _____

5. Why do people in horticultural societies own property?

   _____

Vocabulary

A Synonyms

Read the sentences. Match each word or phrase in bold with its synonym in the box below. Discuss answers with a partner.

_____ 1. Research has shown that a varied diet is a **correlate** of good health.

_____ 2. The harvesting of crops usually begins in the summer. This **coincides** with the opening of outdoor markets so that the fresh fruit and vegetables can be sold.

_____ 3. The move from one location to another is carefully **orchestrated** by mapping out the changing of seasons and best location to find food.

_____ 4. In horticultural societies the **procurement** of food is much easier because crops are planted in specific and easy-to-reach locations near family homes.

_____ 5. Horticultural societies have **extensive** knowledge of how to grow crops. This knowledge allows them to successfully provide food for their people every year.

_____ 6. The foragers traveled many miles to pick fruit because the trees were **dispersed** throughout the region.

_____ 7. When food is **scarce**, people often go hungry.

a. acquisition	**e.** planned
b. co-occurs	**f.** scattered
c. complement	**g.** wide-ranging
d. limited	

B Using the Dictionary

Read the dictionary entry and the sentences that follow. Then match the number of the definition with the appropriate sentence. Compare answers with a partner.

> **cultivation** *n.* **1** the preparation and use of land for growing crops   **2** the process of planting and growing plants and crops   **3** the deliberate development of a particular quality or skill   **4** the process of developing a friendly relationship with someone

_____ a. All parents value the cultivation of social skills in their children.

_____ b. The cultivation of the fields needs to happen at a specific time of year to improve the quality of the crops.

_____ c. Time spent together helps the cultivation of long-lasting friendships.

_____ d. The cultivation of corn is very important to the local people. They use this crop in many different ways.

C Word Forms

Fill in the chart with the correct word forms. Use a dictionary if necessary. An **X** indicates there is no form in that category.

	Noun	Verb	Adjective	Adverb
1.		X	abundant	
2.	adornment		X	X
3.		distribute		X
4.			extensive	
5.	interdependency	X		
6.		manipulate		X
7.	procurement			X

Complete the sentences with the correct form of one of the words above. Be sure to use the correct tense of the verbs and the singular or plural form of the nouns. Compare answers with a partner.

1. Horticulturalists plant seeds but don't _____ the land. They don't use fertilizer or irrigation.

2. Today, as in the past, many cultural groups _____ what they need by exchanging goods with other cultures, for example by trading food for tools.

3. Societies that plant and store food are able to settle down in one place for long periods of time. The _____ of food makes traveling unnecessary.

4. The tradition calls for decorating the outside of the home during harvest season. Everyone _____ their doors with dried corn and flowers from the previous season.

5. People in foraging societies have an _____ relationship with others in their band. They rely on each other for the things they need.

6. Franz Boas was a famous anthropologist who studied and wrote _____ on the languages of Native Americans during his lifetime.

7. The family gave the most food to the members who did physical work because they needed the most calories. The _____ of food was based on need.

GRAMMAR FOR READING

Gerunds

Gerunds are **nouns made from verbs**. A gerund is formed by adding *-ing* to the base form of a verb. It is sometimes easy to confuse gerunds for other words that end in *-ing,* such as the progressive form of a verb or a present participle used as an adjective.

EXAMPLE:
Foraging represents a spectrum, or range, of *food-getting* activities.

In the sentence above *foraging* is a gerund, but *food-getting* is a present participle used as an adjective.

Read the sentences from the reading and circle the gerunds. Not all sentences include a gerund. Discuss your answers with a partner.

1. (Foraging) is food procurement that involves (collecting) wild plant and animal foods and was the earliest adaptive strategy used by humans.

2. We will examine how foraging and horticultural societies acquire and use their resources to obtain or produce food and how food and resources are distributed.

(continued on next page)

3. Sharing, giving, receiving, and no one keeping track of what is given or received is the custom—a custom that is enculturated from infancy.

4. Most access to tools occurs by sharing and borrowing rather than everyone having one of his or her own.

5. The giving of one's time in the form of helping to build a hut or watching someone's child also illustrates something of value.

6. The technology—knowledge, skills, and tools—used in simple cultivation is complex and requires understanding of plant cycles, seasonal weather conditions, soils, when and how to harvest, and how to select and store seeds for the next season's planting.

7. Extended living in one place, plus the need for tools to produce, harvest, store, and process the crops, results in more artifacts.

8. Thus, alliances and interdependencies are formed outside of one's own lineage, and clan and status or reputation may be enhanced by participating in reciprocal exchanges.

NOTE-TAKING: Creating a Comparison Chart

Go back to the reading and read it again. Then fill in the chart below. Compare answers with a partner.

THE NATURE OF FORAGING AND HORTICULTURAL SOCIETIES		
POINTS OF COMPARISON	FORAGING SOCIETIES	HORTICULTURAL SOCIETIES
Social Groups	organized into bands; for example, a family band (several nuclear families—parents and offspring)	
Food Procurement		
Property and Ownership		
Distribution of Resources		

CRITICAL THINKING

Discuss the questions in a small group. Be prepared to share your answers with the class.

1. Why do you think the rules of reciprocity differ between the foraging and horticultural societies?

2. Which society do you think has the healthier diet, the foragers or the horticulturalists? Explain your answer.

LINKING READINGS ONE AND TWO

Discuss the questions in a small group. Be prepared to share your answers with the class.

1. Reading One discusses several components of culture: cognitive processes such as learning, knowing and perceiving, and behaviors, including traditions and social interactions. Describe some examples of components of culture from Reading Two.

2. What artifacts might a nomadic, foraging society create? What might they do without?

3. Foraging societies are often described as sharing and egalitarian (that is, believing that everyone is equal and has equal rights). Why might these particular characteristics be common among these particular societies? Use concepts from Reading One to explain your answer.

READING THREE: Night Flying Woman: An Ojibway Narrative

Ⓐ Warm-Up

Discuss the questions in a small group. Share your answers with the class.

1. Consider the title of the reading. What do you think the narrative might be about?

2. Do you think it is important to pass cultural traditions on to younger generations? If so, why? If not, why not?

Ⓑ Reading Strategy

Recognizing Point of View

The **point of view** of a reading can be **objective or subjective**. A reading that has an objective point of view focuses on **factual** information. An objective reading presents the information in a neutral way. A reading that has a subjective point of view focuses on **feelings, beliefs, and opinions**. You can tell if a reading has a subjective point of view because the words used suggest strong emotions.

Recognizing the point of view of a reading can help you to better understand the author's message, which aids in overall comprehension of the text.

EXAMPLE:
> It is well that they are asking, for the Ojibway young must learn their cycle. These children are again honoring the Old People by asking them to speak.

The sentence above is subjective because the underlined words indicate the opinion of the speaker.

> The two girls poked holes in the ground in the many open spaces in the forest. Then Aunt On-da-g dropped in the seed. She had saved much seed from the last harvest, so there would be a big crop of pumpkins, squash, beans, and ma-da-min, the corn.

The sentence above is objective because the speaker is presenting the factual events of the story without expressing emotions or opinions.

Consider the following sentences from the reading. Indicate whether the author's point of view is *Subjective* or *Objective*. If you choose *Subjective*, underline the words that make the sentence subjective.

	SUBJECTIVE	OBJECTIVE
1. We did not own the land acre by acre as is done today, but we <u>respected the right</u> of all people to share in the gifts given by the Great Being to the Anishinabe.	☑	☐
2. A-wa-sa-si was the oldest person in the village. She had no children or grandchildren there, for her two sons lived far to the east.	☐	☐
3. We believe in the sharing of the harvest and gifts. It is an honor to have the sharing accepted, and it is your joy when the sharing gives joy.	☐	☐
4. When these Ojibway children who went to the boarding schools became the young adults and then the older people, they could not teach their own children the old ways. Their children too went to the government boarding schools, and so a cycle began that made the Ojibway forget their past. The spirit of the Ojibway was far from the spirit of the beginning.	☐	☐
5. Oona thought about the Ojibway children. It had been a long, long time since a child had come to hear the legends and the stories of the old life. "Maybe they do not care," thought Oona. "If this is so, then our history will be lost."	☐	☐
6. Oona felt a joy in her spirit and a light on her face. She knew that the Ojibway ways would forever be known in future years.	☐	☐

Now read the narrative and try to identify additional objective and subjective passages.

Night Flying Woman: An Ojibway Narrative

Foreword by Paulette Fairbanks Molin

1   *Night Flying Woman* is a story in the tradition of the Ojibway people. In *Night Flying Woman* we meet several generations of one family group; through their lives we learn the traditions, beliefs, customs, and some history of the Ojibway in Minnesota. The Ojibway are known in their own language as Anishinabe, **original people**. Their language and culture are based on an **oral tradition**. Children were taught the importance of listening to the Old Ones, for "it has always been the custom for us to tell what must be passed on so that our ways will be known to the Ojibway children of the future."

2   Ignatia Broker (1919–1987) is uniquely **qualified** to tell this story. An Ojibway **elder** and storyteller and an enrolled member of White Earth Reservation, she has experienced both reservation[1] and urban life. She is familiar with the old ways as well as the new.

By Ignatia Broker

3   *My children are urging me to recall all the stories and bits of information that I ever heard my grandparents or any of the older Ojibway tell. It is important, they say, because now their children are asking them. Others are saying the same thing. It is well that they are asking, for the Ojibway young must learn their cycle. These children are again* **honoring** *the Old People by asking them to speak, and I, like other older people, will search my memory and tell what I know. I, myself, shall tell you what I have heard my grandmother tell me, and I shall try to speak in the way she did and use the words that were hers.*

4   We, the Ojibway, are a forest people. A long time before a strange people[2] came to this country, we lived east and north of this land now called Minnesota. We did not own the land acre by acre as is done today, but we respected the right of all people to share in the gifts given by the Great Being to the Anishinabe, which means us, the original people. I shall tell you of my great-great-grandmother (born in the mid-nineteenth century), who is your grandmother five times removed. Her name was Ni-bo-wi-se-gwe, which means Night Flying Woman.

Her nickname was Oona. The time of her birth was after the blueberry gathering and before the wild-rice harvesting.

5   For five years Oona's **cycle of life** was the same. Summer camp to ricing camp to winter village to sugar bush to planting time to summer camp. These years were filled with love and laughter, and this cycle was the cycle of our people, the Ojibway.

6   When it was time to start the planting, E-quay, Oona's cousin, came for her. The two girls poked holes in the ground in the many open spaces in the forest. Then Aunt On-da-g dropped in the seed. She had saved much seed from the last harvest, so there would be a big crop of

---

[1] **reservation:** an area of land in the United States kept separate for Native Americans to live on

[2] **strange people:** white people

pumpkins, squash, beans, and ma-da-min, the corn. Then they went to mark the places where the wild food might grow. In the summer, when On-da-g said the time was right, Oona and E-quay went blueberry picking with Mother, On-da-g and the many cousins.

7   A-wa-sa-si was the oldest person in the village. She had no children or grandchildren there, for her two sons lived far to the east, but she was considered the Grandmother to all. Because A-wa-sa-si was very old, it was she who told the **legends** and the history of the people to the children. Oona went many times to the lodge of A-wa-sa-si and sat before her. One day A-wa-sa-si said, "I wish to tell you of many things, and these I wish you to tell my grandchildren, whom I have never seen."

8   "The Anishabe have always been a **thriving** people born to the **woodland** way of life. We know the secrets of the forest and receive the gifts of a Generous Spirit. These we repay by honoring and respecting the living things in the forests: the animal people and the plant life which in itself is life-giving. We do not waste the **precious** gifts but share them with our brothers. We believe in the sharing of the harvest and gifts. It is an honor to have the sharing accepted, and it is your joy when the sharing gives joy."

9   Then the government built boarding schools[3] hundreds of miles from the Ojibway villages. Each fall the children, five to fifteen years old, were taken to these faraway schools. When they returned home in the summer, there was

---
[3] **boarding school:** a school where students live as well as study

little time to teach them the old ways. When these Ojibway children who went to the boarding schools became the young adults and then the older people, they could not teach their own children the old ways. Their children too went to the government boarding schools, and so a cycle began that made the Ojibway forget their past. The **spirit** of the Ojibway was far from the spirit of the beginning.

10   Oona, in her eightieth year, remembered the feeling of belonging to the past and how it was when there were only Ojibway in the land. Oona thought about the Ojibway children. It had been a long, long time since a child had come to hear the legends and the stories of the old life. "Maybe they do not care," thought Oona. "If this is so, then our history will be lost." Oona rocked and rocked, and she **gazed** out at the trees. She heard the si-si-gaw-d, the **murmuring** that the trees make, and it seemed their hearts were crying, too.

11   There was a knock, and Oona turned and saw a small girl in the doorway. The child stood with eyes cast down just as Oona had stood before her grandmother. Oona said, "Come in, my child, and speak if you wish to do so." The child said, "My name is Mary in the English way, but in the language of our people, I am called A-wa-sa-si." "And what is it you wish, my child?" asked Oona. "I should like," said the child, "to hear the stories of our people." Oona felt a joy in her spirit and a light on her face. She knew that the Ojibway ways would forever be known in future years. "My name is Ni-bo-wi-se-gwe," said Oona, "and I shall tell you of our people."

Work with a partner. Compare your answers. How did thinking about the author's point of view help you understand the narrative?

COMPREHENSION

A Main Ideas

Read each question. Circle the correct answer. Compare answers with a partner.

1. What is the main idea of the reading?

   a. The Ojibway culture includes oral traditions and legends that are being lost.

   b. The Ojibway culture has experienced many challenges but has thrived and survived into the present day.

   c. The Ojibway culture and way of life have not changed despite outside influences.

2. Why might oral tradition be such an essential component of the Ojibway culture?

   a. because this is how the Ojibway language and culture are passed on to the next generation

   b. because the Ojibway don't believe in writing down any of the legends and stories

   c. because the Ojibway wanted their children to share their customs at the government boarding schools

3. Why were the Ojibway's traditions, customs, language, legends, and stories in danger of being lost?

   a. because the children did not want to continue living in the traditional way and were not interested in the old stories and legends

   b. because there was no one left to help the children learn their traditions, language, stories, and legends

   c. because the children were taken away most of the year, and were not home long enough to live their traditional lives and to learn their legends and stories

B Close Reading

Read each question. Write your answer in a complete sentence. Compare answers with a partner.

1. Why did Ignatia Broker write *Night Flying Woman*?

   _____

2. What are important values among the Ojibway?

   _____

3. Why did Oona feel so happy when the little girl came to her home?

   _____

4. What type of food-procurement system did the the Ojibway use in the past?

   _____

Vocabulary

 A **Understanding Content-Specific Vocabulary**

> This reading contains vocabulary that is often used in stories about Native American culture. It is easier to learn such vocabulary altogether, within the context of a text.

Read the words and definitions below. Match the words with their meanings.

_____ 1. elder

_____ 2. cycle of life

_____ 3. legends

_____ 4. oral tradition

_____ 5. original people

_____ 6. woodland

a. the way that older people pass on stories and customs to younger people by speaking to them

b. in many native peoples' beliefs, the concept that they were the very first people

c. a member of a tribe or other social group who is important and respected because he or she is old

d. land that is covered with trees

e. the passage of time as a series of events or seasons that happen again and again

f. old, well-known stories, often about brave people, adventures, or magical events

Complete each sentence with one of the words listed above.

1. All cultures have _____. Johnny Appleseed, a man who planted hundreds of apple trees, is featured in one such story.

2. Some Native Americans live in _____ areas, while others live on the Great Plains or on the sea coast.

3. In societies where experience is highly valued, when a problem arises, a(n) _____ is always asked for advice.

4. Although Europeans claim to have discovered the Americas, the Native Americans are truly the _____, having arrived many thousands of years ago.

5. The _____ is the same among all human groups: birth, growth, aging, and death.

6. Virtually all preliterate cultures have a(n) _____ that helps children learn about their culture.

B Using the Dictionary

Read the dictionary entries and the sentences that follow. Then match the number of the definition with the appropriate sentence. Compare answers with a partner.

1.

> **spirit** *n.* **1** the qualities that make someone live or behave the way they do, and make them different from other people   **2** the way someone feels at a particular time   **3** the part of someone that you cannot see that many people believe continues to live after the person dies

_____ **a.** Oona felt a joy in her spirit and a light on her face. She knew that the Ojibway ways would forever be known in future years.

_____ **b.** The child had an independent spirit, which was unusual for someone so young.

_____ **c.** When the leader of the tribe died, the Ojibway community was unhappy, but they knew that his spirit was in a better place.

2.

> **precious** *adj.* **1** valuable and important to everyone   **2** valuable and important for personal reasons   **3** rare and worth a lot of money

_____ **a.** Oona has no photographs of her grandmother, but she does have precious memories of her that she often recalls and shares with her own grandchildren.

_____ **b.** Many Native American cultures did not have access to precious metals such as gold or silver.

_____ **c.** The Ojibway did not waste the precious gifts given to them by the Great Spirit. They shared them.

 **Synonyms**

Complete each sentence with a word from the box. Use the synonym in parentheses to help you select the correct word. Compare answers with a partner.

gazed	murmur	qualified
honored	precious	thriving

1. The elders of the tribe were the most _____ to pass on the
(suitable)
customs to the younger generation because they had lived the longest and knew

the most about the culture.

2. In many cultures in the past, families _____ their ancestors
(recognized)
by naming their children after them.

3. The farmers' new crops were _____. The soil and the
(flourishing)
weather provided the perfect conditions.

4. The child _____ into the woods for a long time, hoping to
(stared)
see a deer or some other woodland creature.

5. The clan could hear the _____ of the stream as the water
(low sound)
flowed over the rocks.

6. Among horticultural societies, a steel knife was a man's most

_____ possession.
(prized)

CRITICAL THINKING

Discuss the questions in a small group. Be prepared to share your answers with the class.

1. Like the people in some other cultures, the Ojibway did not own land as individuals. How might such cultures share the land if they do not own it? How might they decide to share what is on the land, such as plants they might grow and animals they might hunt?

2. What might have been some consequences of the Ojibway children being sent away to boarding school and not learning their culture's old ways from their village elders?

3. How might a culture such as the Ojibway's survive, even thrive, in the 21st century? How can they pass along their legends, songs, and history to the next generation? How might they maintain their values of sharing and respecting what they receive?

BRINGING IT ALL TOGETHER

Discuss the questions in a small group. Then share your group's answers with the class. Use the vocabulary you studied in the chapter (for a complete list, go to page 87).

1. In Readings One and Two, you read about the components of culture and learned about the nature of foraging and horticultural societies. Reading Three describes the Ojibway culture. Using what you learned in Readings One and Two, discuss the Ojibway values, and the behaviors that reflect those values. Which values and behaviors reflect a foraging society? Which reflect a horticultural society?

2. What are some different ways that culture is transmitted from one generation to the next? Use examples from all three readings.

3. What might happen to a society if its culture is weakened or forgotten in future generations? Use examples from all three readings.

WRITING ACTIVITY

Consider the following statement: *Culture is what makes us strangers when we are away from home.* Write about a time you were away from home, in a different culture, and felt like a stranger. In the first paragraph, tell where you went, why you went, and how long you were there. In the second paragraph, write about the other culture. In the third paragraph, describe why you felt like a stranger.

DISCUSSION AND WRITING TOPICS

Discuss these topics in a small group. Choose one of them and write two or three paragraphs about it. Use the vocabulary from the chapter.

1. Think of a situation where an ethnographer might be helpful in learning something or solving a problem. Describe the situation briefly. Then describe what the ethnographer might do, and what solution the ethnographer might come up with.

2. What components of your culture are especially important to you? How can these components be preserved and passed on to future generations in your culture?

3. Select a culture. Work by yourself and write a short description of the culture you have chosen. Use some of the components outlined in Reading One and Reading Two—behaviors and artifacts—as well as kinship terms.

VOCABULARY

Nouns	Verbs	Adjectives	Adverb
adornment	coincide*	abundant	primarily*
ceremony	correlate	cognitive	
component*	disperse	extensive	**Idioms**
cultivation	distribute*	periodic*	trial and error
cycle of life	gaze	precious	
elder	honor	qualified	
framework*	manipulate*	scarce	
imitation	murmur	symbolic*	
interdependency	orchestrate	woodland	
interval*	thrive		
legend			
oral tradition			
original people			
perspective*			
procurement			
setting			
spirit			

* = AWL (Academic Word List) item

SELF-ASSESSMENT

In this chapter you learned to:

○ Create concept maps and use textual clues to aid comprehension

○ Identify point of view as objective or subjective

○ Identify gerunds

○ Guess the meaning of words from the context and understand word usage

○ Use dictionary entries to learn different meanings of words

○ Understand and use synonyms, idioms, content-specific vocabulary, and different word forms

○ Use headings and subheadings to write notes

○ Create a comparison chart

What can you do well? ✓

What do you need to practice more? ✓

CHAPTER 4

SCIENCE: Human Achievements over Time

SCIENCE: knowledge about the physical world, especially based on examining, testing, and proving facts

OBJECTIVES

To read academic texts, you need to master certain skills.

In this chapter, you will:

- Use a text box to enhance understanding

- Skim for the main idea by reading topic sentences

- Use visuals to understand important terms and concepts

- Identify parallel structures used for emphasis

- Use dictionary entries to learn different meanings of words and understand word usage

- Guess the meaning of words from the context

- Understand and use synonyms, roots, word forms, and collocations

- Organize information chronologically and list problems and solutions

Medieval workers constructing a building.

Consider These Questions

Discuss the questions in a small group. Share your answers with the class.

1. Science is comprised of many different disciplines, or fields, of study. Make a list of disciplines that are included in science. When you are finished, create a single list with your class.

2. Read the title of this chapter: *Science: Human Achievements over Time*. What are some major scientific human achievements over the past 1,000 years?

3. Which branches of science would you need to know and draw on in order to construct a tall building? To build and launch a spacecraft? To navigate on Earth or in space?

4. Examine the photograph on page 88. How would you describe the technology of 12th-century stonemasons compared with that of 21st-century builders?

READING ONE: A Great Human Endeavor: Building the Gothic Cathedrals

A Warm-Up

Work with a partner. Examine the examples below of Romanesque (6th–10th centuries) and Gothic (12th–16th centuries) architecture. What are some differences between the two types of architecture?

Romanesque architecture

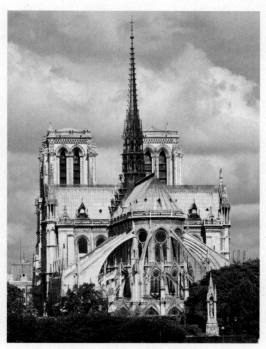

Gothic architecture

Using a Text Box to Enhance Understanding

A reading may be accompanied by a **text box**. The information in the text box usually provides **additional details** not included in the reading itself but which help you understand a **difficult or related concept**.

Read the text box in the reading on page 92 and examine the illustration of the structure of a Gothic cathedral. Then complete the sentences with the correct words. Compare answers with a partner.

1. Weight pushing downward is caused by _____.

2. Weight pushing outward is caused by _____.

3. Gravity and thrust are _____, which if not balanced properly could lead a structure to collapse.

4. The flying buttresses _____ the outward thrust created by the weight of the Gothic arches.

Now read the text and refer to the illustration and the physics principles presented in the text box. Consider how they help you understand what you are reading about the making of the cathedrals.

A Great Human Endeavor: Building the Gothic Cathedrals

By Robert A. Scott

Robert A. Scott is the author of The Gothic Enterprise: A Guide to Understanding the Medieval Cathedral. *In this excerpt from his book, Dr. Scott explains his fascination with Gothic cathedrals and tells some of what he has learned about them.*

1   Awe. Inspiration. Humility. These words just hint at the powerful responses **evoked** by the great Gothic cathedrals of Europe. How, we may wonder, did ordinary people manage these **feats** of tremendous physical and creative effort? Technology in the twelfth to sixteenth centuries was **rudimentary**, famine and disease were rampant, the climate was often harsh, and communal life was unstable and incessantly violent. Yet communities with only a **meager** standard of living managed to make the immense investment of **capital** demanded by the construction of these great **edifices**. They mobilized the spiritual and civic determination needed to sustain building projects that sometimes **spanned** centuries. And they created buildings whose exquisite beauty continues to amaze us today.

What Is the Gothic Enterprise?

2   The movement I call the Gothic **enterprise** began in the first half of the twelfth century in the Greater Paris Basin. It continued for the next four hundred years throughout Europe. Cathedral-building was an impressive **undertaking**. Consider the case of England. Its population during the period of building was about six million. One-third of these people were young (under 5) and another seven percent were old or otherwise unproductive. Planting, tending, and harvesting crops represented the primary occupation of up to 95 percent of the population, whose survival literally depended on their crops. The average life expectancy for those fortunate enough to survive to the age of twenty was only twenty-five to thirty years more.

How Were the Cathedrals Built?

3   The process was enormously complex. Before work could begin, an overall plan was needed. Next, a site had to be found and cleared. Building materials had to be located, delivered to the site, and assembled there. To do all of this, a workforce with the necessary skills had to be found and hired. This workforce had to be instructed, supervised, and paid, and the work checked for quality. In addition, because a main aim of the Gothic style was to flood the interior with light, builders had to **devise** new ways of constructing vaults,[1] buttresses, and arches that would allow them to open the side walls for windows.

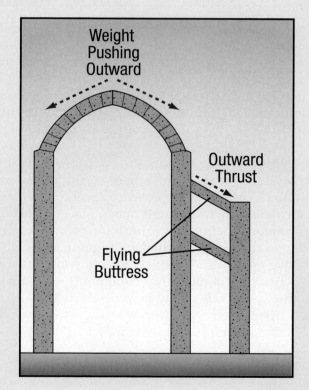

(continued on next page)

---

[1] **vault:** a ceiling that consists of several arches that are joined together and that creates a feeling of height

The Science Behind the Cathedrals

The builders of the Gothic cathedrals wanted to build churches that were much larger than previously built churches, with bigger windows to allow more light inside. They created innovative architectural features by understanding two important principles of physics: gravity and thrust. **Gravity** is the force that pulls an object toward the surface of the Earth. **Thrust** is the force that pushes on something and causes it to move.

The builders of the Gothic cathedrals used heavy stones stacked on top of each other to create tall arches. The downward pull of gravity helps keep the stones in place. However, the weight of the arches creates thrust, which pushes the stones in the columns outward. The taller the arch the more likely it is to collapse because of the opposing forces of gravity and thrust. The Gothic builders had to figure out a way to counteract the force of the top stones to prevent the arch from collapsing.

Pointed arches: In order to make arches taller, the builders began to use pointed arches. The pointed shape redirects the thrust and allows for a taller arch.

Buttresses: Builders added buttresses and flying buttresses to provide more support for the stone columns. Buttresses make higher arches possible because they **counteract** the outward force of the stones in the columns by pushing back against the column.

4   Gothic cathedrals took a very long time to complete. It could take a good half century or more to build such a structure. Some took hundreds of years to build. Initiating and bringing to completion a project of such scope and **magnitude** as the building of a Gothic cathedral obviously could not have occurred without having an enormous impact on the community that built it. Inevitably, a grand cathedral became a focus for communal identity on the part of the cathedral chapter[2] responsible for building it.

5   A cathedral-building project provided a potentially defining focus for **collective** identity among members of the community in which it was built, not unlike the sense of collective pride in achievement that so many Americans felt after the United States placed a man on the moon. Such accomplishments help foster a profound sense of communal **efficacy**.

6   Building a cathedral **entailed** an ongoing, difficult, yet energizing form of collective enterprise in which people could take enormous pride and around which they could rally a community. One imagines that those who built Gothic cathedrals would be pleased to know that future generations who gaze upon them do so with wonder, asking how human beings could possibly have accomplished what they had done.

---

[2] *chapter:* the local members of an organization

Review the text box and the questions you answered before reading. Discuss how the text box helped enhance your understanding of the reading.

COMPREHENSION

A **Main Ideas**

Read each statement. Decide if it is *True* or *False* according to the reading. Check (✓) the appropriate box. If it is false, change it to make it true. Discuss your answers with a partner.

	TRUE	FALSE
1. The process of building cathedrals in Europe was very complex.	☐	☐
2. During the 12th century, the entire population of Europe suffered from famine and disease.	☐	☐
3. While a cathedral was being constructed, the local people often felt a sense of pride and community.	☐	☐
4. The process of building cathedrals in Europe began over 1,000 years ago but lasted only 400 years.	☐	☐
5. During the 12th to the 16th centuries, life was generally violent and unstable.	☐	☐
6. The process of building cathedrals in Europe involved a large number of workers.	☐	☐
7. The local people were unhappy that constructing the cathedrals took such a long time.	☐	☐
8. During the 12th to the 16th centuries, most people did not live to be more than 25 or 30 years old.	☐	☐
9. Large windows that let in light were an important part of Gothic cathedral design.	☐	☐

B **Close Reading**

Go back to the reading and read it again. List the steps that were required to build a cathedral. Compare answers with a partner.

1. An overall plan was created.
2. _____
3. _____
4. _____
5. _____
6. _____

VOCABULARY

 A **Synonyms**

Complete each sentence with a word from the box. Use the synonym or phrase in parentheses to help you select the correct word. Be sure to use the correct tense of the verbs. Compare answers with a partner.

collective	efficacy	feat	span
counteract	entail	magnitude	rudimentary
devise	evoke	meager	undertaking
edifice			

1. Although architects are aware of physical limitations, they are constantly trying to

   _____ new ways of creating taller buildings.
   (come up with)

2. Building a structure as large and complex as a cathedral _____
   (necessitated)

   a lot of planning. There were many details to consider.

3. In many cases, the people involved in building the cathedrals were poor farmers

   with _____ resources.
   (insufficient)

4. Some of the tallest cathedrals have collapsed over time. This has caused modern-

   day architects to question the _____ of methods used by
   (effectiveness)

   medieval builders.

5. The city is planning to build a new church in my neighborhood. Unlike the

   building of the cathedrals in medieval times, this construction project will

   _____ only five years.
   (take place over)

6. The Cologne Cathedral in Germany is an impressive _____.
   (structure)

   Its towers are over 500 feet tall, and it is 284 feet wide and 474 feet long.

7. Even with the most up-to-date technology and equipment, lifting massive pieces

   of stone off the ground is a difficult and dangerous _____.
   (endeavor)

   Historians are still amazed at how medieval builders were able to accomplish

   such a(n) _____.
   (achievement)

8. The architects responsible for planning the Gothic cathedrals had a _____
   (shared)

   vision for creating a dramatic new architectural design.

9. Builders of the cathedrals used _____ tools and methods
   (simple)
   compared to what we have available today.

10. Being involved in a cathedral-building project must have _____
    (elicited)
    feelings of pride for the workers as they saw the results of their labor over time.

11. The cathedrals were structures of such complexity and _____
    (vastness)
    it required the effort of thousands of people working over hundreds of years to
    complete them.

12. In order to _____ the extra weight at the end of the
    (offset)
    building, the architects constructed a strong wall.

B **Roots**

> A **root** is a form of a word that is used as a base to make other words. Longer
> words are made by adding a prefix or a suffix to the root.
>   *voc-, vok-* means "voice" or "to call"
>   *magn-* means "great or large"

Complete each sentence with a word from the box. Use the synonym or phrase in
parentheses to help you select the correct word. Be sure to use the correct tense of
the verbs. Compare answers with a partner.

advocate	magnanimous	magnitude	vocal
convocation	magnificent	provoke	vocation
evoke	magnify	revoke	

1. Visiting a great Gothic cathedral such as the one at Chartres, Rouen, or Amiens in
   France _____ a strong feeling in many people.
   (produces)

2. Compared with the smaller size of the Romanesque structures that preceded
   them, the _____ of the Gothic cathedrals was truly
   (great size)
   awe-inspiring.

3. The suggestion to replace the church's stained glass windows with clear glass
   _____ the people into protesting.
   (angered)

4. The shape of the glass can _____ the intensity of the light
   (enlarge)
   passing through it.

(continued on next page)

5. The government _____ the company's contract to restore

    (took back)

the church because of the company's unsafe work practices.

6. Some very wealthy people are _____ in giving millions of

    (generous)

dollars to renovate Gothic cathedrals and other historic structures.

C **Word Usage**

Read the group of sentences for *capital* and *enterprise*. The words are used with a different meaning in each sentence. Match the word as used in each sentence with the appropriate meaning. Compare answers with a partner.

1. capital

_____ **1.** In Spanish, the days of the week do not begin with a capital letter, but in English they do.

_____ **2.** A person who is proven guilty of the planned murder of another person faces capital punishment in many countries.

_____ **3.** Communities with only a meager standard of living managed to make the immense investment of capital demanded by the construction of these great edifices.

> **a.** money or property that you use to start a business or project
> **b.** a letter that is written or printed in its large form
> **c.** relating to an offense, crime etc. that may be punished by death

2. enterprise

_____ **1.** The movement I call the Gothic enterprise began in the first half of the twelfth century in the Greater Paris Basin.

_____ **2.** Thomas Edison, who is credited with hundreds of inventions including the light bulb, was a man of great enterprise.

_____ **3.** The new company has been successful in its latest enterprise to provide technical support for people who want to repair damage to old buildings.

_____ **4.** Although the name of the company is State Electronics, the business is a private enterprise, not a public one.

> **a.** the ability to think of new activities or ideas and make them work
> **b.** a company, organization, or business, especially a new one
> **c.** the activity of starting and running a business
> **d.** a large and complicated plan or process that is done with other people or groups

Fact or Opinion?

Recognizing the **difference between a fact and an opinion** is an important reading skill because it helps you decide which statements are factual, and which statements are someone's views or personal perspective. A **fact** is something that can be **proven with evidence**. An **opinion** is **something that a person believes**. It may or may not be true, but it has not been proven.

EXAMPLES:

Gothic cathedrals were constructed in the first half of the twelfth century.

This is a fact because it can be confirmed using historical records.

One imagines that those who built Gothic cathedrals would be pleased to know that we admire them today.

This is an opinion because we do not know for sure whether people hundreds of years ago would have thought this way.

Read these statements. Decide if each one expresses a fact or an opinion. Check (✓) the appropriate box. Compare answers with a partner.

	FACT	OPINION
1. Before work could begin, a site had to be found and cleared.	☐	☐
2. During the period of cathedral building, the population of England was about six million.	☐	☐
3. Everyone in the community that built a cathedral was united in their pride for the achievement.	☐	☐
4. Gothic cathedrals evoke awe, humility, and inspiration.	☐	☐
5. It could take 100 years or more to build a cathedral.	☐	☐

A Warm-Up

Think of different places that you go. How do you find the way to your destination? Check (✓) all the ways that apply.

- ☐ **a.** use a map (street map, subway map, road map)
- ☐ **b.** ask someone
- ☐ **c.** rely on personal experience
- ☐ **d.** use a compass
- ☐ **e.** go with someone who knows the way
- ☐ **f.** use a GPS system
- ☐ **g.** just wander around until I find where I want to go

B Reading Strategy

Skimming for the Main Idea by Reading Topic Sentences

In academic writing, the topic sentence is often, but not always, the first sentence in a paragraph. The **topic sentence gives the main idea** of the paragraph. Reading the topic sentence of each paragraph will help you to understand the entire passage better. Writing down each topic sentence will also give you a summary of the entire passage.

Skim the reading and write the topic sentence of each paragraph below. Remember that the topic sentence may or may not be the first sentence. Compare answers with a partner.

PARAGRAPH 1: _____

PARAGRAPH 2: _____

PARAGRAPH 3: _____

PARAGRAPH 4: _____

PARAGRAPH 5: _____

PARAGRAPH 6: _____

Now read the article and connect the main ideas with the information in the paragraphs. As you read, underline the details that support the topic sentences.

From Stone to Satellite: Finding Our Way

1   The origins of the magnetic compass are shrouded in mystery.[1] No one knows who discovered the magnetic[2] **property** of the lodestone.[3] Nor does anyone know who discovered that the stone's attractive power could be **imparted** to steel or hardened iron, or that the magnet could be used in determining geographic directions. The Chinese may have been the first, as early as the 11th century, to use a magnetic needle for indicating direction.

a Compass Rose

2   The original magnetic compass simply pointed North, but was eventually **refined** to indicate several directions, and a printed card was added under the needle to show these directions. It is believed Flavio Gioia first invented the refined compass[4] circa 1300. In those days, even though ancient astronomers had learned to divide the circle mathematically, directions were not marked by degrees, but in terms of winds. Every experienced seaman, however untutored, knew his winds. They meant more to him than any number from 0 to 360. Since the ancients recognized 12 primary winds, at first the medieval compass cards were circles divided into 12 directional points. Later, for greater precision the card eventually had 32 points—eight primary winds, eight "half-winds," and 16 "quarter-winds." And the way they were drawn, often with artistic **flair**, reminded sailors of a 32-petaled flower. **Hence** the compass cards became known as wind roses.

3   The refined magnetic compass with its wind rose **evolved** even further over time. The wind rose was glued to the top of a lodestone and placed in a covered container of water. Later, oils were used instead of water to **stabilize** the compass disk from **erratic** movement. Then it was found you could magnetize needles and glue them to the bottom of the disk. These needles had to be re-magnetized periodically to maintain a sufficient level of magnetism.

4   In the 21st century, a simple compass, while accurate, is inadequate for today's modern needs. Over time, with satellite technology now in place, highly accurate methods of **navigation** are common. The most accurate system is GPS, Global Positioning System. GPS is a satellite-based navigation system made up of a **network** of 24 satellites placed into orbit by the U.S. Department of Defense. GPS was originally intended for military applications, but in the 1980s, the government

(continued on next page)

---

[1] *shrouded in mystery:* an expression that means mysterious

[2] *magnetic:* refers to the physical force by which a piece of iron or steel can make other metal objects move toward it

[3] *lodestone:* a naturally magnetized piece of the mineral magnetite

[4] *refined compass:* a compass that divides directions into 16 directional points instead of simply indicating North and South

made the system available for civilian[5] use. GPS works in any weather conditions, anywhere in the world, 24 hours a day. There are no subscription fees or setup charges to use GPS.

5   GPS satellites circle the Earth twice a day in a very precise orbit and **transmit** signal information to Earth. GPS receivers take this information and use triangulation[6] to **calculate** the user's exact location. Essentially, the GPS receiver compares the time a signal was transmitted by a satellite with the time it was received. The time difference tells the GPS receiver how far away the satellite is. Now, with distance measurements from a few more satellites, the receiver can determine the user's position and display it on the unit's electronic map.

6   A GPS receiver must be locked on to the signal of at least three satellites to calculate a 2D position (latitude[7] and longitude[8]) and track movement. With four or more satellites in view, the receiver can determine the user's 3D position (latitude, longitude, and altitude). Once the user's position has been determined, the GPS unit can calculate other information, such as speed, **bearing**, track, trip distance, distance to destination, sunrise and sunset time, and more. Today's GPS receivers are accurate to within 15 meters on average. Science has come a long way since people first charted their courses with the compass.

---

[5] *civilian*: anyone who is not a member of the military forces or the police

[6] *triangulation:* a method of finding a location by taking measurements from at least three sources

[7] *latitude:* the distance north or south of the equator. 0° latitude is at the equator.

[8] *longitude:* the position on the earth east or west of a meridian (a line drawn from the top to the bottom of the earth). 0° longitude is at Greenwich, England.

Review what you underlined as details supporting each of the topic sentences. Compare with a partner.

COMPREHENSION

A   **Main Ideas**

Read each statement. Decide if it is *True* or *False* according to the reading. Check (✓) the appropriate box. If it is false, change it to make it true. Discuss your answers with a partner.

	TRUE	FALSE
1. A lodestone is magnetized.	☐	☐
2. Flavio Gioia's compass marked direction by degrees.	☐	☐
3. The first refined compass showed 12 directional points based on wind direction.	☐	☐
4. Magnetic compasses eventually used oil instead of water for more stability.	☐	☐
5. In the 21st century, GPS signals make compasses inaccurate.	☐	☐

6. Anyone can use the Global Positioning System (GPS), not just the military.   ☐   ☐

7. A GPS can do much more than calculate an exact position.   ☐   ☐

B **Close Reading**

Read each statement. Circle the correct answer. Compare answers with a partner.

1. Magnetic needles, refined compasses, and magnetic compasses
   a. all indicated the four directions: north, south, east, and west.
   b. all indicated the directions of the winds.
   c. all depended on a magnetized needle or stone, which points north.

2. Lodestones were first used to indicate direction but were later used
   a. so that the compass always pointed north.
   b. to stabilize the compass disk.
   c. to magnetize needles.

3. The original purpose of the Global Positioning System (GPS) was
   a. to help the military.
   b. to help predict the weather.
   c. to help civilians.

4. Using GPS
   a. is free for everyone.
   b. involves a subscription fee.
   c. is free only for the military.

5. GPS satellites work by
   a. calculating the distance between two or more satellites.
   b. taking accurate photographs.
   c. sending signals to a receiver on Earth.

6. To calculate a geographic location accurately, a GPS receiver on Earth
   a. requires a minimum of two satellites.
   b. requires a minimum of three satellites.
   c. requires only one satellite.

VOCABULARY

A **Guessing from Context**

Read each quote from the reading. Try to guess the meaning of the words in bold from the context. Write the clues that helped you guess and your guess. Then consult a dictionary and write the definition.

1. "Nor does anyone know who discovered that the stone's attractive power could be **imparted** to steel or hardened iron, or that the magnet could be used in determining geographic directions."

   Clues: _the stone's attractive power to steel or hardened iron_

   Guess: _given_

   Dictionary: _to give a particular quality to something_

2. "The refined magnet compass with its wind rose **evolved** even further over time."

   Clues: _____

   Guess: _____

   Dictionary: _____

3. "And the way they were drawn, often with artistic **flair**, reminded sailors of a 32-petaled flower."

   Clues: _____

   Guess: _____

   Dictionary: _____

4. "And the way [compass cards] were drawn, often with artistic flair, reminded sailors of a 32-petaled flower. **Hence** the compass cards became known as wind roses."

   Clues: _____

   Guess: _____

   Dictionary: _____

5. "With satellite technology, highly accurate methods of **navigation** are common. The most accurate system is GPS, Global Positioning System."

   Clues: _____

   Guess: _____

   Dictionary: _____

6. "GPS satellites circle the Earth twice a day in a very precise orbit and **transmit** signal information to Earth."

Clues: _____

Guess: _____

Dictionary: _____

7. "GPS receivers take this information and use triangulation to **calculate** the user's exact location."

Clues: _____

Guess: _____

Dictionary: _____

B Using the Dictionary

Read the dictionary entries and the sentences that follow. Then match the number of the definition with the appropriate sentence. Compare answers with a partner.

1.

> **property** *n.* **1** a building, a piece of land, or both together   **2** the thing or things that someone owns   **3** a quality or power that belongs naturally to something

_____ **a.** No one knows who discovered the magnetic property of the lodestone.

_____ **b.** The government bought property in an unpopulated area and built an experimental station for testing rockets to launch satellites.

_____ **c.** Astronauts sometimes brought back rocks from the moon. However, the rocks were not their personal property.

2.

> **network** *n.* **1** a group of radio or television stations, which broadcasts many of the same programs in different parts of the country   **2** a system of lines, tubes, wires, roads, etc. that are connected to each other   **3** a set of computers that are connected to each other so that they can share information   **4** a group of people, organizations, etc. that communicate with each other and can help each other

_____ **a.** The most accurate system is GPS, Global Positioning System. GPS is a satellite-based navigation system made up of a network of 24 satellites placed into orbit by the U.S. Department of Defense.

_____ **b.** There are several major television networks in the metropolitan area.

_____ **c.** Many scientific organizations are part of a large network of professionals who conduct research and share information.

_____ **d.** In the main office, all the computers are wired to the same network, which is very secure.

(continued on next page)

3.

> bearing *n.* **1** an effect or influence on something, or no effect or influence   **2** sense of direction   **3** a direction or angle that is shown by a navigational device

_____ **a.** The billionaire's interest in the sciences had a great bearing on his decision to donate money to astronomical research.

_____ **b.** Once the user's position has been determined, the GPS unit can calculate other information, such as speed, bearing, track, trip distance, distance to destination, sunrise and sunset time and more.

_____ **c.** Without a GPS system, the travelers quickly lost their bearings on the mountain road.

C Word Forms

Fill in the chart with the correct word forms. Use a dictionary if necessary. An X indicates there is no form in that category.

	NOUN	VERB	ADJECTIVE	ADVERB
1.		calculate		X
2.	X	X	erratic	
3.		evolve		X
4.	navigation			X
5.		refine		X
6.		stabilize		X
7.		transmit		X

Complete the sentences with the correct form of one of the words above. Be sure to use the correct tense of the verbs and the singular or plural form of the nouns. Compare answers with a partner.

1. The engineers will need to make precise _____ to determine the length of the new bridge.

2. Throughout human history, people have witnessed the _____ of technology in order to meet today's needs.

3. NASA's new spacecraft has very modern _____ equipment that will be needed for the project to succeed.

4. The GPS receiver must be working properly in order to pick up on the _____ of signals from the satellites.

5. This part of the mechanism makes the manned spacecraft _____ so the people in it do not become disoriented.

6. The _____ of the computer from a machine that filled an entire room to a small hand-held device happened over the course of several decades.

7. The unmanned vehicle moved very _____ during the experiment. Its guidance system required adjustment

NOTE-TAKING: Organizing Information Chronologically

Go back to the reading and read it again. Use information from the reading to help you organize events in chronological order.

1. _The Chinese used a magnetic needle for indicating direction as early as the_
   eleventh century.

2. _____
   _____

3. _____
   _____

4. _____
   _____

5. _____
   _____

CRITICAL THINKING

Discuss the questions in a small group. Be prepared to share your answers with the class.

1. Why are people so interested in navigating? What does this ability help people do?

2. What advantages are there to using a compass? What disadvantages are there?

3. What might be some disadvantages to using GPS systems?

Discuss the questions in a small group. Be prepared to share your answers with the class.

1. "Necessity is the mother of invention" is a well-known expression. What does this saying mean? How is it relevant to the building of Gothic cathedrals? To the development of the compass and GPS technology?

2. Building the Gothic cathedrals involved creating technology that allowed the planners to build tall arches and high walls. The development of technology to create increasingly sophisticated tools for the accurate location of position has taken us from the simple compass to the GPS system. How have people benefited from the technology that developed as a result of these endeavors?

READING THREE: Reaching for the Stars: The 100-Year Starship Project

A Warm-Up

Discuss the questions in a small group.

1. Refer to Reading One. During the 12th to the 16th centuries, people started construction on cathedrals that often took several lifetimes to complete. Do you think people in the 21st century could initiate a project that would take more than a lifetime to complete? Why or why not?

2. What are some other endeavors from the past that took 100 years or more to complete?

3. Consider the title of Reading Three. What would make a century-long, expensive space project worthwhile?

B Reading Strategy

Using Visuals to Understand Important Terms and Concepts

As you saw in Chapter 2, **examining visuals** before reading can help you better understand the text. The visuals in the text sometimes **illustrate important terms** and concepts that are key to understanding the overall reading.

Read paragraph 2 and look at the diagram on page 107. Choose the correct word for each sentence from the box.

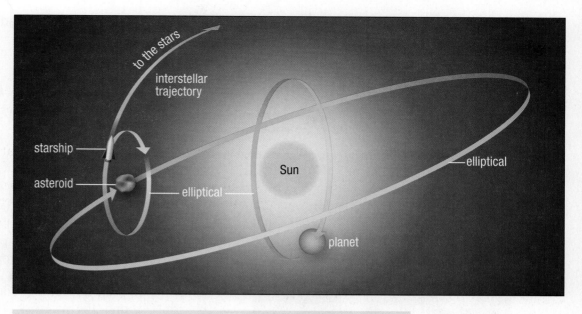

asteroid	interstellar trajectory	starship

1. A(n) _____ is a spacecraft that can travel to the stars.

2. A(n) _____ is the curved path of an object as it is moved

   or driven out to space.

3. A(n) _____ is a small rocky object in space that travels in a

   large elliptical orbit.

Read each statement. Then choose the correct answer. Compare answers with a partner. Take notes on your discussion.

1. What is one difference between a planet and an asteroid?

   a. A planet is much larger than an asteroid.

   b. Planets have elliptical orbits, but asteroids do not.

   c. Asteroids orbit planets as they travel through space.

2. What do the starship, the asteroid, and the planet have in common?

   a. They are all moving at the same speed.

   b. They are all very small objects in space.

   c. They are all in elliptical orbits around another object.

3. What is happening to the starship and the asteroid in the illustration?

   a. The starship and the asteroid are leaving their orbit around the star and going into space.

   b. The starship is leaving its orbit around the asteroid and is being thrown out into space, but the asteroid is remaining in orbit around the star.

   c. The starship is continuing to orbit around the asteroid, and the asteroid is continuing to orbit around the star.

Reaching for the Stars: The 100-Year Starship Project

By Kenneth Chang

1 It may seem a fantastical notion, but hardly more so than the idea of building a starship of any kind. Yet in Orlando, Florida, not far from the launching site of the space program's most **triumphant** achievements, the government's Defense Advanced Research Projects Agency, or DARPA, drew hundreds in October to a symposium[1] on the 100-Year Starship Study, which is devoted to ideas for visiting the stars. Participants—an **eclectic** mix of engineers, scientists, science fiction fans, students, and dreamers—explored a mix of ideas, including how to organize and finance a century-long project; whether civilization would survive, because an engine to propel a starship could also be used for a weapon to **obliterate** the planet; and whether people need to go along for the trip.

A Starship without an Engine?

2 "The space program, any space program, needs a dream," said one participant, Joseph Breeden. "If there are no dreamers, we'll never get anywhere." It was Dr. Breeden who offered the idea of an engineless starship. From his doctoral thesis, Dr. Breeden remembered that in a **chaotic** gravitational dance, stars are sometimes ejected at high speeds. The same effect, he believes, could propel starships. First, find an asteroid in an elliptical orbit that passes close to the Sun. Second, put a starship in orbit around the asteroid. If the asteroid could be captured into a new orbit that clings close to the Sun, the starship would be flung, or thrown, on an interstellar trajectory. "The chaotic **dynamics** of those two allow all the energy of one to be transferred to the other," said Dr. Breeden. "It's a unique type of gravity assist."

Challenges Facing the Project

3 In the talks, speakers laid out challenges that, while **herculean**, did not seem out of the realm of the possible. Still, the sheer distances are **daunting**. "The problem of the stars is larger than most people realize," said James Benford, a physicist who organized sessions on starship propulsion.

4 The first steps, however, are easy to imagine. Even in the 1950s, rocket scientists realized that the current engines—burning kerosene or hydrogen and spewing flames out the nozzle—are the rocket **equivalent** of gas guzzlers.[2] They designed nuclear engines that use reactors to heat liquid hydrogen into a fast-moving stream of gas. NASA had such engines ready for a **hypothetical** manned mission to Mars to follow the Moon landings.

[1] **symposium:** a formal meeting in which people who know a lot about a particular subject have discussions about it

[2] **gas guzzler:** a car that uses a lot of gasoline

5 Today, the space agency has **revived** that work, beginning with studies on an ideal fuel for a space reactor, and new nuclear engines could be ready by the end of the decade. "Space is a wonderful place to use nuclear power, because it is already radioactive," said Geoffrey Landis, a scientist at the NASA Glenn Research Center in Ohio. More advanced nuclear engines could use reactors to **generate** electric fields that **accelerated** charged ions for the thrust. Then fusion engines—producing energy through the combining of hydrogen atoms—could finally be powerful enough for interstellar travel.

6 The British Interplanetary Society put together a concept for a fusion-powered starship in the 1970s called Daedalus, **extrapolating** from known physics and technology. Dr. Richard Obousy, president of Icarus Interstellar, an organization of volunteers that has already spent several years on starship designing, is revisiting the Daedalus design to see if 30-some years of new technology can produce a better starship.

7 Dr. Benford **advocated** another approach, harking back to[3] the era of sailing ships. Giant sails on the starship could billow from photons beamed from Earth by lasers or giant antennae. "Here's a case where we know the physics, and the engineering seems doable," he said.

Vision for the Project

8 "Vision without execution is daydreaming," Mr. Neyland said in his introductory remarks, paraphrasing a Japanese proverb. "And what we're trying to inspire with the 100-Year Starship Study is that first step in establishing a bar that's high enough, with challenges that are hard enough that people will actually go start tackling some of these really hard problems."

9 Some speakers said they thought the first goal over the next century should be colonizing the solar system, starting with Mars. Dr. Obousy, for one, made his preference known in a couplet:

> On to the stars!
> Cowards shoot for Mars.

---

[3] *hark back to:* remind people of something in the past

With a partner, review the illustration, accompanying exercises that you completed, and notes you took as you read. Discuss how examining the illustration and completing the exercises helped you understand the reading. How did the illustration add new information to the reading?

COMPREHENSION

 Main Ideas

Complete the sentences with information from the reading. Discuss your answers with a partner.

1. The goal of the 100-Year Starship Study is to _____.

2. Participants in the symposium on the 100-Year Starship Study represented

_____.

(continued on next page)

Science: *Human Achievements over Time* **109**

3. One way that a starship could be propelled, or powered, is by putting it in orbit around an asteroid near the sun, then _____.

4. The project is probably called the 100-Year Starship Study because

_____.

B Close Reading

Read each question. Circle the correct answer. Compare answers with a partner.

1. In the first paragraph, how many different ideas were mentioned relating to the starship study?

    a. 2

    b. 3

    c. 4

2. What do experts believe about the challenges facing the project?

    a. They believe that overcoming the challenges will be difficult but not impossible.

    b. They believe that the challenges are too difficult to overcome.

    c. They believe that the challenges are minor, but the work involved will be very difficult.

3. What may be one of the biggest challenges facing the 100-Year Starship project?

    a. how to find volunteers to study the project

    b. how to propel an engineless starship through space

    c. how to get people interested in overcoming the problems of space travel

4. What is the ideal type of spacecraft fuel for the proposed project?

    a. Nuclear power, which is radioactive

    b. Fuel that uses sails like a ship

    c. Kerosene and hydrogen

5. What can we understand from paragraphs 6 and 7?

    a. Several people have the same idea about how to power a spacecraft.

    b. Several people have different ideas about how to power a spacecraft.

    c. Several people advocate using technology from the 1950s.

6. What is Mr. Neyland's vision for the project?

    a. The project should attempt to inspire others to take on the challenges of traveling to the stars.

    b. The project will surely succeed because the bar has been set high.

    c. The project should focus on colonizing the planets.

VOCABULARY

A **Guessing from Context**

Read each quote from the reading. Try to guess the meaning of the words in bold from the context. Write the clues that helped you guess and your guess. Then consult a dictionary and write the definition.

1. "Participants—an **eclectic** mix of engineers, scientists, science fiction fans, students, and dreamers—explored a mix of ideas, including how to organize and finance a century-long project." *(paragraph 1)*

   Clues: _mix of engineers, scientists, etc._

   Guess: _varied_

   Dictionary: _including a mixture of many different things or people_

2. "[They explored] whether civilization would survive, because an engine to propel a starship could also be used for a weapon to **obliterate** the planet." *(paragraph 1)*

   Clues: _____

   Guess: _____

   Dictionary: _____

3. "In the talks, speakers laid out challenges that, while **herculean**, did not seem out of the realm of the possible." *(paragraph 3)*

   Clues: _____

   Guess: _____

   Dictionary: _____

4. "Still, the sheer distances are **daunting**." *(paragraph 3)*

   Clues: _____

   Guess: _____

   Dictionary: _____

5. "The first steps, however, are easy to imagine. Even in the 1950s, rocket scientists realized that the current engines—burning kerosene or hydrogen and spewing flames out the nozzle—are the rocket **equivalent** of gas guzzlers." *(paragraph 4)*

   Clues: _____

   Guess: _____

   Dictionary: _____

(continued on next page)

6. "The British Interplanetary Society put together a concept for a fusion-powered starship in the 1970s called Daedalus, **extrapolating** from known physics and technology." *(paragraph 6)*

Clues: _____

Guess: _____

Dictionary: _____

B Synonyms

Read each sentence. Match the word in bold with the correct synonym or phrase from the box. Compare answers with a partner.

_e_ 1. The government is going to **revive** a research project that it had set aside years ago because there was no budget for it.

____ 2. If a spacecraft swings around a moon or a planet, its speed will **accelerate**.

____ 3. The scientist's idea is interesting, but right now it is only **hypothetical**. She will need to conduct some experiments to prove or disprove it.

____ 4. Many members of Congress **advocate** using public funds to finance another manned expedition to the moon.

____ 5. The sudden tremor of the earthquake caused a **chaotic** situation throughout the area as people ran to find a safe location.

____ 6. The physics students were surprised to learn that the rocket engine could **generate** enough heat to warm an entire office building.

____ 7. The first manned landing on the moon in 1969 was a **triumphant** success after so many years of research and experimentation.

____ 8. The **dynamic** among the members of a manned space mission must be positive, especially since they are in such a small space for such a long time.

a. disordered	**d.** relationship	**g.** support
b. produce	**e.** resurrect	**h.** theoretical
c. proud	**f.** speed up	

C Collocations

> As you learned in previous chapters, **collocations** refer to **word partners** or words that are often used together.
>
> The words *daunting* and *eclectic* appear in the reading. Each of these words has several collocations.
>
> **EXAMPLES:**
>
> daunting challenge   eclectic collection
> daunting problem   eclectic menu
> daunting prospect   eclectic mix
> daunting task

Complete each sentence with the appropriate collocation from the box above. More than one answer is sometimes possible. Compare answers with a partner.

1. Figuring out how to send people on missions that involve spending years in space is a(n) _____.

2. Creating batteries that are small, reliable, and long-lasting is a(n) _____ for the researchers, but they must succeed.

3. Spending six or seven months on the International Space Station with a handful of people is a(n) _____ that many people cannot imagine.

4. Meal planners create a very _____ for astronauts on long missions. They have few diversions, so food is very important to them.

5. The Smithsonian Institution in Washington, D.C., has a(n) _____ of historical airplanes and spacecraft.

Parallel Structure for Emphasis

Parallel structure refers to **repetition of specific grammatical forms**. Writers sometimes use parallel structure for emphasis. The repetition keeps the reader focused on the main points the author wishes to make.

EXAMPLES:

"How, we may wonder, did ordinary people manage these feats of tremendous physical and creative effort? Technology in the 12th to the 16th centuries was rudimentary, famine and disease were rampant, the climate was often harsh, and communal life was unstable and incessantly violent." *(Reading One, paragraph 1)*

The author repeated the past form of "be" four times in one sentence to emphasize the number of challenges facing the builders of the Gothic cathedrals. Essentially, the author wants the four "facts" to form a list in a single sentence in order to heighten our interest in the answer to the question.

Work with a partner. Examine the sentences from Readings One and Three. Underline the repeated forms in each. What does the repeated element emphasize in each passage?

1. "Before work could begin, an overall plan was needed. Next, a site had to be found and cleared. Building materials had to be located, delivered to the site, and assembled there. To do all of this, a workforce with the necessary skills had to be found and hired. This workforce had to be instructed, supervised, and paid, and the work checked for quality." *(Reading One, paragraph 3)*

   What does the repeated element emphasize? _____

   _____

2. "Building a cathedral entailed an ongoing, difficult, yet energizing form of collective enterprise in which people could take enormous pride and around which they could rally a community." *(Reading One, paragraph 6)*

   What does the repeated element emphasize? _____

   _____

3. "No one knows who discovered the magnetic property of the lodestone. Nor does anyone know who discovered that the stone's attractive power could be imparted to steel or hardened iron, or that the magnet could be used in determining geographic directions." *(Reading Two, paragraph 1)*

   What does the repeated element emphasize? _____

   _____

4. "And what we're trying to inspire with the 100-Year Starship Study is that first step in establishing a bar that's high enough, with challenges that are hard enough that people will actually go start tackling some of these really hard problems." (*Reading Three, paragraph 8*)

What does the repeated element emphasize? _____

_____

NOTE-TAKING: Listing Problems and Solutions

Go back to the reading and read it again. Use the chart below to identify the problems involved in traveling to the stars and the possible solutions suggested by those involved in the 100-Year Starship Project. (Note: There may be more problems than solutions, and not all problems have corresponding solutions.)

PROBLEMS	SOLUTIONS
• Danger of having someone use the power of the starship to destroy the world	•
•	•
•	•
•	•

CRITICAL THINKING

Discuss the questions in a small group. Be prepared to share your answers with the class.

1. In the first paragraph of the reading we find a list of people who attended the symposium on the 100-Year Starship Project. What other experts not already in the group would be valuable in helping to come up with more ideas for travel to the stars?

2. Why do you think some people are interested in traveling to the stars?

3. Can you think of any additional ideas that might make it possible to transport a starship into space?

BRINGING IT ALL TOGETHER

Debate the question: Do you think these endeavors are worthwhile pursuits? To prepare for the debate, first, consider the three human endeavors you read about in this chapter: the building of Gothic cathedrals, the invention and development of compasses and ultimately GPS, and the 100-Year Starship Project. Each team will consist of two students on one side of an argument and will write a list of points to support its side.

TOPIC ONE: BUILDING GOTHIC CATHEDRALS	
PRO	CON

TOPIC TWO: FINDING OUR WAY: COMPASS TO GPS	
PRO	CON

TOPIC THREE: DEVELOPING THE 100-YEAR STARSHIP PROJECT	
PRO	CON

When you are finished debating, discuss which team presented the better arguments.

WRITING ACTIVITY

Human beings have always taken on challenges, both as individuals and as groups. Think of a major scientific breakthrough from the distant or recent past. What breakthrough has affected you personally? What impact do you think it has had on other people? Write three paragraphs. In the first paragraph, describe the breakthrough. In the second paragraph, explain the impact the breakthrough has had on you. In the third paragraph, assess what you think the impact of this breakthrough has been on other people or on society as a whole.

DISCUSSION AND WRITING TOPICS

Discuss these topics in a small group. Choose one of them and write two or three paragraphs about it. Use the vocabulary from the chapter (for a complete list, go to page 118).

1. What are some of the reasons people enjoy challenges and problem-solving? Why do people often take the difficult path and try to create or achieve what seems almost impossible to accomplish?

2. Think of a human endeavor that you believe is worth the time, effort, and expense to achieve. Describe this endeavor and explain why you feel it is worthwhile.

3. What do you consider the greatest human endeavor ever attempted? Why do you think so?

VOCABULARY

Nouns	Verbs	Adjectives	Adverb
bearing	accelerate	chaotic	hence*
capital	advocate*	collective	
dynamics*	calculate	daunting	
edifice	counteract	eclectic	
efficacy	devise*	erratic	
enterprise	entail	herculean	
equivalent*	evolve*	hypothetical*	
feat	evoke	meager	
flair	extrapolate	rudimentary	
magnitude	generate*	triumphant	
navigation	impart		
network*	obliterate		
property	refine*		
undertaking*	revive		
	span		
	stabilize*		
	transmit*		

* = AWL (Academic Word List) item

SELF-ASSESSMENT

In this chapter you learned to:

O Use a text box to enhance understanding

O Skim for the main idea by reading topic sentences

O Use visuals to understand important terms and concepts

O Identify parallel structures used for emphasis

O Use dictionary entries to learn different meanings of words and understand word usage

O Guess the meaning of words from the context

O Understand and use synonyms, roots, word forms, and collocations

O Organize information chronologically and list problems and solutions

What can you do well? ✓

What do you need to practice more? ✓

CHAPTER 5

POLITICAL SCIENCE: Managing Hard Times

POLITICAL SCIENCE: the study of politics and government

OBJECTIVES

To read academic texts, you need to master certain skills.

In this chapter, you will:

- Analyze a graph
- Predict content from the first paragraph
- Paraphrase to identify main ideas
- Guess the meaning of words from the context
- Use dictionary entries to learn the meanings of words
- Understand and use synonyms, idioms, prefixes, and word forms
- Use adverb clauses to show time relationships
- Create timelines and make lists

Men wait on a breadline in New York City during the Depression.

Consider These Questions

Discuss the questions in a small group. Share your answers with the class.

1. The American stock market crash of October 29, 1929, meant that many companies lost much of their value or they went out of business. This marked the beginning of the Great Depression. What do you know about the Great Depression in the United States?

2. How do you think the stock market crash and the Great Depression that followed affected people throughout the country?

3. Consider the title of this chapter, *Political Science: Managing Hard Times*. What public services should the government provide for people when a country's economic situation worsens and millions of people are out of work?

READING ONE: The Great Depression: A Nation in Crisis

 Warm-Up

Discuss the questions in a small group. Share your answers with the class.

Oklahoma City Hooverville

Look at the photos on page 119 and above.

1. In the first photo, what are the people standing in line for?

2. Who do you think these people are?

3. In the second photo, what sort of place is being shown?

4. Who do you think is living there?

5. Why do you think they are living there?

Analyzing Graphs

Graphs are **visual ways of presenting statistics** that may be included in a text. Statistics shown in this way can enhance readers' understanding of why the information is significant. Graphs can also serve to highlight any dramatic changes the writer is explaining in the text.

Work in a small group. Examine the graph in the reading on page 123 and answer the questions below.

1. What was the trend in the Dow Jones Industrial Average in the months preceding October 1929?

   a. The industrial average was rising fairly steadily.

   b. The industrial average was rising sharply.

   c. The industrial average was decreasing steadily.

2. When did the Dow Jones Industrial Average reach its highest point during the period shown?

   a. August 1929

   b. September 1929

   c. October 1929

3. When did the Dow Jones reach its lowest point during the period shown?

   a. November 1929

   b. November 1930

   c. July 1932

Now read the text and make connections between paragraph 2 and the graph.

THE GREAT DEPRESSION: A NATION IN CRISIS

By David Goldfield, Carl E. Abbott, Virginia DeJohn Anderson, Jo Ann E. Argersinger, Peter H. Argersinger, William M. Barney, and Robert M. Weir

1   In the United States, the 1920s were a time of great **prosperity**. That prosperity ended in a stock market crash in October, 1929. As the nation slid into a catastrophic depression,[1] factories closed, employment and incomes tumbled, and millions lost their homes, hopes, and dignity.

Crash!

2   During the two years preceding the stock market crash, the market had hit record highs, stimulated by optimism, easy credit, and speculators' **manipulations**. After peaking in September, 1929, the market suffered several sharp checks, and on October 29, "Black Tuesday," panicked investors dumped their stocks, wiping out the previous year's gains in one day. Confidence in the economy disappeared, and the slide continued for months, and then years. The market hit bottom in July 1932. By then, the stock of U.S. Steel had **plunged** from $262 to $22, for example. Much of the paper wealth of America had **evaporated**, and the nation sank into the Great Depression.

3   The Wall Street crash marked the beginning of the depression, but it did not cause it. The depression stemmed from weaknesses in the New Era[2] economy. Most damaging was the unequal **distribution** of wealth and income. Workers' wages and farmers' incomes had fallen far behind industrial productivity and corporate profits; by 1929, the richest 0.1 percent of American families had as much total income as the bottom 42 percent. With more than half the nation's people living at or below the subsistence level,[3] there was not enough purchasing power to maintain the economy.

4   A second factor was that oligopolies[4] dominated American industries. By 1929, the 200 largest corporations (out of 400,000) controlled half the corporate wealth. Their power led to prices kept artificially high and rigid rather than determined by supply and demand. Because it did not respond to purchasing power, this system not only helped bring on economic **collapse** but also dimmed prospects for **recovery**.

The Depression Spreads

5   By early 1930, the effects of financial contraction were painfully evident. Factories shut down or cut back, and industrial production **plummeted**; by 1932, it was scarcely 50 percent of its 1929 level. Steel mills operated at 12 percent of capacity, auto factories at 20 percent. Unemployment **skyrocketed**, as an average of 100,000 workers a week were fired in the first three years after the crash. By 1932, one-fourth of the labor force was out of work and the wages of those Americans lucky enough to work fell sharply. Personal income dropped by more than half between 1929 and 1932. Moreover, the depression began to feed on itself in a vicious circle: shrinking wages and employment cut into purchasing power, causing businesses to slash production again and lay off workers, thereby further reducing purchasing power.

---

[1] *depression:* a long period of seriously reduced business activity and high unemployment

[2] New Era refers to the years 1920 through 1929

[3] *subsistence level:* a very poor standard of living, in which people only have the things that are completely necessary for life and nothing more

[4] *oligopoly:* the control of all or most of a business activity by very few companies so that other organizations cannot easily compete with them

Dow Jones Industrial Average, October 1928–July 1933

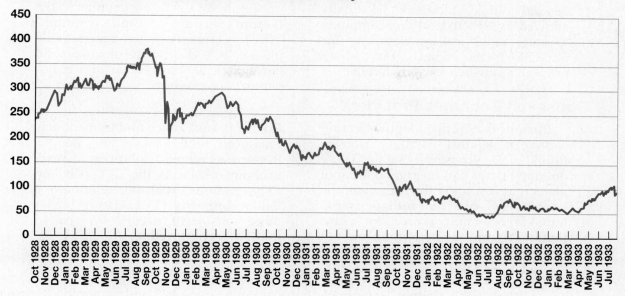

6   The depression particularly battered farmers. Commodity[5] prices fell by 55 percent between 1929 and 1932, **stifling** farm income. Cotton farmers earned only 31 percent of the pittance[6] they had received in 1929. Unable to pay their mortgages, many farm families lost their homes and fields. The **dispossessed** roamed the byways, highways, and railways of a troubled country.

7   Urban families were also evicted when they could not pay their rent. Some moved in with relatives; others lived in Hoovervilles—the name reflects the bitterness directed at the president[7]—shacks where people shivered, suffered, and starved. Oklahoma City's vast Hooverville covered 100 square miles.

8   Soup kitchens became standard features of the urban landscape, with lines of the hungry stretching for blocks. But charities and local communities could not meet the massive needs, and neither the states nor the federal government had welfare or unemployment **compensation** programs. To survive, people planted gardens in vacant lots and back alleys and tore apart empty houses or tapped gas lines for fuel.

President Hoover's Response

9   The president took **unprecedented** steps to resolve the crisis but shrank back from the interventionist policies activists urged. Hoover fought economic depression more vigorously than any previous president, but he believed that voluntary private **relief** was preferable to federal **intervention**. As the depression worsened, Hoover adopted more activist policies. He persuaded Congress to cut taxes to boost consumers' buying power, and he increased the public works[8] budget. In January 1932, he established the Reconstruction Finance Corporation (RFC), which lent federal funds to banks, insurance companies, and railroads so that their recovery could "trickle down" to ordinary Americans.

(continued on next page)

---

[5] *commodity:* a product that is bought and sold and that is the same no matter who produces it, such as oil, metal, and farm products

[6] *pittance:* a very small or unfairly small amount of money

[7] Herbert Hoover was president of the United States from 1929 to 1933.

[8] Public works include buildings, roads, ports, and so on that are built and provided by the government for the public to use.

Hoover still opposed direct aid to the general public, although he finally allowed the RFC to lend small amounts to state and local governments for unemployment relief. But these programs satisfied few Americans.

Roosevelt Becomes President

10   During his 1932 presidential election campaign against Herbert Hoover, Franklin D. Roosevelt said, "These unhappy times call for the building of plans that rest upon the forgotten, the unorganized but the **indispensable** units of economic power; for plans that build from the bottom up and not from the top down, that put their faith once more in the forgotten man at the bottom of the economic pyramid." "The forgotten man" was a memorable phrase. It had a powerful impact. In November, he was elected in a major victory over Hoover.

11   On March 4, 1933, Franklin D. Roosevelt took office and immediately reassured the American people. Roosevelt created a number of work programs, such as the CCC (Civilian Conservation Corps) and the Tennessee Valley Authority (TVA). However, far more jobs were needed for the 15 million unemployed.

Work with a partner. Refer back to the graph on page 123 and paragraph 2. How did the graph help you understand the circumstances described in the paragraph? What conclusions can you draw from the information in the graph and the paragraph?

COMPREHENSION

A **Main Ideas**

Read each statement. Then circle the correct answers. Compare answers with a partner.

1. What is the main idea of the reading?

    a. In 1929, the stock market crashed, and the United States entered a Great Depression, during which time millions of people lost their jobs and blamed the President.

    b. In 1929, the stock market crashed, and the United States entered a Great Depression, during which time no one, including the President, knew what to do.

    c. In 1929, the stock market crashed, and the United States entered a Great Depression, during which time millions of people lost their jobs and two presidents tried to help the country out of the crisis.

2. How was wealth distributed in the period just before the Great Depression began in the United States?

    a. Wealth was fairly evenly spread out among the people.

    b. The greatest amount of wealth was in the hands of a very few people.

    c. Wealth was in the hands of about half the population.

3. When they were each president during the Great Depression Herbert Hoover's and Franklin Roosevelt's actions

   a. reflected very different beliefs about how to help people in need.

   b. reflected almost the same beliefs about how to help people in need with a few key differences.

   c. reflected exactly the same beliefs about how to help people in need.

B Close Reading

Read the quotes from the reading. Write a paraphrase for each quote. Discuss your answers with a partner.

1. "After peaking in September, 1929, the market suffered several sharp checks, and on October 29, 'Black Tuesday,' panicked investors dumped their stocks, wiping out the previous year's gains in one day." *(paragraph 2)*

   Paraphrase: _____

   _____

2. "Much of the paper wealth of America had evaporated, and the nation sank into the Great Depression." *(paragraph 2)*

   Paraphrase: _____

   _____

3. "By early 1930, the effects of financial contraction were painfully evident." *(paragraph 5)*

   Paraphrase: _____

   _____

4. "The President took unprecedented steps to resolve the crisis but shrank back from the interventionist policies activists urged." *(paragraph 9)*

   Paraphrase: _____

   _____

5. "In January 1932, [Hoover] established the Reconstruction Finance Corporation (RFC), which lent federal funds to banks, insurance companies, and railroads so that their recovery could 'trickle down' to ordinary Americans." *(paragraph 9)*

   Paraphrase: _____

   _____

VOCABULARY

A Guessing from Context

Read each quote from the reading. Try to guess the meaning of the words in bold from the context. Write the clues that helped you guess and your guess. Then consult a dictionary and write the definition.

1. "By early 1930, the effects of financial contraction were painfully evident. Factories shut down or cut back, and industrial production **plummeted**; by 1932, it was scarcely 50 percent of its 1929 level." *(paragraph 5)*

   Clues: _By 1932 industrial production was scarcely 50% of its 1929 level_

   Guess: _dropped sharply_

   Dictionary: _to suddenly and quickly decrease in value or amount_

2. "Unemployment **skyrocketed**, as an average of 100,000 workers a week were fired in the first three years after the crash. By 1932, one-fourth of the labor force was out of work and the wages of those Americans lucky enough to work fell sharply." *(paragraph 5)*

   Clues: _____

   Guess: _____

   Dictionary: _____

3. "Commodity prices fell by 55 percent between 1929 and 1932, **stifling** farm income. Cotton farmers earned only 31 percent of the pittance they had received in 1929." *(paragraph 6)*

   Clues: _____

   Guess: _____

   Dictionary: _____

4. "Unable to pay their mortgages, many farm families lost their homes and fields. The **dispossessed** roamed the byways, highways, and railways of a troubled country." *(paragraph 6)*

   Clues: _____

   Guess: _____

   Dictionary: _____

5. "Hoover fought economic depression more vigorously than any previous president, but he believed that voluntary private relief was preferable to federal **intervention**." *(paragraph 9)*

Clues: _____

Guess: _____

Dictionary: _____

B Synonyms

Complete each sentence with a word from the box. Use the synonym or phrase in parentheses to help you select the correct word. Compare answers with a partner.

compensation	plunged	recovery
indispensable	prosperity	unprecedented

1. After Black Tuesday and the Great Depression, U.S. economic

_____ took several years.
       (restoration)

2. The measures Franklin D. Roosevelt proposed for helping Americans during the

Great Depression were _____.
       (unheard of)

3. Franklin D. Roosevelt believed that the average worker was a(n)

_____ part of his plan to strengthen the weak economy.
       (essential)

4. Stock market prices _____ as investors panicked over
       (dropped sharply)
recent political decisions.

5. During Franklin D. Roosevelt's presidency Congress passed an act that provided

_____ for unemployed workers to temporarily make up
       (pay)
for lost wages.

6. When a person has lived a life of _____, suddenly losing
       (abundance)
one's job and being poor is a great shock. Many people experienced this change in

circumstances during the Great Depression.

C Word Forms

Fill in the chart with the correct word forms. Use a dictionary if necessary. An **X** indicates there is no form in that category.

	NOUN	VERB	ADJECTIVE	ADVERB
1.	manipulation			X
2.	X	stifle		
3.	collapse			X
4.		evaporate		X
5.	recovery			X
6.	intervention			X

Complete the sentences with the correct form of one of the words above. Be sure to use the correct tense of the verbs and the singular or plural form of the nouns. Compare answers with a partner.

1. Once the housing market fell, homeowners realized that most of the value of their homes had _____.

2. The government refused to _____ on behalf of the homeowners who were faced with foreclosure.

3. In many of the areas affected by the depressed housing market, prices have still not _____.

4. Getting a mortgage became more difficult, and this _____ home sales for a number of years.

5. _____ lending practices led to the housing bubble. Borrowers were falsely led to believe that they could borrow more than they could actually afford.

6. The recent housing downturn was not the first time homeowners saw dropping home prices. Many homeowners still remember how the housing market _____ in the 1980s.

GRAMMAR FOR READING

Using Adverb Clauses to Show Time Relationships

Clauses that begin with adverbs of **time** such as *when, as,* and *by the time* indicate **time relationships** and help you understand when events occur in a reading.

EXAMPLES:
1. **As** more and more people lost their homes, Hoovervilles grew in number.
2. The Great Depression lasted almost **until** the United States entered World War II.
3. **By the time** Hoover left office, the Great Depression had gotten much worse.

- *As* conveys the idea of while or when something is happening.
- *Until* means "up to the time that"
- *By the time* indicates that one event occurred before a certain time or before another event took place.

Read each statement. Insert the correct adverb of time. More than one adverb may be possible. Compare answers with a partner.

1. I can't leave _____ I finish my homework.

2. _____ Roosevelt took office, the unemployment rate was over 20 percent.

3. _____ the Great Depression continued, many people lost hope for a better life.

4. _____ work programs such as the CCC and the TVA went into action, many people remained out of work.

5. _____ World War II ended in 1945, the United States had recovered almost completely from the Great Depression.

6. _____ they face the future, people who grew up during a depression often fear a recurrence of hard times.

NOTE-TAKING: Creating a Timeline

Go back to the reading and read it again. Chart the important information on the timeline.

1920 _____

1921 _____

1922 _____

1923 _____

1924 _____

1925 _____

1926 _____

1927 _____

1928 _____

1929 _____

1930 _____

1931 _____

1932 _____

1933 _____

CRITICAL THINKING

Discuss the questions in a small group. Be prepared to share your points of view with the class.

1. Consider the following quote from the reading: "[Hoover] believed that voluntary private relief was preferable to federal intervention." Why do you think voluntary private relief didn't work during the Great Depression?

2. Why do you think President Hoover was against federal intervention or giving direct assistance to people?

A Warm-Up

Discuss this question in a small group. Make a list of arguments for both sides of the question.

QUESTION: When a nation is in a depression, should people take whatever work they can get or should they refuse work unless it is in their chosen field? For example, should an unemployed teacher be expected to work in construction?	
PEOPLE SHOULD TAKE WHATEVER WORK THEY CAN GET. REASONS:	PEOPLE SHOULD TRY TO WORK IN THEIR CHOSEN FIELD. REASONS:

B Reading Strategy

Predicting Content from the First Paragraph

The **first paragraph** of a reading not only serves as the **introduction** to the rest of the text but also **stimulates our interest** in, and curiosity about, what we are going to read. The first paragraph presents ideas that are expanded upon later in the reading. Taking the time to think about and try to predict what we are going to read engages us as active participants in the text. It also gives a preview of what is to come, allowing us to know what details to focus on as we read.

Read the first paragraph of the reading. Answer the question below.

1. What types of emergency public works projects do you think the writer will focus on? Be specific.

   _____

2. What do you think Roosevelt meant by "a single new and greatly enlarged plan"?

   _____

Now read the text and underline information that provides details about the ideas in the first paragraph.

The Works Progress Administration and the Federal Arts Project

By Nick Taylor

1   In his April 7, 1932 speech, Roosevelt said, "It is my thought that with the exception of certain of the normal public building operations of the government, all emergency public works shall be united in a single new and greatly **enlarged** plan." The overriding **criterion** of the new program, said the president, was that "all work undertaken should be useful—not just for a day, or a year, but useful in the sense that it affords permanent improvement in living conditions or that it creates future new wealth for the nation."

2   In 1935, President Roosevelt was ready to **launch** a three-to-five-year program that would spend as much as six billion dollars on projects that included building housing and highways and carrying electricity deeper into rural areas.[1]

The Emergency Relief Appropriations Act

3   In April, 1935, Congress passed the Emergency Relief **Appropriations** Act authorizing $4.8 billion to be spent on work **relief**. Roosevelt called the effort that was about to start "the most **comprehensive** work plan in the history of the nation." On May 6, Roosevelt signed the executive[2] order creating the Works Progress Administration (WPA). WPA labor would be used for building roads, public buildings, water and sewer lines, and a variety of other projects.

4   Project proposals were submitted to the WPA for approval. For example, projects approved by the WPA for Oakland, California, included rat control, book repairs at public libraries, park and playground improvements, painting and repairs to schools and other public buildings. Applications for projects like these had come from virtually every local government around the country. These projects had the **virtue** of being labor-intensive and quick to start, and they did improve the infrastructure[3] in small ways, as well as improve people's lives.

---

[1] In 1929 only 2 percent of American farms had electricity.

[2] The president has the power, given to him by Congress and the U.S. Constitution, to issue an executive order. Such orders are administrative in nature.

[3] *infrastructure:* the basic systems and structures that a country or organization needs in order to work well, for example roads and banking systems

5   Roosevelt named Harry Hopkins head of the WPA. Hopkins stated that the new work program "would give the nation's resources in wages to the unemployed, in return for which they would help build and improve America."

Federal One: The WPA's Federal Arts Project

6   During a speech in Iowa City, Hopkins announced that the government would sponsor a national theater and other arts projects under the WPA. Before long it had painters, sculptors, musicians and composers, actors and stagehands, and playwrights and writers all around the country applauding their good fortune.

7   The WPA's Federal One had freed the arts from their need to please commercial tastes and elite **patrons**. With the government funding artists, actors, playwrights, and musicians, their work had spilled into parks, schools, churches, and community centers. Millions of Americans, many for the first time in their lives, **thronged** to concerts and plays and studied paintings and drawings, much of the time without having to take a penny from their pockets. They were sending their children to free art and music classes and attending these classes on their own. After a year and a half, the WPA's **mission** to take the arts to the people and keep arts workers out of breadlines was by most measures a complete success.

8   Federal One had by now spent approximately $40 million and employed a total of some 40,000 workers. Both figures were **minuscule** portions of the WPA's total funding and jobs,[4] but the arts projects had already received an outsized share of attention and publicity—and **notoriety**. Some critics, among them the *New York Times,* objected on principle to the idea of paying artists to create art rather than build roads. "Their usefulness has been widely doubted," the newspaper wrote in a September 1, 1936 editorial.

9   Artists had had high expectations when the projects started. Douglas Lynch, in Portland, Oregon, had been **eking out** a living painting scenic backdrops for department store window displays. When he heard the news it was as if "we artists had received a **commission** from the Medicis."[5] Printmaker and lithographer Will Barnet viewed Federal One as overdue recognition by the government that the arts deserved public support. "It was one of the greatest efforts in history to make a democracy a democracy," he said years later. Artists took it as a natural evolutionary stage in the nation's development; it was finally following the lead of European countries in providing the arts with public **subsidies**.

---

[4] During the course of its existence, the WPA's total funding was $13.4 billion, and it provided 8 million jobs. Funding for the Federal One Arts Project represented .003 percent of the total funding, and 40,000 Federal One workers represented .005 percent of all the people employed by the WPA.

[5] *the Medicis*: During the 15th to 18th centuries, the Medicis were a very powerful Italian family in Florence. They were strong supporters of artists

How did underlining information that provides details for the ideas in the first paragraph help you predict and understand what you read ?

COMPREHENSION

A Main Ideas

Read each statement. Decide if it is *True* or *False* according to the reading. Check (✓) the appropriate box. If it is false, change it to make it true. Discuss your answers with a partner.

	TRUE	FALSE
1. Roosevelt had a plan to create projects that would help improve life for many people in the country.	☐	☐
2. The Emergency Relief Appropriations Act gave people money but not jobs.	☐	☐
3. One purpose of the Works Progress Administration was to get people back to work by building roads, public buildings, and so on.	☐	☐
4. Federal One focused on all the arts.	☐	☐
5. Artists were disappointed that so little money had been allocated to the arts.	☐	☐

B Close Reading

Read the quotes from the reading. Circle the statement that best explains each quote. Share your answers with a partner.

1. "Roosevelt called the effort that was about to start 'the most comprehensive work plan in the history of the nation.'" *(paragraph 3)*

   a. Roosevelt was making an effort to create a work plan that would be written about as a historic moment in the United States.

   b. Roosevelt believed that the new effort was going to cover more types of work than any work project before it.

   c. Roosevelt called people and asked them to make an effort with the new work plan he was about to start.

2. "These projects [such as rat control, book repairs at public libraries, repairs to public buildings] had the virtue of being labor-intensive and quick to start." *(paragraph 4)*

   a. These projects were quick to start but involved too much labor.

   b. The advantages of some of the projects were that they could start up fast and employ a lot of people.

   c. Projects like the ones mentioned were very virtuous because they involved the public.

3. "Before long [Federal One] had painters, sculptors, musicians and composers, actors and stagehands, and playwrights and writers all around the country applauding their good fortune." *(paragraph 6)*

   a. Before long, Federal One had contacted painters, musicians, writers, and other people in the arts and applauded the wonderful work they had done.

   b. Federal One was going to create a fortune for artists, writers, and others in a short time.

   c. In a short time, people involved in the arts throughout the country were happy about their good luck in having Federal One.

4. "Some critics, among them the *New York Times*, objected on principle to the idea of paying artists to create art rather than build roads. 'Their usefulness has been widely doubted,' the newspaper wrote." *(paragraph 8)*

   a. Some people criticized the idea of paying artists to create art, because they felt that artists should be doing other work, such as building roads.

   b. Some critics objected to the idea of paying artists, because they thought art was useless.

   c. Some critics felt that artists had no principles, so they should not be paid for the art they created.

VOCABULARY

Ⓐ Using the Dictionary

Read the dictionary entries and the sentences that follow. Then match the number of the definition with the appropriate sentence. Compare answers with a partner.

> **mission** *n.* **1** an important job that involves traveling somewhere, done by a member of the Air Force, Army, etc.   **2** an important job that someone has been given to do, especially when they are sent to another place   **3** a group of important people who are sent by their government to another country to discuss something or collect information   **4** the purpose or the most important aim of an organization

1.

_____ a. After a year and a half, the WPA's mission to take the arts to the people and keep arts workers out of breadlines was by most measures a complete success.

_____ b. The soldiers trained for a secret mission to find and destroy the enemy's supply of weapons.

_____ c. The medical team's mission for the next two years is to establish a hospital in a mountain community in New Guinea.

_____ d. The president assigned five people to go on a fact-finding mission to investigate the unemployment problem in Europe.

(continued on next page)

commission *n.* **1** a group of people who have been given the official job of finding out about something or controlling something **2** an amount of money paid to someone for selling something, according to the value of the goods they have sold **3** a request for an artist, musician etc. to make a piece of art or music, for which they are paid

2.

_____ **a.** The artist received a commission to paint a portrait of a well-known family.

_____ **b.** After the two planes collided, the Federal Transportation Safety Board created an investigatory commission to determine the cause of the crash.

_____ **c.** The real estate agent received a 6-percent commission on the sale of the house.

launch *v.* **1** to start an important activity or a serious attempt to achieve something **2** to send a weapon or spacecraft into the sky or into space **3** to make a new product, book etc. available for sale for the first time **4** to throw something into the air with a lot of force

3.

_____ **a.** In 1935, President Roosevelt was ready to launch a three-to-five-year program that would spend as much as $6 billion on projects that included building housing and highways and carrying electricity deeper into rural areas.

_____ **b.** The company is planning to launch its new line of fall clothing next week.

_____ **c.** A protester launched a huge rock through the government office window and shattered it.

_____ **d.** The company is going to launch a new satellite to replace one that is 20 years old.

B Synonyms

Complete each sentence with a word or phrase from the box. Use the synonym in parentheses to help you select the correct word. Compare answers with a partner.

appropriation	criterion	miniscule	patron	throng
comprehensive	eke out	notoriety	subsidy	virtue

1. The newspaper reported on a man who lost his job and his savings. He had to take various odd jobs to _____ eke out _____ a living.
   (barely sustain)

2. The amount of money the charity was given by the government was _____ compared to what they received through private
   (meager)
   donations. Private donations last year totalled $10 million.

3. Every summer, thousands of people _____ to the outdoor
   (go in large numbers)
   theater in Central Park to enjoy the free entertainment.

4. In the United States, many farmers receive a(n) _____
   (payment)
   from the government to keep their farms in operation.

5. Many governments around the world have created _____
   (extensive)
   plans to guarantee that people without health insurance are provided medical care.

6. The new computer system was intimidating to some but had the _____ of being easy to use.
   (good quality)

7. Hundreds of artists would never have survived the Great Depression without a generous _____ like the U.S. government to help them by
   (benefactor)
   paying them to do their art.

8. Potential employees at the company had to meet one very important _____: the ability to remain calm under pressure.
   (rule)

9. The politician gained considerable _____ for his unethical
   (disrepute)
   behavior.

10. The large anonymous donation, which provided a(n) _____
    (allocation)
    of $50,000 for the purchase of books, was a tremendous help to the university library.

C Prefix en-

> The prefix *en-* means "to make or cause to become." *En-* can be added to an adjective or a noun to create a verb.
>
> **EXAMPLE:**
> *enlarge* v. to make bigger
> We are going to enlarge our house by building additional rooms.

Work with a partner. Complete each sentence with the correct word from the box.

enclose	endanger	endear	enrich	ensure	entrust

1. The government was willing to _____ an inexperienced

   person with the new project.

2. Local officials can _____ the welfare of the people in their

   districts by creating more jobs.

3. President Roosevelt was able to _____ himself to many

   people by providing work to thousands during the Great Depression.

4. Unsafe working conditions can _____ the lives of people

   working on bridges and tunnels.

5. Roosevelt wanted artists to create works that would _____

   people's lives at the time and in the future.

NOTE-TAKING: Making Lists

Go back to the reading and read it again. Then use the chart to list the projects done under the Works Progress Administration (WPA) in general and the Federal Arts Project in particular. Share your work with a partner.

WORKS PROGRESS ADMINISTRATION	FEDERAL ARTS PROJECT

CRITICAL THINKING

Discuss the questions in a small group. Be prepared to share your answers with the class.

1. During the Great Depression, the Federal Arts Project brought concerts, plays, and art for free or at very low cost to millions of people across the country. In what ways was this project a worthwhile use of government funds? How do you think it benefited people during the depression?

2. Federal One supported painters, sculptors, musicians, writers, and others in the arts. Who else outside the field of art might have benefited economically from the artists' work?

3. In 1929 only 2 percent of American farms had electricity. One of the goals of the WPA was to provide electricity to thousands of these people. How do you think not having electricity affected farmers' lives? How did getting electricity change their lives?

LINKING READINGS ONE AND TWO

Discuss the questions in a small group. Be prepared to share your answers with the class.

1. What was the major difference between Hoover's and Roosevelt's approaches to reducing the jobless rate and providing relief to the unemployed?

2. In Reading One, President Roosevelt is quoted as saying, "These unhappy times call for the building of plans that rest upon the forgotten." According to Reading Two, how did Roosevelt keep his promise to the forgotten?

READING THREE: An Artist's Perspective on the Federal Arts Project

 **Warm-Up**

Discuss the questions in a small group.

1. You will recall from Reading Two that during the Great Depression, the Federal Arts Project provided $40 million in funds to support 40,000 artists in their work. If you were an artist—a painter, sculptor, musician, or writer, for example—what would your perspective be on this project? How would you feel about being subsidized to do your art? Would you feel that you had a responsibility to work on public projects such as building roads or repairing buildings instead?

2. The artist Robert Gwathmey describes spending a summer working on a tobacco farm in the American South. Do you think an artist needs to have a direct experience such as this in order to create a work of art?

Paraphrasing to Identify Main Ideas

As you learned in Chapter 2, a **paraphrase is a shorter restatement** of something someone has written. When we paraphrase, we use our own words to **express the general idea** of what we are reading. Paraphrasing each paragraph in a reading will help clarify the main ideas.

EXAMPLE PARAGRAPH:
Richmond, Virginia, didn't feel the Depression to any great extent. It's a tobacco town. A strange thing, I don't care how deep a Depression might be, people seem to insist on smoking. That sort of sustained the city, I'm certain.

EXAMPLE PARAPHRASE:
Richmond, Virginia, wasn't badly affected by the Depression because the tobacco business continued to support it.

Read paragraph 2 and write a paraphrase on the lines below.

_____

_____

_____

Now read the text and write a one-sentence paraphrase in the margin next to each paragraph.

An Artist's Perspective on the Federal Arts Project

By Robert Gwathmey

Robert Gwathmey (1903–1988) was a Virginia-born artist living in New York at the time he was interviewed by Studs Terkel for Terkel's book, *Hard Times: An Oral History of the Great Depression.* In this excerpt, Gwathmey gives his perspective on working for the Federal Arts Project, which was part of the WPA.

1   Richmond, Virginia, didn't feel the Depression to any great extent. It's a tobacco town.[1] A strange thing, I don't care how deep a Depression might be, people seem to **insist** on smoking. That sort of sustained the city, I'm certain.

[1] *tobacco town:* a town or city whose economy is based on growing tobacco and manufacturing tobacco products

2   I got out of art school in 1930. That was the **proper** time for any artist to get out of school. (Laughs.) Everybody was unemployed, and the artist didn't seem strange any more. I got a job teaching at a girls' school in Philadelphia, Beaver College. This was 1932. I taught two days a week and spent the rest of the time painting. The WPA was founded[2] then, '33, '34.

[2] *founded:* established

Tamino gelashvi

3   The total cost of the Federal Arts Project was only $23 million.[3] Many of these paintings, sculptures, and prints were given to museums, courthouses, public buildings. I think that today those in museums alone are worth about $100 million. Not only did this $23 million support young artists just out of school, but artists in **transition**. I'll wager if there were five hundred gallery artists who **made it**, who are represented by dealers, about four hundred were on WPA.

4   Nobody was buying art in those days. The Whitney Museum had $35,000 a year to buy **contemporary** art in the Thirties. We thought that was just the greatest thing ever. Now a man will pay $35,000 for a single painting.

5   Guys on the project made something **in the neighborhood of** $94 a month. Then a guy might have a sweetheart[4] on the project, so that would be almost $200 a month. You could live very well. But the most important thing was: the artist had a **patron** who made no aesthetic judgments. So artists for the first time, I dare say, had a patron—the Government—who made no aesthetic judgments at all.

6   The director of the Federal Arts Project was Edward Bruce. He was a friend of the Roosevelts—from a polite family— who was a painter. He was a man of real **broad** vision. He insisted there be no **restrictions**. You were a painter: Do your work. You were a sculptor: Do your work. You were a printmaker: Do your work. An artist could do anything he **pleased**.

7   I painted this thing called "Tobacco." If I'm going to paint tobacco, let me do

some work on tobacco. It was 1936. I spent a summer on this tobacco farm in North Carolina. I picked tobacco because I wanted to **know the whole story**. An instant observer could do all this surface quality. To be involved, it has to have a deeper meaning, right? We're all total fellows,[5] aren't we? Right. I insist on being a total fellow. I couldn't sit there and make a sort of **representational** and calling it priming tobacco (i.e., pulling the leaves off the tobacco plant), if I hadn't done it myself. I had to.

8   I lost my job at Beaver College. I wouldn't expect a man in 1930 to think like a man in 1968, would you? Of course not. But there are many people who will take a point of view as artists: I'll be an idealist. I'll be a romanticist, I'll be this or that or the other. You've got to be what you are, churning up the day in which you live and pull out of that experience something that is representative in artistic terms.

9   Artists have to live, right? Eat, sleep, breathe, build. The great difference is when you have a government as a patron or anyone else as a patron, who made no **demands** on you at all, there were no enlarged notions of **making that extra buck**.

10   During the Depression, we were all more or less engulfed. Today when people say poverty, they turn their head. They don't want to admit poverty exists. They're living too high, so on-the-fat, right? If you're **living on-the-fat** and see poverty, you simply say: They're no good. In the Depression, there was a little more acceptance of the unemployed guy, because you could be he.

[3] Gwathmey made an error. The total cost was $40 million.

[4] *sweetheart:* girlfriend

[5] *total fellows:* refers to the idea that all men are equal

Compare your paraphrases with those of a classmate. If a classmate wrote a different paraphrase, discuss why you think there were differences.

COMPREHENSION

A Main Ideas

Check (✓) the statements that best express the main ideas in the reading. Discuss your answers with a partner.

☐ 1. Gwathmey thought the WPA was a very beneficial program for artists during the depression.

☐ 2. Gwathmey thought that all the work the artists produced should be in museums.

☐ 3. Gwathmey thought the artwork was later worth far more than the government originally spent to support the artists.

☐ 4. Gwathmey believed that the most positive aspect of the Federal Arts Project was that artists did not have to work building roads or repairing buildings.

☐ 5. Gwathmey believed that the most positive aspect of the Federal Arts Project was that artists were supported by a patron who let them create whatever they wanted.

☐ 6. Gwathmey worked on a tobacco farm because he wanted to help out tobacco farmers in North Carolina.

☐ 7. Gwathmey worked on a tobacco farm because he wanted to gain an understanding of the people who picked tobacco and the work they did.

B Close Reading

Read the quotes from the reading. Circle the statement that best explains each quote. Share your answers with a partner.

1. "I got out of art school in 1930. That was the proper time for any artist to get out of school." (Laughs.) *(paragraph 2)*

   a. Gwathmey laughed because what he said about artists getting out of school in 1930 was very funny.

   b. Gwathmey laughed at the irony of an artist getting out of school at the beginning of the Depression, when there was no work.

   c. Gwathmey laughed because he felt fortunate as an artist to get out of art school in 1930.

2. "I'll wager if there were five hundred gallery artists who made it, who are represented by dealers, about four hundred were on WPA." *(paragraph 3)*

   a. Of the artists whose work was in galleries and who were successful, 80 percent of them had been supported by the WPA.

   b. Of the artists whose work was in galleries and who were successful, 80 percent of them needed dealers to represent them.

   c. Of the artists whose work was in galleries and who were represented by dealers, 80 percent of them needed help from the WPA.

3. "He [Edward Bruce] insisted there be no restrictions. You were a painter: Do your work. You were a sculptor: Do your work. You were a printmaker: Do your work. An artist could do anything he pleased." *(paragraph 6)*

   a. Bruce believed that artists on the project should do their work.

   b. Bruce believed that artists on the project should create only what pleased them.

   c. Bruce believed that artists on the project should not be told what to create.

4. "During the Depression, we were all more or less engulfed. Today when people say poverty, they turn their head. They don't want to admit poverty exists." *(paragraph 10)*

   a. During the Depression, everyone was poor and in the same bad situation, but today economic times are better, and people don't want to think about poverty.

   b. During the Depression, everyone was poor and in a bad situation, but today people aren't poor, so they don't think about it.

   c. During the Depression, everyone was poor and in a bad situation, but today people don't believe that the Great Depression ever took place.

VOCABULARY

 Collocations

> As you learned in previous chapters, **collocations** refer to **word partners** or **words that are often used together.**
>
> The words *contemporary* and *broad* appear in the reading. Each of these words has several collocations.
>
> **EXAMPLES:**
>
> | | |
> |---|---|
> | contemporary art | broad agreement |
> | contemporary debate | broad category |
> | contemporary issue | broad definition |
> | contemporary life | broad range |
> | contemporary society | |

Complete each sentence with the appropriate collocation from the box above. Compare answers with a partner.

1. The term *art* describes a _____ that includes not only mural painting, easel painting, and sculpture, but also architecture and even furniture design.

2. The economic downturn and its probable causes are the subject of _____.

(continued on next page)

3. A _____ of "recovery" is "the process by which something that was taken, damaged, or lost returns to normal."

4. _____ is extremely dependent on computer technology. People rely on it for business, personal matters, and even health issues.

5. This contract does not include many details. It is a _____ based on mutual trust between the two parties.

6. The fast pace of _____ is very stressful. It is important to relax whenever possible.

B Idioms

1 Read the list of idioms found in the reading. Go back to the reading and consider the context of each idiom. Then match each idiom with its meaning. Compare answers with a partner.

_____ 1. know the whole story   **a.** approximately

_____ 2. make an extra buck   **b.** earn additional money

_____ 3. make it   **c.** fully understand a situation

_____ 4. in the neighborhood of   **d.** having a prosperous life

_____ 5. living on-the-fat   **e.** succeed

2 Complete each sentence with an idiom. The phrases in parentheses will help you choose the correct idiom. Be sure to use the correct tense of the verbs. Compare answers with a partner.

1. I'm not sure exactly what I will make on my new job, but it will be

_____ $50,000 per year.
    (about)

2. Bill Gates started out working in his garage, but he eventually _____,
                                                               (became very rich)
and now he is one of the wealthiest people in the world.

3. Several of the artists who benefited from the Federal Arts Project were

_____ after the Depression ended. Their artwork today is
(successful and wealthy)
worth hundreds of thousands of dollars.

4. The employees did not have any details about the company's finances, but the

CEO _____ and told them what was happening.
    (understood the issues)

5. During the Depression some people had steady jobs and _____
                                                                   (earned money)
by taking on a second, part-time job.

C Word Forms

Fill in the chart with the correct word forms. Use a dictionary if necessary. An **X** indicates there is no form in that category.

	NOUN	VERB	ADJECTIVE	ADVERB
1.	demand			X
2.		insist		
3.	X	please		
4.	X	X	proper	
5.	restriction			
6.	transition			

Complete the sentences with the correct form of one of the words above. Be sure to use the correct tense of the verbs. Compare answers with a partner.

1. The government did not _____ the artists in any way. In fact, some artists created work that ridiculed the government, but the government never intervened.

2. Nancy is a very _____ person. She has very high standards and expects things to be done perfectly.

3. Even though they had little or no work, many Depression-era families felt it was important for their children to get a _____ education and not to go to work.

4. It took several years for some writers to gain acceptance in the literary world. They persevered in the face of harsh criticism and were _____ when their work was finally published and read.

5. American farmers experienced a time of _____ beginning in the 1930s. Their lives went from being extremely primitive, with only 2 percent having electricity, to advanced, with modern machinery, over the course of many years.

6. Roosevelt was a very persistent person. He never gave up. His _____ on providing jobs and supporting the arts never failed.

CRITICAL THINKING

Discuss the questions in a small group. Be prepared to share your answers with the class.

1. Many people criticized President Roosevelt for creating the Federal Arts Project, saying that artists should build roads rather than create art. After reading Robert Gwathmey's perspective as an artist, do you agree or disagree with the critics of the Federal Arts Project? Explain your answer.

2. Robert Gwathmey said that today people do not want to admit that poverty exists, in part because they are living well. Do you agree or disagree with his statement? Explain your answer.

AFTER YOU READ

BRINGING IT ALL TOGETHER

In a small group discuss the situations described below. Then share your group's ideas with the class. Use the vocabulary you studied in the chapter (for a complete list go to page 147).

1. Imagine you are advisers to the president during the Great Depression. Create a plan of action to help either President Hoover or President Roosevelt make decisions that will give people work and improve the economic situation.

2. Determine an amount of money you think would be appropriate to spend on the plan you developed in question 1. Decide on the categories of work/jobs, who is qualified to do them, and what percent of your budget you will allocate to each category of work.

WRITING ACTIVITY

Write a narrative. Imagine you are a young man or woman who is out of work during the Great Depression. Describe where you live, what has happened to you, and how you feel. Write about your efforts to find work and to live during these hard times. Describe your response to President Roosevelt's programs, both in terms of helping you find employment, and in providing you with opportunities to learn about art, music, and theater for little or no money.

DISCUSSION AND WRITING TOPICS

Discuss these topics in a small group. Choose one of them and write three paragraphs about it. Use the vocabulary from the chapter.

1. As you have learned, artists were paid by the WPA to create artwork. When the artists completed their work, it belonged to the government. How do you feel about this? Should the artists have been able to keep or to sell their work? Explain your answer.

2. What connections do you see between what happened during the Great Depression and the economic situation at another period of time in the United States or in another country? What are the similarities? What are the differences? Do you think the measures taken by Presidents Hoover and Roosevelt during the Great Depression could be used in the situation you have chosen? Why or why not?

VOCABULARY

Nouns	Verbs	Adjectives	Idioms
appropriation*	eke out	broad	in the
collapse*	enlarge	comprehensive*	neighborhood of
commission*	evaporate	contemporary*	know the whole
compensation*	insist	indispensable	story
criterion*	launch	minuscule	living on-the-fat
demand	please	proper	make an extra
dispossessed	plummet	unprecedented	buck
intervention*	plunge		make it
manipulation*	skyrocket		
mission	stifle		
notoriety	throng		
patron			
prosperity			
recovery*			
restriction*			
subsidy*			
transition*			
virtue			

* = AWL (Academic Word List) item

SELF-ASSESSMENT

In this chapter you learned to:

○ Analyze a graph

○ Predict content from the first paragraph

○ Paraphrase to identify main ideas

○ Guess the meaning of words from the context

○ Use dictionary entries to learn the meanings of words

○ Understand and use synonyms, idioms, prefixes, and word forms

○ Use adverb clauses to show time relationships

○ Create timelines and make lists

What can you do well? ✓

What do you need to practice more? ✓

CHAPTER 6

HEALTH SCIENCES: Medical Mysteries Solved

HEALTH SCIENCES: the study of human health and disease

OBJECTIVES

To read academic texts, you need to master certain skills.

In this chapter, you will:

- Identify tone and point of view
- Draw inferences
- Read the last paragraph first to get an overview
- Understand phrasal verbs
- Guess the meaning of words from the context
- Create a flowchart and a chain of events
- Understand and use content-specific vocabulary, prefixes, suffixes, word forms, and idioms
- Understand the use of the passive voice

Consider These Questions

Discuss the questions in a small group. Share your answers with the class.

1. Read the title of this chapter, *Medical Mysteries Solved,* and the title of this reading, *Solving a Deadly Puzzle*. From these titles what can you predict about the reading? Make a list.

   _____

   _____

   _____

2. Finding causes and cures for diseases in the 19th century and the early 20th century was even more difficult than it is today. Why do you think this is so? List your reasons.

   _____

   _____

   _____

READING ONE: Solving a Deadly Puzzle

A Warm-Up

Answer the questions. Share your answers in a small group.

1. Throughout history, serious diseases such as cholera[1] have spread through human populations. What major diseases do you know of? Make a list of them and include places and dates if you can.

   _____   _____

   _____   _____

   _____   _____

2. Think about how scientists figure out how serious diseases spread among populations. What methods do they use? Make a list.

   _____   _____

   _____   _____

   _____   _____

----

[1] *cholera*: a serious, often fatal disease

Reading the Last Paragraph First to Get an Overview

The **last paragraph** of a reading usually **summarizes** the passage. Reading the last paragraph first gives you an overview of the reading and enhances understanding. It helps you understand how the author arrives at his or her conclusion.

Read the title again, and then read the last paragraph. What does the last paragraph tell you about what the deadly puzzle was, who solved it, and how the puzzle was solved?

Now read the text and refer to questions you answered based on the last paragraph. As you read, highlight the sentences that provide details that support the conclusions given in the last paragraph.

Solving a Deadly Puzzle

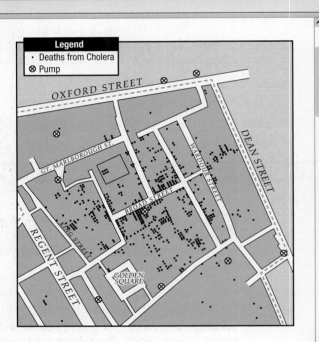

Legend
· Deaths from Cholera
⊗ Pump

1   Pressure on public officials was intense, at times **hysterical**. The **clock was ticking**, and people were dying by the dozens. The year was 1854; the scene was the Soho District of West London. During the stifling heat of August, there had been a handful of deaths from the dreaded disease cholera. On August 31, the situation exploded: In a single evening, within a radius of only blocks, doctors reported 56 new cholera cases. By the next evening there were 143. The death toll had reached 70 and was climbing. Residents started fleeing the district in panic. Medical authorities debated **around the clock** but couldn't **settle on** a plan of action.

Studying the Spread of a Disease

2   Among those not consulted on the subject was a 41-year-old physician named John Snow. Snow was something of a maverick[1] because of his unconventional ideas. At medical conferences in 1849, and again in 1853, Snow had delivered impassioned papers arguing that several diseases (cholera among them) that were thought to be spread via the air were in fact **transmitted** through drinking water. His presentations were politely ignored by the establishment.[2]

3   But the 1854 cholera emergency seemed to **bear out** his waterborne theory: The initial deaths were all within walking distance of a popular water

---

[1] *maverick:* someone who does not follow accepted ways of doing things

[2] *the establishment:* the organizations and people in a society who have a lot of power and influence, and are often opposed to change and new ideas

hand-pump at the intersection of Cambridge and Broad Streets. Snow went to the Register of Deaths and made a detailed list of the past two days' cholera fatalities. But **his heart sank** as the specifics of the deaths seemed to **shoot holes in** his theory. None of the workers at a large brewery **adjacent to** the pump had **contracted** cholera, and a nearby workhouse with more than 500 inmates had reported only five deaths. What's more, fatalities had now been reported several miles away, in the rural villages of Hampstead and Islington.

4   The death toll reached 127. New cases **leveled off**, but only, officials realized, because the area was by now nearly deserted—except for victims and their families.

Disease Detective Delivers Answer

5   Snow redoubled his efforts, going from building to building, house to house, asking questions of the people who remained. Finally, **one piece of the puzzle fit**: He discovered that the workhouse that had largely escaped the epidemic[3] had its own private well. Then, another piece fell into place—at the unaffected brewery, the workers told Snow that they were afraid of the public water supply, so they drank only beer.

6   With a growing sense of excitement and purpose, Snow rode to the outlying homes where the two most recent cholera deaths had occurred. At the house in Hampstead, a surviving relative told him that the lady who died there had a large bottle of water carted to her house every day from the Broad Street pump, because she preferred its taste above all others. Her visiting niece, Snow was told, also drank the Broad Street water and later died at her own home—in Islington.

7   Snow methodically sketched his findings into a rough statistical map of the area. He presented the map and his report to the Board of Guardians of St. James Parish. They were finally convinced, and they **disabled** the infamous pump by removing its handle. Immediately, new cases of cholera started to **dwindle** and then disappeared.

8   A detailed investigation of the pump determined that, more than 20 feet underground, a sewer pipe passed within a few feet of the well. The raw sewage was gradually seeping through the dirt barrier into the drinking water, and **contaminating** it. Scattered witnesses came forward to report a "bad smell" near the pump just before the outbreak[4] began. Snow, the establishment outsider, had, as one historian writes, "used **meticulously** gathered data and the power of statistics to **bring about** the beginning of the end for cholera in Britain." Snow's work eventually helped lead to a **transformation** in medical practices.

---

[3] *epidemic:* a large number of cases of a particular disease happening at the same time; the disease can be passed from one person to another

[4] *outbreak:* sudden appearance of a serious disease

Work with a partner. Discuss how reading the last paragraph first helped you get an overview of the reading, and understand it better.

COMPREHENSION

A Main Ideas

Arrange these events from the reading in chronological order (from 1 to 7). Discuss your answers with a partner.

_6_ Dr. Snow presented his findings to the Board of Guardians of St. James Parish.

_3_ Dr. Snow made a detailed list of deaths that had taken place over two days' time.

_2_ A cholera epidemic broke out in London, and people were dying from the disease.

_7_ The Board of Guardians prevented people from using the Broad Street pump by taking off the pump handle.

_5_ Dr. Snow charted the deaths from cholera on a street map.

_1_ Raw sewage from a sewer pipe was seeping into the drinking water at the Broad Street pump.

_4_ Dr. Snow called on every house and building, asking people about illnesses and deaths from cholera.

B Close Reading

Read the quotes from the reading. Write a paraphrase for each quote. Discuss your answers with a partner.

1. "During the stifling heat of August, there had been a handful of deaths from the dreaded disease cholera. On August 31, the situation exploded: In a single evening, within a radius of only blocks, doctors reported 56 new cholera cases." *(paragraph 1)*

   The number of cholera cases in August increased
   dramatically by the end of the month.

2. "Snow had delivered impassioned papers arguing that several diseases (cholera among them) that were thought to be spread via the air were in fact transmitted through drinking water. His presentations were politely ignored by the establishment." *(paragraph 2)*

   Other people paid no attention to Dr Snow's ideas b/c
   they couldn't accept that was different from what they
   already believed

3. "The initial deaths were all within walking distance of a popular water hand-pump at the intersection of Cambridge and Broad Streets." *(paragraph 3)*

   _____

   _____

4. "[Dr. Snow] discovered that the workhouse that had largely escaped the epidemic had its own private well. [Additionally,] at the unaffected brewery, the workers told Snow that they were afraid of the public water supply, so they drank only beer." (*paragraph 5*)

_____

_____

5. "[Dr. Snow] presented the map and his report to the Board of Guardians of St. James Parish. They were finally convinced, and they disabled the infamous pump by removing its handle" (*paragraph 7*)

_____

_____

VOCABULARY

A Guessing from Context

Read each quote from the reading. Try to guess the meaning of the word in bold from the context. Write the clues that helped you guess and your guess. Then consult a dictionary and write the definition. Compare answers with a partner.

1. "Pressure on public officials was intense, at times **hysterical**. The clock was ticking, and people were dying by the dozens." (*paragraph 1*)

   Clues: _pressure was intense; people were dying by the dozens_

   Guess: _very anxious_

   Dictionary: _unable to control your behavior or emotions because you are very_

   upset, afraid, excited etc.

2. "None of the workers at a large brewery **adjacent to** the pump had contracted cholera, and a nearby workhouse with more than 500 inmates had reported only five deaths." (*paragraph 3*)

   Clues: _____

   Guess: _____

   Dictionary: _next to / near_

(*continued on next page*)

3. "None of the workers at a large brewery adjacent to the pump had **contracted** cholera, and a nearby workhouse with more than 500 inmates had reported only five deaths." *(paragraph 3)*

   Clues: _____

   Guess: _____

   Dictionary: _____

4. "He presented the map and his report to the Board of Guardians of St. James Parish. They were finally convinced, and they **disabled** the infamous pump by removing its handle." *(paragraph 7)*

   Clues: _____

   Guess: _____

   Dictionary: _____

5. "[The Board of Guardians of St. James Parish] disabled the infamous pump by removing its handle. Immediately, new cases of cholera started to **dwindle** and then disappeared." *(paragraph 7)*

   Clues: _____

   Guess: _____

   Dictionary: _____

6. "More than 20 feet underground, a sewer pipe passed within a few feet of the well. The raw sewage was gradually seeping through the dirt barrier into the drinking water, and **contaminating** it." *(paragraph 8)*

   Clues: _____

   Guess: _____

   Dictionary: _____

7. "Snow . . .'used meticulously gathered data and the power of statistics to bring about the beginning of the end for cholera in Britain.' Snow's work eventually helped lead to a **transformation** in medical practices." *(paragraph 8)*

   Clues: _____

   Guess: _____

   Dictionary: _____

B Understanding Phrasal Verbs

Many **verbs** are used together **with certain prepositions**. These phrasal verbs **take on specific meanings** depending on the preposition. For example, we *look for* something when we have lost it, we *look up* a word in the dictionary to learn its meaning, and when we *look up to* someone, we admire that person.

Read the sentences containing phrasal verbs. Match the verbs with their meanings in the box. More than one meaning may be correct.

<u>b</u> **1.** Medical authorities debated around the clock but couldn't **settle on** a plan of action.

<u>d</u> **2.** The 1854 cholera emergency seemed to **bear out** his [Dr. Snow's] waterborne theory.

<u>c</u> **3.** The death toll reached 127. New cases **leveled off**, but only, officials realized, because the area was by now nearly deserted—except for victims and their families.

<u>a</u> **4.** Snow, the establishment outsider, had, as one historian writes, "used meticulously gathered data and the power of statistics to **bring about** the beginning of the end for cholera in Britain."

> **a.** cause something to happen as a result of something else
> **b.** decide on
> **c.** stopped increasing
> **d.** support

Complete each sentence with the correct phrasal verb. Compare answers with a partner.

1. The doctor made every effort to <u>bring about</u> an improvement in her patient's condition though medication and therapy.

2. Hundreds of students protested the proposed increases in tuition, but after a few days, the number of protesters began to <u>level off</u> as the administration agreed to reconsider the issue.

3. After the tornado destroyed the town, government officials quickly gathered to <u>settle on</u> a way to help the survivors.

4. People may think that getting wet in the rain causes colds, but there is no research to <u>bear out</u> this belief.

C Idioms

As you learned in previous chapters, an **idiom** is a **group of words that has a special meaning that is different from the ordinary meaning** of each word. For example, when someone says, "It's raining cats and dogs," we understand that cats and dogs are not really falling from the sky. This idiom actually means that it is raining very hard.

Work with a partner. Match the idioms with their meanings. If you need help, look back at the reading to find the idioms in context.

_d_ 1. the clock was ticking   a. became very discouraged

_e_ 2. around the clock   b. part of a mystery

_a_ 3. heart sank   c. prove wrong

_c_ 4. shoot holes in   d. time was running out

_b_ 5. piece of the puzzle   e. without stopping

Very unpleasant Weather, or the Old saying verified "Raining cats, Dogs, & Pitchforks". !!!

NOTE-TAKING: Creating a Flowchart

The flowchart represents the steps in the scientific method. Use it to chart the steps that Dr. Snow followed to identify the cause of the 1854 cholera outbreak in London.

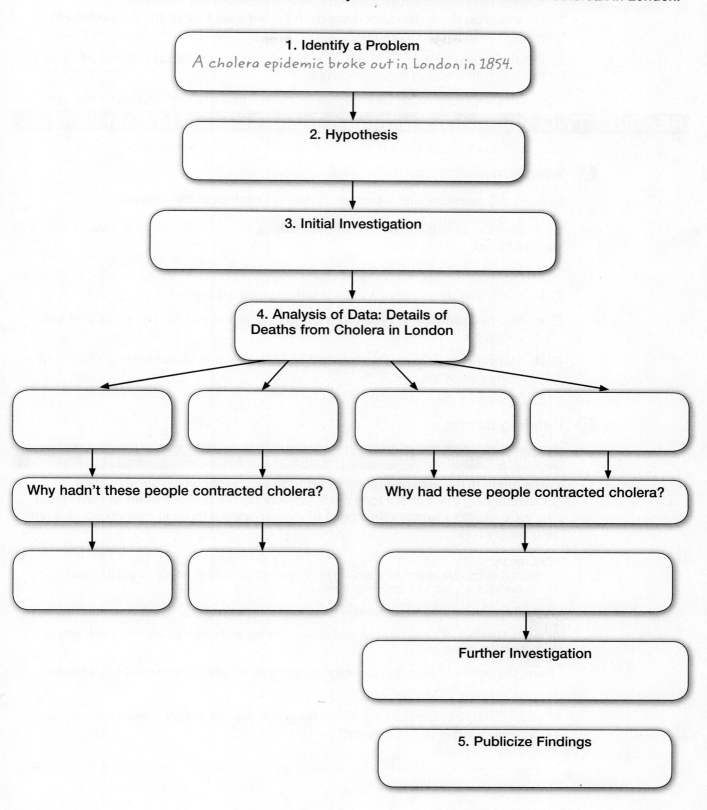

1. Identify a Problem
A cholera epidemic broke out in London in 1854.

2. Hypothesis

3. Initial Investigation

4. Analysis of Data: Details of Deaths from Cholera in London

Why hadn't these people contracted cholera?

Why had these people contracted cholera?

Further Investigation

5. Publicize Findings

Discuss the questions in a small group. Be prepared to share your answers with the class.

1. Why do you think the other doctors and other members of the establishment refused to listen to Dr. Snow?

2. What kinds of transformations, or major changes, in medical practices do you think resulted from Dr. Snow's work?

READING TWO: Imprisoned without a Trial: The Story of Typhoid[2] Mary

A **Warm-Up**

Discuss the question with a partner. Check (✓) each possible answer.

What can you infer from the title of the reading, *Imprisoned without a Trial: The Story of Typhoid Mary*?

☐ **a.** Mary was the name of a person who went to prison.

☐ **b.** Mary was the name of a person who contracted typhoid.

☐ **c.** Mary committed a crime but went to prison without having a trial and being convicted.

☐ **d.** Mary did not commit a crime but went to prison without having a trial and being convicted.

B **Reading Strategy**

Identifying Tone and Identifying Point of View

Tone refers to the general **feeling or attitude expressed** in a piece of writing. Understanding the author's tone helps you identify the author's **point of view** about the topic. Authors express their point of view or opinion through their choice of words and expressions.

EXAMPLES:

Mallon emigrated to America around the age of 15. Like most Irish immigrant women, Mallon found a job as a domestic servant.

Here, the author is being objective and is not expressing any opinion.

Mary Mallon was taken by force and against her will and was held without a trial. She had not broken any laws.

Here, the author is expressing disagreement with what happened to Mary Mallon.

1. Read the title of the reading. What do you think the author's opinion is about Typhoid Mary's imprisonment?

_____

---

[2] *typhoid*: a serious infectious disease that is caused by dirty food or water

2. Read paragraph one. How does the author feel about Mary having to live on North Brother Island?

_____

3. What word or words in the paragraph one help you understand how the author feels?

_____

Now read the article and look for clues to the author's point of view or opinion. Then answer the questions at the end of the article.

Imprisoned without a Trial: The Story of Typhoid Mary
By Jennifer Rosenberg

1   Mary Mallon, now known as Typhoid Mary, seemed a healthy woman when a health inspector knocked on her door in 1907, yet she was the cause of several typhoid outbreaks. In fact, forty-seven illnesses and three deaths were attributed to her. Mary was the first "healthy carrier"[1] of typhoid fever in the United States. She was forced to live in relative **seclusion** upon North Brother Island off New York. Who was Mary Mallon, and how did she spread typhoid fever?

An Investigation

2   For the summer of 1906, New York banker Charles Henry Warren wanted to take his family on vacation. They rented a summer home from George Thompson and his wife in Oyster Bay, Long Island. Also for the summer, the Warrens hired Marry Mallon to be their cook.

3   On August 27, one of the Warren's daughters became ill with typhoid fever. Soon, Mrs. Warren and two maids became ill, followed by the gardener and another Warren daughter. In total, six of the eleven people in the house came down with typhoid. Since the common way typhoid spread was through water or food sources, the owners of the home feared they would not be able to rent the property again without first discovering the source of the outbreak. The Thompsons first hired investigators to find the cause, but they were unsuccessful.

4   Then the Thompsons hired George Soper, a civil engineer with experience in typhoid fever outbreaks. It was Soper who believed the recently hired cook,

(continued on next page)

_____

[1] _carrier:_ someone who passes a disease to other people without actually having the disease

Mary Mallon, was the cause. Mallon had left the Warren's approximately three weeks after the outbreak. Soper began to research her employment history for more clues.

5 Mary Mallon was born on September 23, 1869 in Cookstown, Ireland. According to what she told friends, Mallon emigrated to America around the age of 15. Like most Irish immigrant women, Mallon found a job as a domestic servant. Finding she had a talent for cooking, Mallon became a cook, which paid better wages than many other domestic service positions.

6 Soper was able to **trace** Mallon's employment history back to 1900. He found that typhoid outbreaks had followed Mallon from job to job. From 1900 to 1907, Soper found that Mallon had worked at seven jobs in which 22 people had become ill, including one young girl who died with typhoid fever shortly after Mallon had come to work for them. Soper was satisfied that this was much more than a **coincidence**; yet, he needed to scientifically prove she was the carrier.

Capture and Isolation of Typhoid Mary

7 In March 1907, Soper found Mallon working as a cook in the home of Walter Bowen and his family. Soper handed his research and hypothesis over to Hermann Biggs at the New York City Health Department. Mallon was taken to the Willard Parker Hospital in New York. There, samples were taken and examined; typhoid bacilli[2] were found. The health department then transferred Mallon to an **isolated** cottage (part of the Riverside Hospital) on North Brother Island (in the East River near the Bronx).

8 Mary Mallon was taken by force and against her will and was held without a trial. She had not broken any laws. Mary Mallon believed she was being unfairly **persecuted**. Wasn't she healthy? She could not understand how she could have spread disease and caused a death when she, herself, seemed healthy. In 1909, after having been isolated for two years on North Brother Island, Mallon sued the health department.

9 Mallon did not understand a lot about typhoid fever and, unfortunately, no one tried to explain it to her. Not all people have a strong bout of typhoid fever; some people can have such a weak case that they only experience flu-like symptoms. Thus, Mallon could have had typhoid fever but never known it. Though commonly known at the time that typhoid could be spread by water or food products, people who are **infected** by the typhoid bacillus could also pass the disease via unwashed hands. For this reason, infected persons who were cooks (like Mallon) or food handlers had the most likelihood of spreading the disease.

10 The judge ruled in favor of the health officials, and Mallon, now popularly known as "Typhoid Mary," "was remanded to the custody of the Board of Health of the City of New York." Mallon went back to the isolated cottage on North Brother Island with little hope of being released. In February of 1910, a new health commissioner decided that Mallon could go free as long as she agreed never to work as a cook again. Anxious to regain her freedom, Mallon accepted the conditions. On February 19, 1910, Mary Mallon agreed that she

---

[2] *bacilli*: bacteria

"is prepared to change her occupation (that of cook), and will give assurance by affidavit[3] that she will upon her release take such **hygienic precautions** as will protect those with whom she comes in contact, from infection." She was let free.

Recapture of Typhoid Mary

11   Some people believe that Mallon never had any **intention** of following the health officials' rules. Feeling healthy, Mallon still did not really believe that she could spread typhoid. Though in the beginning Mallon tried to be a laundress as well as worked at other jobs, for a reason that has not been left in any documents, Mallon eventually went back to working as a cook.

12   In January of 1915 (nearly five years after Mallon's release), the Sloane Maternity Hospital in Manhattan suffered a typhoid fever outbreak. Twenty-five people became ill, and two of them died. Soon, evidence pointed to a recently-hired cook, Mrs. Brown. Mrs. Brown was really Mary Mallon, using a pseudonym.

13   Mallon was again sent to North Brother Island to live in the same isolated cottage that she had inhabited during her last **confinement**. For twenty-three more years, Mary Mallon remained imprisoned on the island. In December 1932, Mary Mallon suffered a large stroke that left her **paralyzed**. She was then transferred from her cottage to a bed in the children's ward of the hospital on the island, where she stayed until her death six years later, on November 11, 1938.

Typhoid Mary Lives On

14   Since Mary Mallon's death, the name "Typhoid Mary" has grown into a term **disassociated** from the person. Anyone who has a **contagious** illness can be termed, sometimes jokingly, a "Typhoid Mary." If someone changes their jobs frequently, they are sometimes referred to as a "Typhoid Mary." (Mary Mallon changed jobs frequently.) During her life, Mary Mallon experienced extreme punishment for something in which she had no control and, for whatever reason, has gone down in history as the **evasive** and **malicious** "Typhoid Mary."

---

[3] *affidavit:* a written statement made after promising to tell the truth, for use as proof in a court of law

Work with a partner. Compare the instances of author's tone and point of view that you found in the text. What instances did your partner find that you can add to your own?

COMPREHENSION

A **Main Ideas**

Read each statement. Decide if it is *True* or *False* according to the reading. Check (✓) the appropriate box. If it is false, change it to make it true. Discuss your answers with a partner.

	TRUE	FALSE
1. Mary Mallon knew she had once been ill with typhoid.	☐	☐
2. The Warren family never discovered how members of their household had contracted typhoid.	☐	☐
3. George Soper discovered that people became ill with typhoid in many places where Mary Mallon had been working at the time.	☐	☐
4. Mary Mallon deliberately made people ill with typhoid by not washing her hands.	☐	☐
5. Mary Mallon did not report her condition to health officials because she did not want to be arrested.	☐	☐
6. Mary Mallon was held in isolation to prevent her from passing typhoid fever on to others.	☐	☐
7. Mary Mallon never believed she could pass typhoid on to other people.	☐	☐
8. Altogether, Mary Mallon was confined to North Brother Island for over 30 years.	☐	☐

B **Close Reading**

Read the quotes from the reading. Write a paraphrase for each quote. Discuss your answers with a partner.

1. "Though commonly known at the time that typhoid could be spread by water or food products, people who are infected by the typhoid bacillus could also pass the disease via unwashed hands." *(paragraph 9)*

_____

_____

2. "The judge ruled in favor of the health officials, and Mallon, now popularly known as 'Typhoid Mary,' 'was remanded to the custody of the Board of Health of the City of New York.'" *(paragraph 10)*

_____

_____

3. "On February 19, 1910, Mary Mallon agreed that she 'is prepared to change her occupation (that of cook), and will give assurance by affidavit that she will upon her release take such hygienic precautions as will protect those with whom she comes in contact, from infection.'" *(paragraph 10)*

_____

_____

4. "Though in the beginning Mallon tried to be a laundress as well as worked at other jobs, for a reason that has not been left in any documents, Mallon eventually went back to working as a cook." *(paragraph 11)*

_____

_____

VOCABULARY

Ⓐ Categorizing Words

Work with a partner. Put the words listed into two categories in the box below, and then label each category.

| confinement | hygienic | isolate | precaution |
| contagious | infected | paralyzed | seclusion |

B Prefix *dis-*

The **prefix *dis-*** means **"not"**—for example, when someone disapproves of something, he or she does not approve. It also means **"the opposite of"**—for example, when someone disappears, he or she does the opposite of appearing.

disabled 2	disassociate 4	disability 1
disappearance 5	discomfort 3	

Complete each sentence with the correct word from the box. Compare answers with a partner.

1. Some infections can lead to the loss of a leg, resulting in a lifelong

   _____ .

2. Many people who are deaf do not consider themselves _____ .

   They believe they are normal and can live normal lives.

3. Patients in hospitals often experience considerable _____

   when they have to remain in bed for days or weeks at a time.

4. The doctors had to _____ themselves from that medical

   group because of its bad reputation for patient care.

5. Although Molly Mallon staged a _____ by changing her

   name and taking on different jobs, she was discovered anyway.

C Word Forms

Fill in the chart with the correct word forms. Use a dictionary if necessary. An *X* indicates there is no form in that category.

	NOUN	VERB	ADJECTIVE	ADVERB
1.	confinement	confine	confined	X
2.	association	disassociate	disassociated	X
3.	evasion	evade	evasive	evasively
4.	isolation	isolate	isolated	X
5.	malice	X	malicious	maliciously
6.	persecution	persecute	persecuted	X
7.	trace	trace		X

Complete the sentences with the correct form of one of the words in the chart. Be sure to use the correct tense of the verbs in the affirmative or negative. Compare answers with a partner.

1. The little boy was kept in ___isolation___ because his disease was so contagious.

2. The surgeon feels that the medical community _has persecuted_ him because of his radical ideas and practices.

3. Even though their child could not be cured, the parents held no ___malice___ toward the doctor, because he did his best to save her.

4. The nurses ___disassociated___ themselves from that medical group because the leaders appeared to have little respect for their work.

5. The researchers eventually ___traced___ the cause of the epidemic to a single infected individual.

6. The hospital ___didn't confine___ the small child to an isolated room because he needed the company of other children as part of his recovery process.

7. Mary Mallon temporarily ___evaded___ capture by changing her name.

GRAMMAR FOR READING

Understanding the Use of the Passive Voice

Passive sentences are formed by using **be + past participle**.
The passive voice is used for various reasons including:

- When the performer of the action (agent) is not known.

EXAMPLE: *Yesterday a bank **was robbed** on Main Street.*

- When the focus is on the object of the action instead of the agent.

EXAMPLE: *The bank robbers **were caught** yesterday by the police.*

Read the sentences. Underline *be* + past participle in each sentence. Then circle the agent. Not all sentences include an agent.

1. People who <u>are infected</u> by the (typhoid bacillus) could also pass the disease via unwashed hands.

2. In fact, forty-seven illnesses and three deaths were attributed to her.

(continued on next page)

3. She was forced to live in relative seclusion on North Brother Island off New York.

4. Mary Mallon was taken by force and against her will and was held without a trial.

5. Mallon was taken to the Willard Parker Hospital in New York.

6. In 1909, after having been isolated for two years on North Brother Island, Mallon sued the health department.

7. Though commonly known at the time that typhoid could be spread by water or food products, people who are infected by the typhoid bacillus could also pass the disease via unwashed hands.

8. If someone changes their jobs frequently, that person is sometimes referred to as a "Typhoid Mary."

Complete each sentence with the most likely performer of the action from the choices in the box. Compare answers with a partner.

_C_ 1. now know(s) Mary Mallon as Typhoid Mary.

_B_ 2. took Mallon to the Willard Parker Hospital in New York.

_A_ 3. isolated Mallon for two years on North Brother Island.

_D_ 4. spread typhoid.

_A_ 5. remanded Mallon to the custody of the board of Health of the City of New York.

_C_ 6. refer(s) to those who change jobs frequently as a "Typhoid Mary."

> a. A court judge
> b. Health Department officials
> c. People in general
> d. Water or food products

NOTE-TAKING: Creating a Chain of Events

Go back to the reading and read it again. Follow the chain of events in the story of Typhoid Mary. Write the events on the lines.

1. _____ ⟶ 2. _____ ⟶

3. _____ ⟶ 4. _____ ⟶

5. _____ ⟶ 6. _____

CRITICAL THINKING

Discuss the questions in a small group. Be prepared to share your answers with the class.

1. Mary Mallon never believed she had made other people ill with typhoid. How might Mary's condition as a carrier, once it was discovered, have been handled differently so Mary would not have had to spend over 30 years of her life confined to North Brother Island, believing to her death that she had done nothing wrong?

2. Mary Mallon was taken by force and isolated on North Brother Island to prevent her spreading typhoid to others. Do you think the Board of Health had the right to put her in seclusion for decades in order to protect the health of the general population? Explain your reasons for your answer.

LINKING READINGS ONE AND TWO

Use the chart below to compare the methods that Dr. Snow and George Soper used to find the cause of the diseases they were investigating. Be prepared to share your answers with the class.

NAME	STEPS EACH MAN TOOK
Dr. John Snow	• He investigated every death from cholera and charted it on a map. • • • •
George Soper	• • • • •
SIMILARITIES BETWEEN SNOW'S AND SOPER'S METHODS	

A **Warm-Up**

Discuss the questions in a small group.

1. What are some of the most effective drugs that help cure illnesses and diseases? Make a list.

   _____   _____

   _____   _____

   _____   _____

2. In your opinion, what are the most important drugs on your list? List the drugs you chose in order of importance, with 1 being the most important drug of all.

   1. _____   4. _____

   2. _____   5. _____

   3. _____   6. _____

B **Reading Strategy**

Drawing Inferences

Drawing inferences as you read is an important component of reading comprehension. An inference is **something that you think is probably true based on information that you already know.** In readings, information is not always directly stated, but we can still draw conclusions from the information presented.

EXAMPLE:
In 1928, while sorting through his pile of dishes, Fleming's former lab assistant, D. Merlin Pryce stopped by to visit with Fleming. Fleming took this opportunity to gripe about the amount of extra work he had to do since Pryce had transferred from his lab. *(paragraph 4)*

POSSIBLE INFERENCE: Pryce had done a good job when he worked in Fleming's lab, and no one had replaced him.

Read the quotes from the reading and write an inference you can draw from them. Compare answers with a partner.

1. "Alexander Fleming sat at his work bench at St. Mary's Hospital after having just returned from a vacation. Before he had left, Fleming had piled a number of his Petri dishes to the side of the bench. Back from vacation, Fleming was sorting through the long–unattended stacks." *(paragraph 2)*

   Inference: _____

2. "Back from vacation, Fleming was sorting through the long-unattended stacks to determine which ones could be salvaged." *(paragraph 2)*

   Inference: _____

3. "Most likely, the mold came from La Touche's room downstairs. La Touche had been collecting a large sampling of molds for John Freeman, who was researching asthma [a respiratory disease], and it is likely that some floated up to Fleming's lab." *(paragraph 7)*

Inference: _____

Now read the article and draw inferences as you read.

The Discovery of a Miracle Drug
By Jennifer Rosenberg

1   In 1928, **bacteriologist** Alexander Fleming made a **chance** discovery from an already discarded, **contaminated** Petri dish.[1] The **mold** that had contaminated the experiment turned out to contain a powerful **antibiotic**, penicillin. However, although Fleming was credited with the discovery, it was over a decade before someone else turned penicillin into the miracle drug for the 20th century. How did this Petri dish almost get cleaned before being noticed? How did the mold get onto the dish? Who **transformed** penicillin into a useful drug?

The Chance Discovery

2   On a September morning in 1928, Alexander Fleming sat at his work bench at St. Mary's Hospital after having just returned from a vacation. Before he had left, Fleming had piled a number of his Petri dishes to the side of the bench. Back from vacation, Fleming was sorting through the long-unattended stacks to **determine** which ones could be **salvaged**. Many of the dishes had been contaminated. Fleming placed each of these in an ever-growing pile in a tray of Lysol.[2]

3   Much of Fleming's work focused on the search for a "wonder drug." Though the concept of bacteria had been around since Antoine van Leeuwenhoek first described it in 1683, it wasn't until the late 19th century that Louis Pasteur confirmed that bacteria caused diseases. However, though they had this knowledge, no one had yet been able to find a chemical that would kill **harmful** bacteria but also not harm the human body.

4   In 1928, while sorting through his pile of dishes, Fleming's former lab assistant, D. Merlin Pryce stopped by to visit with Fleming. Fleming took this opportunity to gripe[3] about the amount of extra work he had to do since Pryce had transferred from his lab. To demonstrate, Fleming rummaged through the large pile of plates he had

(continued on next page)

---

[1] **Petri dish**: a small clear dish with a cover which is used by scientists, especially for growing bacteria

[2] **Lysol**: a disinfectant (a chemical that destroys bacteria)

[3] **gripe**: complain

placed in the Lysol tray and pulled out several that had remained safely above the Lysol. Had there not been so many, each would have been submerged in Lysol, killing the bacteria to make the plates safe to clean and then reuse.

5   While picking up one particular dish to show Pryce, Fleming noticed something strange about it. While he had been away, a mold had grown on the dish. That in itself was not strange. However, this particular mold seemed to have killed the *Staphylococcus aureus* that had been growing in the dish. Fleming realized that this mold had **potential**.

What Was That Mold?

6   Fleming spent several weeks growing more mold and trying to determine the particular **substance** in the mold that killed the bacteria. After discussing the mold with mycologist (mold expert) C. J. La Touche, they determined the mold to be a *Penicillium* mold. Fleming then called the active antibacterial **agent** in the mold, penicillin.

7   But where did the mold come from? Most likely, the mold came from La Touche's room downstairs. La Touche had been collecting a large sampling of molds for John Freeman, who was researching asthma, and it is likely that some floated up to Fleming's lab. Fleming continued to run numerous experiments to determine the effect of the mold on other harmful bacteria. Surprisingly, the mold killed a large number of them. Fleming then ran further tests and found the mold to be **non-toxic**.

8   Could this be the "wonder drug"? To Fleming, it was not. Though he saw its potential, Fleming was not a chemist and thus was unable to **isolate** the active antibacterial **element**, penicillin, and could not keep the element active long enough to be used in humans. In 1929, Fleming wrote a paper on his findings, which did not garner any scientific interest.

Twelve Years Later

9   In 1940, the second year of World War II, two scientists at Oxford University were researching promising projects in bacteriology that could possibly be **enhanced** or continued with chemistry. Australian Howard Florey and German refugee Ernst Chain began working with penicillin. Using new chemical **techniques**, they were able to produce a brown powder that kept its antibacterial power for longer than a few days. They experimented with the powder and found it to be safe. The availability of penicillin during World War II saved many lives that otherwise would have been lost due to bacterial **infections** in even minor **wounds**.

Recognition

10   Although Fleming discovered penicillin, it took Florey and Chain to make it a usable product. Though both Fleming and Florey were knighted in 1944, and all three of them (Fleming, Florey and Chain) were awarded the 1945 Nobel Prize in Physiology or Medicine, Fleming is still credited with discovering penicillin.

Work with a partner. Discuss the inferences you found in the reading. What additional inferences did you draw from the reading?

COMPREHENSION

A Main Ideas

Read each question. Then circle the correct answer. Compare answers with a partner.

1. What effect did the Lysol have on the bacteria in the Petri dishes?
   a. The Lysol preserved the bacteria.
   b. The Lysol killed the bacteria.
   c. The Lysol transformed the bacteria into a mold.

2. What was Fleming's main research project?
   a. finding a drug that would kill bacteria but not be harmful to people
   b. finding a drug that would cure all illnesses
   c. finding a drug that could be developed from mold

3. What was Fleming successful in doing?
   a. discovering that Lysol killed bacteria
   b. determining that the mold was a *Penicillium* mold
   c. trying to improve Lysol

4. What did Florey and Chain succeed in doing that Fleming had not been able to accomplish?
   a. isolating the antibacterial element and creating a useful drug
   b. creating a harmless *Penicillium* mold
   c. writing a paper on their research findings

B Close Reading

Read each question. Write your answer in a complete sentence. Compare answers with a partner.

1. Why was Fleming unable to isolate the antibacterial substance in the mold?

   _____

2. Why were Florey and Chain interested in working with penicillin?

   _____

3. In what ways is penicillin a "wonder drug"?

   _____

VOCABULARY

A Synonyms

Read the sentences. Match each word or phrase in bold with its synonym in the box. Compare answers with a partner.

___D___ 1. This new drug has considerable **promise**. It may cure a number of diseases in the future.

___E___ 2. The researcher decided to **recover** the Petri dishes he had thrown away because he discovered that he still needed them.

___A___ 3. The water pollution was due to an **accidental** leak in an old underground pipe.

___B___ 4. Peanuts have an **ingredient** that can cause illness in some people, or even death.

___C___ 5. Using computer databases to track the spread of disease can **improve** the way the public is informed about health threats.

> a. chance
> b. element
> c. enhance
> d. potential
> e. salvage

B Suffix -ful

> **Suffixes** are added to the end of words and **change or modify their meanings.** They also change the part of speech of words when added to them.
>
> • The suffix *-ful* means "notable for"— for example, when something such as a toothache is painful, it is known for causing pain.

| careful 4 | peaceful 1 | useful 2 |
| harmful 3 | powerful | wonderful 6 |

Read each sentence. Complete it with the correct word. Compare answers with a partner.

1. The hospital provides a _____ environment for its patients so they can relax and feel less anxiety.

2. Chemotherapy is a _____ and often effective treatment for cancer.

3. Infections that worsen can be quite _____ to your health.

4. Patients should be _____ when taking any medication. They should always read the directions and warnings that come with it.

5. Aspirin is a very _____ drug. Not only can it help relieve pain, it can also help reduce the risk of a stroke.

6. People generally feel that a physician who is not only knowledgeable but also caring is a _____ doctor.

C Understanding Content-Specific Vocabulary

> This reading contains **vocabulary** specific to science. It is often much easier to learn such vocabulary **as a group, within the context of the field** itself.

Read paragraphs 1, 6, 7, and 9, and guess the meaning of the words in bold. Then match the words with their meanings below. Compare answers with a partner.

___c___ 1. agent
___A___ 2. antibiotic
___G___ 3. bacteriologist
___F___ 4. mold
___E___ 5. non-toxic
___B___ 6. wound
___D___ 7. substance

a. a drug that kills bacteria
b. an injury, especially one that breaks through the skin
c. a chemical or substance that makes other substances change
d. a material of some kind with particular qualities
e. not poisonous or harmful to one's health
f. a substance that grows on certain food such as old bread
g. a scientist who researches bacteria

CRITICAL THINKING

Discuss the questions in a small group. Be prepared to share your answers with the class.

1. Prior to the discovery of penicillin, bacterial infections ranked as a leading cause of death. Even a simple cut that became infected could lead to death. What were some of the consequences of the discovery of penicillin?

2. Although Fleming discovered penicillin, he could not isolate the active antibacterial element, and he could not keep the element active long enough to be used in humans. However, through their experiments and research, Florey and Chain were able to make penicillin a usable product. Should Fleming have shared the Nobel Prize with Florey and Chain? Explain your answer.

BRINGING IT ALL TOGETHER

Work in a small group. Then share your group's answers with the class. Use some of the vocabulary you studied in the chapter (for a complete list, go to page 175).

1. Set up a panel discussion. Establish two sides to the issue of Mary Mallon's forced seclusion on North Brother Island. Mary Mallon was discovered to be a carrier of the typhoid bacteria. Although she was never charged with a crime, she was detained on North Brother Island for decades, essentially imprisoned, for the sake of protecting the public. Was this action legal? Was it right?

2. The members of the medical and scientific community responded differently to Dr. Snow's theory and evidence than they responded to Soper's evidence. Describe their response to each, and explain why you think their responses were different.

WRITING ACTIVITY

In this chapter you learned about three threats to human health and three ways these threats were addressed. Write a three-paragraph paper on a health threat.

- In the first paragraph, describe a major health threat that exists today. How is it caused? Where is it most prevalent?
- In the second paragraph, describe what is being done to eliminate this health threat.
- In the third paragraph, write about the actions you recommend taking to prevent health threats in the future.

DISCUSSION AND WRITING TOPICS

Discuss these topics in a small group. Choose one of them and write three paragraphs about it. Use the vocabulary from the chapter.

1. What are some ways that doctors, scientists, and researchers discover the causes of diseases?

2. What are some ways that they discover the cures for diseases?

3. What are some of the most serious illnesses and diseases of the past 150 years? Which ones have a cure? Which ones do not yet have a cure?

VOCABULARY

Nouns
agent
antibiotic
bacteriologist
confinement*
element*
mold
potential*
precaution
seclusion
substance
transformation*
wound

Verbs
contaminate
contract*
disable
dwindle
enhance*
infect
persecute
salvage
trace*

Phrasal Verbs
bear out
bring about
level off
settle on

Adjectives
adjacent to*
chance
contagious
(dis)associated
evasive
harmful
hygienic
hysterical
isolated*
malicious
non-toxic
paralyzed

Idioms
around the clock
the clock was
  ticking
his heart sank
one piece of the
  puzzle fit
shot holes in

* = AWL (Academic Word List) item

SELF-ASSESSMENT

In this chapter you learned to:

○ Identify tone and point of view

○ Draw inferences

○ Read the last paragraph first to get an overview

○ Understand phrasal verbs

○ Guess the meaning of words from the context

○ Create a flowchart and a chain of events

○ Understand and use content-specific vocabulary, prefixes, suffixes, word forms, and idioms

○ Understand the use of the passive voice

What can you do well? ☑

What do you need to practice more? ☑

CHAPTER 7

LITERATURE: Storytelling through Poetry

LITERATURE: the study of books, short stories, plays, and poems that are generally considered to have value, and that are worth reading and studying

OBJECTIVES

To read academic texts, you need to master certain skills.

In this chapter, you will:

- Understand literary terms
- Identify allegorical references
- Paraphrase poetry
- Create a literary semantic web
- Guess the meaning of words from the context, categorize words, and understand familiar words with unfamiliar meanings
- Understand and use synonyms and prefixes
- Understand literary meaning
- Make double-entry notes

Consider These Questions

Complete the chart below. Share your notes in a small group.

YOUR NAME	WHAT IS THE TITLE OF YOUR FAVORITE POEM?	WHO IS THE AUTHOR? IN WHAT LANGUAGE AND IN WHAT YEAR WAS IT WRITTEN?	WHY DO YOU LIKE THIS POEM? DO YOU HAVE A FAVORITE QUOTE? WHAT IS IT AND WHY DO YOU LIKE IT?

READING ONE: Themes and Characters in *The Rime*[1] *of the Ancient Mariner*

A Warm-Up

Discuss the questions in a small group.

1. What are some common themes in poetry (for example, love)?

2. What characters often appear in poems?

3. What kinds of stories do poems usually tell?

_____

[1] *rime:* "rhyme" is the modern spellimg

Understanding Literary Terms

Knowing **specialized terms** is critical to **understanding literature**. In this chapter, you will read about a poem, and parts of the poem. The poem in this chapter is a *ballad*—a poem that tells a story. Some of the essential terms used to analyze the poem in this chapter are *theme*, *subtheme*, *character*, *figure*, and *moral*. The *theme* is the main subject or idea of the poem, and the *subthemes* are secondary ideas. The *characters* are the people in the poem, and the *figures* are characters that are not necessarily people. The *moral* refers to the lesson taught by the poem.

Read the questions. Be sure you understand the italicized word.

1. What is the *theme* of the poem, and what are its *subthemes?*

2. What *characters* and *figures* are introduced in the poem?

Now read the article and underline the answers to the questions.

Themes and Characters in
The Rime of the Ancient Mariner

1   Samuel Taylor Coleridge wrote during the Romantic period (1798–1832) along with such famous poets as William Wordsworth and Charles Lamb. The Romantic period occurred during a time of radical thinking, social unrest, wars, and economic **turbulence** across Europe. The Romantic-era poets experimented with a radical kind of poetry, a style **embedded** in their intellectual creative power. Coleridge **embraced** these new ideas. In "The Rime of the Ancient Mariner," Coleridge develops the supernatural themes that allow the mariner to navigate the consequences of his **rash** act. "The Rime" was the last poem Coleridge wrote before his declining health affected his writing style. He died in 1834 at age 62. His death was considered a great loss to the Romantic movement.

2   There are two primary themes and several subthemes that relate to the **supernatural** in "The Rime of the Ancient Mariner." The first primary theme concerns the potential consequences of a single unthinking act. When the mariner shoots an albatross,[1] he does it casually and without **animosity**.

3   The mariner gradually comes to realize the enormous consequences of his casual act, even as he struggles to accept responsibility for it. To do this he must comprehend that all things in nature are of equal value. Everything, as a part of nature, has its own beauty and is to be cherished[2] for its own sake.

_____

[1] *albatross:* a very large white sea bird

[2] *cherished:* loved

4   This realization is suddenly apparent when the mariner spontaneously appreciates the beauty of the sea snakes; his heart fills with love for them, and he can bless them "unaware." The **moral** of the tale is manifest in the ancient mariner's final words to the wedding guest: "He prayeth best, who loveth best/ All things both great and small;/ For the dear God who loveth us,/He made and loveth all."

5   The major character in "The Rime of the Ancient Mariner" is the mariner who relates his chilling experiences. It is he who kills the albatross, suffers the consequences, learns from his sufferings, and earns his **redemption**. As part of his **penance**, he spends his life telling his tale to others as a warning and as instruction. At first terrifying in looks and manner, the mariner is so intense that the wedding guest is **compelled** to listen. As the tale unfolds, the wedding guest's reactions to the mariner change from scorn to sympathy, and finally even to pity. The wedding guest serves as a plot device to frame and advance the story, but he also undergoes a transformation of his own. Startled by the mariner who accosts him, the wedding guest first appears as a devil-may-care gallant.[3] But after he hears the mariner's dreadful tale, he is thoughtful and **subdued**.

6   The mariner's shipmates are innocent victims of his rash act. Like the members of the wedding party, the sailors are purposefully kept vague and undeveloped, for Coleridge's intent is that the audience focus their full attention on the plight of the mariner.

7   Supernatural beings appear in the poem as **symbolic** or **allegorical** figures, representing the forces of nature, life, death, and **retribution**. The mariner confronts these figures and must ultimately **appease** them in order to obtain his salvation.

---

[3] *a devil-may-care gallant:* a cheerful and carefree young man

Review the elements of the poem presented in the article (theme, subtheme, characters, and figures). Compare what you underlined with what your partner underlined. Discuss how identifying these components helped you prepare for reading the poem.

COMPREHENSION

Ⓐ Main Ideas

Check (✓) the statements that best express the main ideas in the reading. Discuss your answers with a partner.

- ☐ **1.** A primary theme involves the consequences of the mariner's careless killing of a bird.

- ☐ **2.** The mariner needs to understand the value of all living things.

- ☐ **3.** A lesson to be learned from this poem is never to kill any living things.

(continued on next page)

□ 4. The wedding guest provides a means for the mariner to tell his story.

□ 5. The wedding guest's attitude toward the mariner changes from the beginning to the end of the story.

□ 6. The mariner's shipmates are guilty of helping to kill the albatross.

□ 7. Readers should pay more attention to the mariner than to any other character.

□ 8. The mariner needs to deal with the supernatural figures he encounters.

B Close Reading

Read each question. Write your answer in a complete sentence. Compare answers with a partner.

1. What was the social and historical context of the Romantic period?

_____

2. What did Coleridge draw on when he wrote his poetry?

_____

3. Why doesn't Coleridge develop the characters of the ship's crew, or the people who come to attend the wedding?

_____

VOCABULARY

A Guessing from Context

Go back to the reading and reread the sentences in which these words appear. Be sure that you understand what they mean in the context. Then match them with their meanings.

__e__ 1. appease

_____ 2. compelled

_____ 3. moral

_____ 4. penance

_____ 5. redemption

_____ 6. subdued

_____ 7. supernatural

a. punishment or suffering that you accept to show you are sorry for having behaved badly

b. state of doing something to improve what people think of you after you have done something bad

c. events, powers, or creatures that cannot be explained, and that seem to involve magic

d. unusually quiet and possibly unhappy

e. make someone less angry by giving them what they want

f. to the lesson regarding the principles of right and wrong

g. driven or urged forcefully or irresistibly

B Synonyms

Read the sentences. Match each word or phrase in parentheses with its synonym in the box below. Compare answers with a partner.

allegorical	embedded	rash	turbulence
animosity	embrace	retribution	

1. Several of William Shakespeare's plays include the theme of punishment as a result of a _____ action.
   (reckless)

2. Themes of social unrest are often _____ in prose as well as poetry.
   (integrated)

3. According to the legend, King Midas was granted his wish that everything he touched be turned to gold. As _____ for his greed, his
   (severe punishment)
   daughter turned to gold when he touched her.

4. In *The Rime of the Ancient Mariner*, one of the supernatural beings is Death. This figure is a(n) _____ character, because it represents the
   (symbolic)
   idea of death.

5. William Wordsworth (1770–1850) and Samuel Coleridge were the first writers to _____ the concepts that became known as Romanticism.
   (adopt)

6. Many of the French felt considerable _____ toward the
   (hostility)
   Romantic movement.

7. The Napoleonic Wars, which lasted from 1799 to 1815, caused considerable _____ in many European countries.
   (disturbance)

C   The Prefix *super-*

As you have learned, when prefixes are added to the beginning of words, they change or modify the words' meanings.

- *Super-* means "over" or "above"—for example, a plane that flies at supersonic speed flies above, or faster than, the speed of sound.

Complete each sentence with the correct word from the box. Compare answers with a partner.

supercompetitive	supercomputer	superimpose	supernatural	superscript

1. People often use a _____ for tasks involving a very large database, especially tasks involving math or science.

2. The professors in the university's English department are _____. They all try to write and publish more articles than anyone else, and to present papers at as many conferences as possible each year.

3. In writing, people often use a(n) _____ to express an ordinal number. For example, someone may write *15th* instead of *fifteenth*.

4. Be careful not to _____ one picture on top of another in your presentation, or the second picture will show through.

5. _____ beings often appear in poetry and prose.

NOTE-TAKING: Creating a Literary Semantic Web

Use the literary semantic web to organize the information you read in the text. Discuss your answers with a partner.

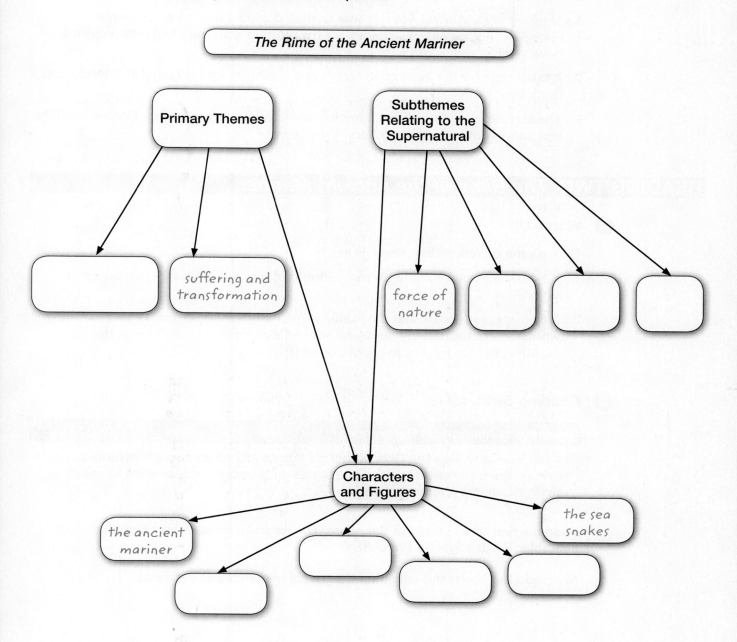

CRITICAL THINKING

Discuss the questions in a small group. Be prepared to share your answers with the class.

1. *The Rime of the Ancient Mariner* was written during a time of social unrest and wars. Given this context, what might the mariner's killing of an innocent bird have symbolized?

2. It takes time for the mariner to accept responsibility for his rash act. Why do you think this is so?

3. The mariner spends his life telling his tale to others as a warning. Do you think he was successful in warning others? Why or why not?

READING TWO: *The Rime of the Ancient Mariner*

A Warm-Up

Discuss the questions in a small group.

1. If a person does something wrong, should others suffer for that person's bad action?

2. A concept of justice is that the punishment should fit the crime. What punishment would be appropriate for someone who kills an animal for no reason (for example, not for food or to protect oneself)?

B Reading Strategy

Identifying Allegorical References

As you learned in Reading One, allegorical figures and characters are **symbolic.** For example, the supernatural beings that appear in the poem represent the forces of nature, life, death, and retribution.

Read the first four stanzas of the poem. The wedding guest is an allegorical character. What might he symbolize?

Now read the poem and underline allegorical references as you read.

The Rime of the Ancient Mariner

By Samuel Coleridge

Part the First

1 It is an ancient Mariner,
    And he stoppeth one of three.
    "By thy[1] long grey beard and **glittering** eye,
    Now wherefore stopp'st thou[2] me?

2 "The Bridegroom's doors are opened wide,
    And I am next of kin[3]
    The guests are met, the feast is set:
    May'st hear the merry din."[4]

3 He holds him with his skinny hand,
    "There was a ship," quoth he.
    "Hold off! unhand me, grey-beard loon!"[5]
    Eftsoons[6] his hand dropt he.

4 He holds him with his glittering eye—
    The Wedding-Guest stood still,
    And listens like a three years child:
    The Mariner hath his **will**.

5 The ship was cheered, the harbour cleared,
    Merrily did we drop
    Below the kirk,[7] below the hill,
    Below the light-house top.

6 The Sun came up upon the left,
    Out of the sea came he!
    And he shone bright, and on the right
    Went down into the sea.

7 And now there came both mist and snow,
    And it grew wondrous cold:
    And ice, mast-high, came floating by,
    As green as emerald.

(continued on next page)

---

[1] thy means "your," it is used as a possessive adjective

[2] thou means "you" (see stanzas 11 and 62); it is used as a subject pronoun.

[3] *next of kin:* a relative

[4] *din:* noise

[5] *loon:* strange person

[6] *eftsoons:* immediately

[7] *kirk:* church

8   The ice was here, the ice was there,
      The ice was all around:
      It cracked and growled, and roared and howled,
      Like noises in a swound!

9   At length did cross an Albatross:
      Through the fog it came;
      As if it had been a Christian **soul**,
      We hailed[8] it in God's name.

10   And a good south wind sprung up behind;
      The Albatross did follow,
      And every day, for food or play,
      Came to the mariners' hollo!

11   "God save thee,[9] ancient Mariner!
      From the fiends[10] that plague[11] thee thus!—
      Why look'st thou so?"—With my cross-bow[12]
      I shot the ALBATROSS.

Part the Second

12   And I had done an hellish thing,
      And it would work 'em **woe**:
      For all averred,[13] I had killed the bird
      That made the breeze to blow.
      Ah **wretch**! said they, the bird to **slay**
      That made the breeze to blow!

13   Nor dim nor red, like God's own head,
      The glorious Sun uprist:[14]
      Then all averred, I had killed the bird
      That brought the fog and mist.
      'Twas right, said they, such birds to slay,
      That bring the fog and mist.

14   Down dropt the breeze, the sails dropt down,
      'Twas sad as sad could be;
      And we did speak only to break
      The silence of the sea!

---

[8] *hail:* greet

[9] thee means "you" (see stanzas 57 and 62); it is used as an object pronoun

[10] *fiends:* evil spirits

[11] *plague:* cause suffering

[12] *cross-bow:* a powerful type of bow; used for shooting arrows with a lot of force

[13] *averred:* affirmed

[14] *uprist:* rose up

15 Day after day, day after day,
    We stuck, nor breath nor motion;
    As **idle** as a painted ship
    Upon a painted ocean.

16 Water, water, every where,
    And all the boards did shrink;
    Water, water, every where,
    Nor any drop to drink.

17 And every tongue, through utter drought,[15]
    Was withered at the root;
    We could not speak, no more than if
    We had been choked with soot.

18 Ah! well a-day! what **evil** looks
    Had I from old and young!
    Instead of the cross, the Albatross
    About my neck was hung.

Part the Third

19 There passed a weary time. Each throat
    Was **parched**, and glazed each eye.
    A **weary** time! a weary time!
    How glazed each weary eye,
    When looking westward, I beheld
    A something in the sky.

20 With throats unslaked,[16] with black lips baked,
    We could not laugh nor wail;
    Through utter drought all dumb we stood!
    I bit my arm, I sucked the blood,
    And cried, A sail! a sail!

21 Alas! (thought I, and my heart beat loud)
    How fast she nears and nears!
    Are those her sails that glance in the Sun,
    Like restless gossameres![17]

22 Are those her ribs through which the Sun
    Did peer, as through a grate?
    And is that Woman all her crew?
    Is that a DEATH? and are there two?
    Is DEATH that woman's mate?

(continued on next page)

---

[15] *drought:* a period of dry weather when there is not enough water

[16] *throats unslaked:* thirst unsatisfied

[17] *gossamer:* light, thin material

23 Four times fifty living men,
    (And I heard nor sigh nor groan)
    With heavy thump, a lifeless lump,
    They dropped down one by one.

24 The souls did from their bodies fly,—
    They fled to bliss or woe!
    And every soul, it passed me by,
    Like the whizz of my CROSS-BOW!

Part the Fourth

25 Alone, alone, all, all alone,
    Alone on a wide wide sea!
    And never a saint took pity on
    My soul in **agony**.

26 I looked upon the rotting sea,
    And drew my eyes away;
    I looked upon the rotting deck,
    And there the dead men lay.

27 An orphan's **curse** would drag to Hell
    A spirit from on high;
    But oh! more horrible than that
    Is a curse in a dead man's eye!
    Seven days, seven nights, I saw that curse,
    And yet I could not die.

28 Beyond the shadow of the ship,
    I watched the water-snakes:
    They moved in tracks of shining white,
    And when they reared, the elfish light
    Fell off in hoary[18] flakes.

29 O happy living things! no tongue
    Their beauty might declare:
    A spring of love gushed[19] from my heart,
    And I blessed them unaware:
    Sure my kind saint took **pity** on me,
    And I blessed them unaware.

30 The self same moment I could pray;
    And from my neck so free
    The Albatross fell off, and sank
    Like lead into the sea.

---

[18] *hoary:* frosty; white
[19] *gushed:* poured quickly

Work with a partner. Compare the allegorical references you underlined. Discuss what they represent. How did identifying these allegorical figures and characters help you better understand the poem?

COMPREHENSION

Ⓐ Main Ideas

Read each statement. Decide if it is *True* or *False* according to the reading. Check (✓) the appropriate box. If it is false, change it to make it true. Discuss your answers with a partner.

	TRUE	FALSE
1. The wedding guest was compelled to listen to the mariner's story.	☐	☐
2. The mariner killed the albatross because he didn't like it.	☐	☐
3. The crew believed the albatross brought either good weather or bad weather.	☐	☐
4. The ship that appeared had real people on it.	☐	☐
5. The albatross fell off the mariner's neck because he had blessed the water-snakes.	☐	☐

Ⓑ Close Reading

Read the questions. Circle the correct answers. Discuss your answers with a partner.

1. What is the purpose of the young man in the poem?

   a. He is a judge of the mariner's moral or immoral behavior.

   b. He provides a listener so the mariner can tell his story.

   c. He is there to remember and retell the story to others.

2. What can we understand about the sailors' beliefs about the albatross and the weather?

   a. The sailors know that the albatross appears only when the weather is good.

   b. The sailors know that the albatross appears only when the weather is bad.

   c. The sailors are superstitious and believe that the albatross can influence the winds.

3. Why do the men hang the dead albatross on the mariner's neck?

   a. as a reminder never to kill any living thing

   b. because the albatross is a holy object

   c. to punish the mariner for bringing them bad luck

(continued on next page)

4. Why does the mariner bless the water-snakes?

    a. because the mariner has just understood the value of all living things

    b. because he thinks the water-snakes are very beautiful

    c. because the water-snakes moved around the ship

VOCABULARY

A **Guessing from Context**

Go back to the reading and guess the meaning of the words in bold. Then match the words with their meanings on the right. Compare answers with a partner.

_e_ 1. glittering	a. what someone wants
___ 2. will	b. motionless
___ 3. slay	c. a swear word, or words
___ 4. idle	d. vicious
___ 5. curse	e. shining with strong emotion
___ 6. evil	f. very tiring
___ 7. parched	g. a very sad or emotionally difficult situation
___ 8. weary	h. sympathy
___ 9. agony	i. kill
___ 10. pity	j. very dry from lack of water

B **Literary Meanings**

The reading contains vocabulary with meanings specific to the context of literature. Match each word as used in the poem with the appropriate literary meaning. Compare answers with a partner.

> **soul** *n.* **1** the part of a person that is not physical and contains their thoughts, feelings, character etc., that many people believe continues to exist after they die.   **2** the part of a person that contains their true character, where their deepest thoughts and feelings come from   **3** LITERARY a person   **4** soul music   **5** a special quality of a painting, piece of music, performance, etc. that makes people feel strong emotions.

At length did cross an Albatross:
Through the fog it came;
As if it had been a Christian **soul**,
We hailed it in God's name.

definition of *soul:* _____

woe *n.* **1** the problems and troubles affecting someone **2** LITERARY great sadness

wretch *n.* **1** someone you feel sorry for because their condition is so bad **2** someone you are annoyed or angry with **3** LITERARY an evil person

And I had done an hellish thing,
And it would work 'em **woe**:
For all averred, I had killed the bird
That made the breeze to blow.
Ah **wretch**! said they, the bird to slay
That made the breeze to blow!

definition of *woe*: _____

definition of *wretch*: _____

Ⓒ Categorizing Words

The vocabulary in Readings One, Two, and Three can be categorized within various themes and subthemes present in the poem. Use the categories in the chart to organize the words in the box. Review the meanings of the words on pages 190–191 if necessary.

agony	glittering	parched	weary	woe
evil	idle	pity	will	wretch

MORAL / MORAL LESSON	SUFFERING / PUNISHMENT	EMOTIONS	POWER / POWERLESSNESS
	agony		

Verb Forms and Word Order

Samuel Taylor Coleridge wrote *The Rime of the Ancient Mariner* using forms of English grammar that are no longer in use. The **verb forms and word order** he used **need to be examined closely in order to understand** the poem.

EXAMPLE: Now wherefore stopp'st thou me?

In modern English, this sentence is: Now why do you stop me?
- Verb Forms
  The third person singular ends in -*eth*, for example, "And he stoppeth one of three."
  The second person singular ends in -*est* or -'*st*, for example, "Why look'st thou so?"
- Word Order
  The subject may come after the verb, as in the example "Why look'st thou so?"

Read the lines from the reading. Match each with the correct sentence in today's English.

___d___ 1. **At length did cross an Albatross.**

_____ 2. **May'st hear the merry din.**

_____ 3. **What evil looks had I from old and young.**

_____ 4. **Eftsoons his hand dropt he.**

_____ 5. **Down dropt the breeze.**

a. The breeze weakened.

b. Soon after he let his hand fall.

c. You can hear the happy noise.

d. Eventually an Albatross passed overhead.

e. Everyone looked at me angrily.

NOTE-TAKING: Making Double-Entry Notes

Copy three or four stanzas from the first part of *The Rime of the Ancient Mariner*. Write your response to each stanza. Your responses might include what the characters or figures symbolize, or your emotional reaction to what you read. Share your notes with a partner.

Stanza	Your Response

CRITICAL THINKING

Discuss the questions in a small group. Be prepared to share your answers with the class.

1. The mariner told his tale again and again as part of his ongoing penance. Why do people have the need to talk about their bad or immoral actions?

2. The expression "having an albatross around one's neck" is still used today. What does it symbolize? Why do you think so?

3. When the mariner blessed the water-snakes, he was pitied, and the albatross was released from his neck. Why did loving and blessing the water-snakes have this effect?

4. After he had listened to the mariner's story, the wedding guest was very subdued. Why did he feel this way? What do you think he felt or did afterward?

The left column lists elements of the poem that were introduced in Reading One. Fill in the stanza numbers and details about these elements that you noted when you were reading the poem.

READING ONE: INTRODUCTION TO THE POEM'S THEMES AND CHARACTERS	READING TWO: PART ONE OF THE POEM
the mariner's careless, unthinking act	stanzas: details:
the consequences of the mariner's act	stanzas: details:
what the mariner learns from his sufferings	stanzas: details:

A Warm-Up

What do you think will happen in the second part of the poem? Write your predictions. Share your predictions with a partner.

1. _____

2. _____

3. _____

4. _____

B Reading Strategy

Paraphrasing Poetry

Paraphrasing the stanzas in a poem **facilitates comprehension**. You can paraphrase more than one or two stanzas together if they focus on the same main idea.

EXAMPLE:

31 Oh sleep! it is a gentle thing,
Beloved from pole to pole!
To Mary Queen the praise be given!
She sent the gentle sleep from Heaven,
That slid into my soul.

32 The silly buckets on the deck,
That had so long remained,
I dreamt that they were filled with dew;
And when I awoke, it rained.

33 My lips were wet, my throat was cold,
My garments all were dank;
Sure I had drunken in my dreams,
And still my body drank.

34 And the coming wind did roar more loud,
And the sails did sigh like sedge;
And the rain poured down from one black cloud;
The Moon was at its edge.

PARAPHRASE: I fell into a gentle sleep and dreamed that the buckets filled with water. When I woke up, it rained and wet my clothes, and I drank the water as the rain poured and the wind roared loudly.

Now read the second half of the poem.

The Rime of the
Ancient Mariner (continued)

Part the Fifth

31   Oh sleep! it is a gentle thing,
Beloved from pole to pole!
To Mary Queen the praise be given!
She sent the gentle sleep from Heaven,
That slid into my soul.

32   The silly buckets on the deck,
That had so long remained,
I dreamt that they were filled with dew;[20]
And when I awoke, it rained.

33   My lips were wet, my throat was cold,
My garments[21] all were dank;[22]
Sure I had drunken in my dreams,
And still my body drank.

34   And the coming wind did roar more loud,
And the sails did sigh like sedge;[23]
And the rain poured down from one black cloud;
The Moon was at its edge.

35   The loud wind never reached the ship,
Yet now the ship moved on!
Beneath the lightning and the Moon
The dead men gave a groan.

36   They groaned, they **stirred**, they all uprose,
Nor spake,[24] nor moved their eyes;
It had been strange, even in a dream,
To have seen those dead men rise.

37   The helmsman steered, the ship moved on;
Yet never a breeze up blew;
The mariners all 'gan[25] work the ropes,
Where they were wont[26] to do:
They raised their limbs like lifeless tools—
We were a **ghastly** crew.

---

[20] *dew:* drops of water

[21] *garments:* clothes

[22] *dank:* wet and cold

[23] *sedge:* a plant similar to grass

[24] *spake:* spoke

[25] *'gan:* began

[26] *wont:* accustomed

38 Till noon we quietly sailed on,
   Yet never a breeze did breathe:
   Slowly and smoothly went the ship,
   Moved onward from beneath.

39 The Sun, right up above the mast,
   Had **fixed** her[27] to the ocean:
   But in a minute she 'gan stir,
   With a short **uneasy** motion—
   Backwards and forwards half her length
   With a short uneasy motion.

40 Then like a pawing horse let go,
   She made a sudden bound:
   It flung the blood into my head,
   And I fell down in a swound.[28]

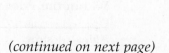

41 How long in that same fit I lay,
   I have not to declare;
   But ere[29] my living life returned,
   I heard and in my soul **discerned**
   Two VOICES in the air.

42 "Is it he?" quoth one, "Is this the man?
   By him who died on cross,
   With his cruel bow he laid full low,
   The harmless Albatross."

43 The other was a softer voice,
   As soft as honey-dew:
   Quoth he, "The man hath penance done,
   And penance more will do."

Part the Sixth

44 I woke, and we were sailing on
   As in a gentle weather:
   'Twas night, calm night, the Moon was high;
   The dead men stood together.

45 And now this **spell** was snapt: once more
   I viewed the ocean green.
   And looked far forth, yet little saw
   Of what had else been seen—

(continued on next page)

---

[27] *her:* In English, a ship is always referred to in the feminine.
[28] *fell down in a swound:* fainted
[29] *ere:* before

46   Swiftly, swiftly flew the ship,
Yet she sailed softly too:
Sweetly, sweetly blew the breeze—
On me alone it blew.

47   Oh! dream of joy! is this indeed
The light-house top I see?
Is this the hill? is this the kirk?
Is this mine own countree!

48   We **drifted** o'er the harbour-bar,
And I with sobs did pray—
O let me be awake, my God!
Or let me sleep alway.

49   The Pilot, and the Pilot's boy,
I heard them coming fast:
Dear Lord in Heaven! it was a joy
The dead men could not blast.[30]

50   I saw a third—I heard his voice:
It is the Hermit good!
He singeth loud his godly hymns
That he makes in the wood.
He'll shrieve[31] my soul, he'll wash away
The Albatross's blood.

Part the Seventh

51   The boat came closer to the ship,
But I nor spake nor stirred;
The boat came close beneath the ship,
And straight a sound was heard.

52   Under the water it rumbled on,
Still louder and more **dread**:
It reached the ship, it split the bay;
The ship went down like lead.

53   **Stunned** by that loud and dreadful sound,
Which sky and ocean smote,[32]
Like one that hath been seven days drowned
My body lay afloat;
But swift as dreams, myself I found
Within the Pilot's boat.

---

[30] *blast:* destroy

[31] *shrieve my soul:* clean my soul of guilt

[32] *smote:* the past form of *smite*, which means "to strike"

54 I moved my lips—the Pilot **shrieked**
    And fell down in a fit;
    The holy Hermit raised his eyes,
    And prayed where he did sit.

55 I took the oars: the Pilot's boy,
    Who now doth crazy go,
    Laughed loud and long, and all the while
    His eyes went to and fro.
    "Ha! ha!" quoth he, "full plain I see,
    The Devil knows how to row."

56 And now, all in my own countree,
    I stood on the firm land!
    The Hermit stepped forth from the boat,
    And scarcely he could stand.

57 "O shrieve me, shrieve me, holy man!"
    The Hermit crossed his brow.
    "Say quick," quoth he, "I bid thee say—
    What manner of man art thou?"

58 Forthwith[33] this **frame** of mine was **wrenched**
    With a woeful agony,
    Which **forced** me to begin my tale;
    And then it left me free.

59 Since then, at an uncertain hour,
    That agony returns;
    And till my ghastly tale is told,
    This heart within me burns.

60 I pass, like night, from land to land;
    I have strange power of speech;
    That moment that his face I see,
    I know the man that must hear me:
    To him my tale I teach.

61 O Wedding-Guest! this soul hath been
    Alone on a wide wide sea:
    So lonely 'twas, that God himself
    Scarce seemed there to be.

(continued on next page)

_____

[33] *forthwith:* immediately

62   Farewell, farewell! but this I tell
      To thee, thou Wedding-Guest!
      He prayeth well, who loveth well
      Both man and bird and beast.

63   He prayeth best, who loveth best
      All things both great and small;
      For the dear God who loveth us
      He made and loveth all.

64   The Mariner, whose eye is bright,
      Whose beard with age is hoar,
      Is gone: and now the Wedding-Guest
      Turned from the bridegroom's door.

65   He went like one that hath been stunned,
      And is of sense forlorn:[34]
      A sadder and a wiser man,
      He rose the morrow morn.

      ⎯⎯⎯⎯⎯⎯⎯⎯⎯⎯
      [34] *forlorn:* lost

Write a sentence summarizing one or more stanzas.

STANZAS	PARAPHRASE
31, 32, 33, 34	I fell asleep and dreamed that the buckets filled with water. When I woke up, it rained, and I drank the water.
35, 36, 37, 38, 39	
40, 41, 42, 43	
44, 45, 46, 47, 48	
49, 50, 51, 52, 53, 54, 55	
56, 57, 58	
59, 60	
61, 62, 63	
64, 65	

With a partner, review the paraphrases you wrote for stanzas 31 through 65. Discuss how paraphrasing helped you understand the reading. Connect your paraphrases to the themes, subthemes, characters, and figures you outlined earlier.

COMPREHENSION

Ⓐ Main Ideas

Read each statement. Decide if it is *True* or *False* according to the reading. Check (✓) the appropriate box. If it is false, change it to make it true. Discuss your answers with a partner.

	TRUE	FALSE
1. A strong wind came up, but the wind did not move the ship.	☐	☐
2. The ship moved because it had an engine.	☐	☐
3. The two voices that the mariner heard were those of other crew members.	☐	☐
4. The mariner asked the hermit to free him of his guilt for his bad actions and their consequences.	☐	☐
5. The mariner tells his tale again and again because he enjoys telling it to others.	☐	☐
6. The wedding guest is a wiser but an unhappier man after listening to the mariner's tale.	☐	☐

Ⓑ Close Reading

Read the questions. Circle the correct answers. Share your answers with a partner.

1. What actually moved the ship?
   a. the wind
   b. a supernatural force
   c. an engine

2. Who were the two voices in the air?
   a. supernatural beings
   b. voices of the crew
   c. voices in the mariner's mind

3. What is the purpose of the hermit in the poem?
   a. He is a witness to the sinking of the mariner's ship.
   b. He provides a listener so the mariner can ask for redemption.
   c. He is there to remember and retell the story to others.

(continued on next page)

4. Why does the mariner look for people to tell his story to?

  a. because he enjoys telling the story

  b. because he wants others to learn something

  c. because he must tell the story as part of his penance

VOCABULARY

 Familiar Words with Unfamiliar Meanings

> Words such as *fixed*, *spell*, and *stir* are familiar. For example, we can say that a mechanic will *fix* our car. We learn how to *spell* words. When we add sugar to our coffee, we *stir* the coffee.
>
> These three words have **unfamiliar meanings when they are used in the context** of *The Rime of the Ancient Mariner*.

Read the stanzas below. Then match each word with its meaning.

1. The Sun, right up above the mast,
  Had **fixed** her to the ocean:
  But in a minute she 'gan stir,
  With a short uneasy motion—
  Backwards and forwards half her length
  With a short uneasy motion.

2. And now this **spell** was snapt: once more
  I viewed the ocean green.
  And looked far forth, yet little saw
  Of what had else been seen—

3. They groaned, they **stirred**, they all uprose,
  Nor spake, nor moved their eyes;
  It had been strange, even in a dream,
  To have seen those dead men rise.

_____ **1. spell**   **a.** hold firmly in place

_____ **2. fix**   **b.** move slightly, especially because you are about to wake up

_____ **3. stir**   **c.** a piece of magic that someone does or the special words or
          ceremonies used in doing it

B Synonyms

Read the sentences. Match each word or phrase in parentheses with its synonym in the box. Compare answers with a partner.

discerned	frame	shrieked	uneasy
drifted	ghastly	stunned	wrenched

1. The mariner felt very _____ about being alone on the ship
   (anxious)
   with a crew of dead men.

2. The wedding guest's feelings were _____ as he listened to
   (strained)
   the mariner's tale. He could not help but feel pity for the man.

3. The supernatural beings _____ that the mariner was alone
   (noticed)
   among the dead crew.

4. The mariner was probably _____ to see all his crew
   (shocked)
   members die before his eyes.

5. Being surrounded by dead men on the deck of a motionless ship must have been

   a(n) _____ experience.
   (extremely upsetting)

6. Many of the people on shore _____ in horror when they
   (cried out loudly)
   saw the death ship approach.

7. After telling his tale, the mariner continued to _____
   (move aimlessly)
   throughout the countryside until he was compelled to tell his story again.

8. The mariner had a very slim _____. His arms and legs
   (body)
   were thin, too.

C Word Forms

Fill in the chart with the correct word forms. Use a dictionary if necessary. An **X** indicates there is no form in that category.

	Noun	Verb	Adjective	Adverb
1.			dread / dreadful	
2.	X	drift		X
3.		fix		X
4.		force		
5.	X	stun		X
6.		X	uneasy	

Complete the sentences with the correct form of one of the words above. Be sure to use the correct tense of the verbs in the affirmative or negative. Compare answers with a partner.

1. When the mariner saw the dead members of the crew rise and move, he was too

   _____ to speak.

2. In the poem, the _____ of nature combined with the

   supernatural to create a strange experience for the mariner.

3. Many people _____ the unknown, while others have little

   fear at all.

4. The crew _____ the torn sail to the ship with rope.

5. The mariner looked _____ at the dead crew all

   around him.

6. Because there was no wind, the ship _____ on the water,

   moving with the waves.

CRITICAL THINKING

Discuss the questions in a small group. Be prepared to share your answers with the class.

1. The mariner unthinkingly and carelessly killed an innocent animal. As a result of his act, all his shipmates died. However, the mariner seems more upset by being forced to tell his tale again and again than he is by having caused his shipmates' deaths. Why do you think this is so?

2. The mariner was forced to spend the rest of his life wandering and telling his story to others. Do you think his penance is too severe? Should the mariner eventually be freed from the agony he feels? Explain your answer.

AFTER YOU READ

BRINGING IT ALL TOGETHER

Work in a small group to fill in the chart. Use the vocabulary you studied in the chapter.

As you learned in Reading One, *The Rime of the Ancient Mariner* is very well known and is often quoted. Read the two best-known quotes from the poem. In a small group, discuss the deeper meaning of each quote, and why it might be so popular. Share your answers with the class.

QUOTE	DEEPER MEANING AND WHY YOU THINK IT IS SO OFTEN QUOTED
Water, water, every where, And all the boards did shrink; Water, water, every where, Nor any drop to drink.	
He prayeth best, who loveth best All things both great and small; For the dear God who loveth us He made and loveth all.	

WRITING ACTIVITY

Write a three-paragraph paper in which you focus on one of the themes or subthemes in *The Rime of the Ancient Mariner*. Use vocabulary from the chapter (for a complete list, go to page 207). Follow these instructions, and use the questions below as a guide.

What are the supernatural forces at work in the poem? How do they affect the action in the story? How does the mariner respond to them? What do you think is the main lesson of the poem? What are other lessons to be learned from the poem?

1. The first paragraph should introduce the theme or subtheme.

2. The second paragraph should describe how the theme or subtheme is woven, or worked, into the poem.

3. The third paragraph should describe why you chose this particular theme or subtheme, and what it means to you.

DISCUSSION AND WRITING TOPICS

Discuss these topics in a small group. Choose one of them and write a short essay about it. Use the vocabulary from the chapter.

1. English speakers sometimes say that a person or situation is like an albatross around his or her neck. Explain why someone might refer to a person or situation in this way, and describe what the albatross might represent.

2. In a careless moment, the mariner killed an albatross. As a consequence of his unthinking act, his shipmates died, and the mariner was made to undergo severe suffering, as well as a penance that lasted the rest of his life. Why do you think Coleridge had the mariner suffer his whole life for that one act of killing an innocent animal?

3. The ancient mariner relates his tale to the wedding guest. Who does the wedding guest represent? What is the moral that Coleridge wants the reader to learn from his poem?

4. What does *The Rime of the Ancient Mariner* mean to you? What lessons did you draw from this poem?

VOCABULARY

Nouns	Verbs	Adjectives
agony	appease	allegorical
animosity	compel	dread
curse	discern	evil
frame*	drift	ghastly
moral	embed	glittering
penance	embrace	idle
pity	fix	parched
redemption	force	rash
retribution	shriek	stunned
soul	slay	subdued
spell	stir	uneasy
supernatural	wrench	weary
turbulence		
will		
woe		
wretch		

* = AWL (Academic Word List) item

SELF-ASSESSMENT

In this chapter you learned to:

○ Understand literary terms

○ Identify allegorical references

○ Paraphrase poetry

○ Create a literary semantic web

○ Guess the meaning of words from the context, categorize words, and understand familiar words with unfamiliar meanings

○ Understand and use synonyms and prefixes

○ Understand literary meaning

○ Make double-entry notes

What can you do well? ☑

What do you need to practice more? ☑

CHAPTER 8

HISTORY: Encountering New Worlds

OBJECTIVES

To read academic texts, you need to master certain skills.

In this chapter, you will:

- Make connections between sentences
- Draw inferences
- Summarize
- Guess the meaning of words from the context and understand word usage
- Use dictionary entries to learn different meanings of words
- Understand and use synonyms, collocations, word forms, and content-specific vocabulary
- Use the adverb *even*
- Create a semantic map and an outline

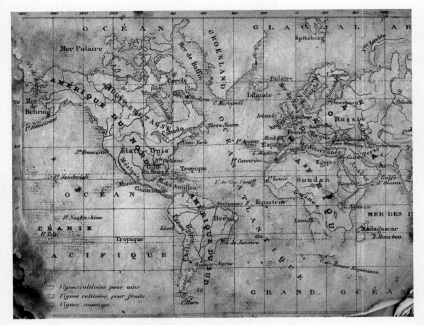

Seventeenth century map of the world

Consider These Questions

Think of a historical event you are familiar with. Answer the questions. Discuss your answers with a partner.

1. What was the event (a war, an expedition, new legislation, a social or cultural movement)?

2. What happened? Describe the event or movement in a few sentences.

3. Why do you think this event or movement succeeded or failed?

Now share your answers with the class. What similarities do you notice among the events you have described? Are there any common elements among the causes or the results? Were similar conditions involved?

READING ONE: Europe on the Eve of Conquest

 Warm-Up

Discuss the questions in a small group.

1. What new worlds did Europeans record having encountered in past centuries?

2. The term *conquest* can refer to the act of taking land by force. It can also mean the act of dealing successfully with something difficult or dangerous. Based on these meanings and the title of the reading, what do you think the reading will be about?

Making Connections between Sentences

Sentences are written in a specific order within a paragraph because they follow a flow of logic. The sentences may indicate:

a. a compare/contrast relationship

b. a statement followed by an example

c. a statement followed by an explanation

Keep in mind that these connections can occur even when the comparison, example, or explanation does not immediately follow the statement.

EXAMPLE:
> Columbus's discovery of America was completely accidental. He had been expecting to sail to Asia.

The second sentence provides an explanation of why Columbus's discovery of America was accidental.

Read the sentences from the reading. Write *comparison, example,* **or** *explanation* **on the line to indicate what the connection between the two sentences is.**

_____*Example*_____ **1.** "In the tenth century, Scandinavian seafarers known as Vikings actually established settlements in the New World. In the year 984, a band of Vikings led by Eric the Red sailed west from Iceland to a large island in the North Atlantic." *(paragraph 2)*

_____ **2.** "At the time of the Viking settlement, other Europeans were unprepared to sponsor transatlantic exploration. Medieval kingdoms were loosely organized, and until the early fifteenth century, fierce provincial loyalties, widespread ignorance of classical learning, and dreadful plagues such as the Black Death discouraged people from thinking expansively about the world beyond their own immediate communities." *(paragraph 2)*

_____ **3.** "Ptolemy (second-century A.D.) and other ancient geographers had mapped the known world and had even demonstrated that the world was round. During the Middle Ages, however, Europeans lost effective contact with classical tradition." *(paragraph 5)*

_____ **4.** "By 1500, centralization of political authority and advances in geographic knowledge brought Spain to the first rank as a world power. In the early fifteenth century, though, Spain consisted of several autonomous kingdoms." *(paragraph 6)*

Now read the text and highlight sentences where you find logical connections.

EUROPE ON THE EVE OF[1] CONQUEST

By Robert A. Divine, T. H. H. Breen, George M. Fredrickson, R. Hal Williams, Ariela J. Gross, and H. W. A. Brands

1   In the tenth century, Scandinavian seafarers known as Vikings actually established **settlements** in the New World. In the year 984, a band of Vikings led by Eric the Red sailed west from Iceland to a large island in the North Atlantic. A few years later, Eric's son Leif[2] founded a small settlement he named Vinland at a location in northern Newfoundland. At the time, the Norse voyages went unnoticed by other Europeans. The **hostility** of Native Americans, poor lines of communication, climatic cooling, and political **upheavals** in Scandinavia made maintenance of these distant outposts impossible. At the time of his first voyage in 1492, Columbus seemed to have been unaware of these earlier **exploits**.

Building New Nation-States

2   At the time of the Viking settlement, other Europeans were unprepared to sponsor transatlantic exploration.

Medieval[3] kingdoms were loosely organized, and until the early fifteenth century, fierce provincial loyalties, widespread ignorance of classical learning, and **dreadful** plagues[4] such as the Black Death discouraged people from thinking **expansively** about the world beyond their own immediate communities.

3   In the fifteenth century, however, these conditions began to change. Europe became more **prosperous**, political authority was more **centralized**, and the Renaissance[5] **fostered** a more expansive outlook among literate people in the arts and sciences. The Renaissance

(continued on next page)

[1] *on the eve of:* just before

[2] *Leif:* known today as Leif Ericson

[3] *medieval:* relating to a period in Europe also called the Middle Ages; from 476 to 1453 A.D.

[4] *plague:* a very infectious disease that often causes death

[5] *Renaissance:* a period in Europe from the early 1300s to 1600 marked by great artistic and scientific achievements and discoveries

encouraged—first in Italy and later throughout Europe—bold new creative thinking. A major element in the shift was the slow but steady growth of population after 1450. The result was a substantial rise in the price of land, since there were more mouths to feed. Landlords profited from these trends, and as their income expanded, they demanded more of the luxury items, such as spices, silks, and jewels, that came from distant Asian ports. Economic prosperity created powerful new **incentives** for exploration and trade.

4   This period also witnessed the centralization of political authority under a group of rulers whom historians refer to collectively as the New Monarchs. Before the mid-fifteenth century, feudal[6] nobles dominated small districts throughout Europe. The New Monarchs challenged the nobles' **autonomy**. The changes that accompanied the challenges came slowly, and in many areas violently, but the results **altered** traditional political relationships between the nobility and the crown, and between the citizen and the state. The New Monarchs of Europe recruited armies and supported these expensive organizations with revenues from national taxes. Strong-willed monarchs **forged** nations out of groups of independent kingdoms. If political centralization had not occurred, the major European countries could not possibly have generated the financial and military resources necessary for worldwide exploration.

5   A final **prerequisite** to exploration was reliable technical knowledge. Ptolemy[7] (second century A.D.) and

---

[6] *feudal:* relating to feudalism, a social system that existed in the Middle Ages

[7] *Ptolemy:* a Roman who lived in Egypt and who wrote in Greek

other ancient geographers had mapped the known world and had even demonstrated that the world was round. During the Middle Ages, however, Europeans lost effective contact with classical tradition. Within Arab societies, the old learning had survived, indeed flourished, and when Europeans eventually rediscovered the classical texts during the Renaissance, they drew heavily on the work of Arab scholars. This "new" learning generated great intellectual curiosity about the globe and about the world that existed beyond the Mediterranean.

Imagining a New World

6   By 1500, centralization of political authority and advances in geographic knowledge brought Spain to the first rank as a world power. In the early fifteenth century, though, Spain consisted of several autonomous kingdoms. It lacked rich natural resources and possessed few good seaports. In fact, there was little about this land to suggest its people would take the lead in conquering and colonizing the New World. By the end of the century, however, Spain suddenly came alive with creative energy. The union of Ferdinand and Isabella sparked a drive for political **consolidation** that, because of the monarchs' fervid Catholicism, took on the characteristics of a religious crusade.

7   From this **volatile** social and political environment came the conquistadores, men eager for personal glory and material gain, uncompromising in matters of religion, and unswerving in their loyalty to the crown. They were prepared to employ fire and sword in any cause **sanctioned** by God and king, and these adventurers carried European culture to the most populous regions of the New World.

Work with a partner. Review the sentences you highlighted. Decide whether the connection indicates a compare/contrast relationship, a statement followed by an example, or a statement followed by an explanation.

COMPREHENSION

A **Main Ideas**

Read each statement. Decide if it is *True* or *False* according to the reading. Check (✓) the appropriate box. If it is false, change it to make it true. Discuss your answers with a partner.

	TRUE	FALSE
1. The Vikings did not maintain their settlements in the New World because Leif Ericson's settlement was too small.	☐	☐
2. Between the tenth and the fifteenth century, Europeans did not explore the New World because several factors prevented them from considering such large expeditions.	☐	☐
3. In the fifteenth century, Europeans began exploring the world because they finally learned about the Vikings' expeditions and wanted to settle the New World, too.	☐	☐
4. In the second century A.D., Europeans knew the world was round, but during the Middle Ages, this knowledge was lost.	☐	☐
5. In the sixteenth century, Spain unexpectedly became a great power, in part because of the political and religious environment.	☐	☐

B **Close Reading**

Answer the questions. Check (✓) all the answers that apply. Discuss your answers with a partner.

1. What conditions existed prior to the European expeditions that prevented Europeans from exploring outside their immediate communities?

   ☐ **a.** lack of knowledge of classical learning

   ☐ **b.** the hostility of Native Americans

   ☐ **c.** the high price of land

   ☐ **d.** the loose organization of European kingdoms

   ☐ **e.** widespread instances of dreadful plagues

2. In what ways did conditions in Europe begin to change?

   ☐ **a.** Europeans learned about the Viking (Norse) settlements.

   ☐ **b.** Europe became more prosperous.

   ☐ **c.** The Native Americans became friendlier.

   ☐ **d.** Literate Europeans began to have a more expansive outlook.

   ☐ **e.** Political authority became more centralized.

   ☐ **f.** The nobles wanted more land.

   ☐ **g.** Land in Europe became more expensive as the population increased.

(continued on next page)

3. What were some of the political changes that took place after the mid-fifteenth century?

    ☐ **a.** Political power became more centralized.

    ☐ **b.** The New Monarchs destroyed the nobility's independence.

    ☐ **c.** Political relationships between nobility and kings began to change.

    ☐ **d.** Political relationships between the people and the government began to change.

    ☐ **e.** The New Monarchs created armies and supported them with their own wealth.

4. What were some conditions that led to Spain becoming a world power?

    ☐ **a.** Spain had many natural resources.

    ☐ **b.** Spain's many kingdoms were united.

    ☐ **c.** The country experienced a great increase in creative energy.

    ☐ **d.** Good seaports were built.

    ☐ **e.** Men loyal to the king were willing to engage in exploration.

VOCABULARY

Ⓐ Guessing from Context

Read each quote from the reading. Try to guess the meaning of the word in bold from the context. Write the clues that helped you guess and your guess. Then consult a dictionary and write the definition. Compare answers with a partner.

1. "In the tenth century, Scandinavian seafarers known as Vikings actually established **settlements** in the New World. In the year 984, a band of Vikings led by Eric the Red sailed west from Iceland to a large island in the North Atlantic. A few years later, Eric's son Leif founded a small **settlement** he named Vinland at a location in northern Newfoundland." *(paragraph 1)*

    Clues: _____

    Guess: _____

    Dictionary: _____

2. "Europe became more prosperous, political authority was more centralized, and the Renaissance **fostered** a more expansive outlook among literate people in the arts and sciences. The Renaissance encouraged—first in Italy and later throughout Europe—bold new creative thinking." *(paragraph 3)*

    Clues: _____

    Guess: _____

    Dictionary: _____

3. "Landlords profited from these trends, and as their income expanded, they demanded more of the luxury items, such as spices, silks, and jewels, that came from distant Asian ports. Economic prosperity created powerful new **incentives** for exploration and trade." (*paragraph 3*)

Clues: _____

Guess: _____

Dictionary: _____

4. "Before the mid-fifteenth century, feudal nobles dominated small districts throughout Europe. The New Monarchs challenged the nobles' **autonomy**." (*paragraph 4*)

Clues: _____

Guess: _____

Dictionary: _____

5. "The New Monarchs challenged the nobles' autonomy. The changes that accompanied the challenges came slowly, and in many areas violently, but the results **altered** traditional political relationships between the nobility and the crown, and between the citizen and the state." (*paragraph 4*)

Clues: _____

Guess: _____

Dictionary: _____

B Synonyms

Read the sentences. Match each word or phrase in parentheses with its synonym in the box. Compare answers with a partner.

centralized	expansively	prerequisite	volatile
consolidation	exploits	upheaval	

1. Government leaders need to think more _____ if they

   (broadly)

   want to foster their countries' economic growth.

2. The political situation between the two countries is very

   _____. War may break out any day.

   (unstable)

3. The city's historical records used to be spread out across the city, but recently they

   were _____ in one location downtown.

   (organized in one place)

(*continued on next page*)

4. Being born in the United States is a _____ for being president.
(requirement)

5. The historian used to store her research notes in several files, but after their

_____ in one file she found information much easier to
(merging)
locate.

6. Christopher Columbus and others who came to the New World often recorded

their _____ in logs and journals.
(ventures)

7. After the revolution a new government was established, but the

_____ caused by the revolution lasted for many years.
(disruption)

C Word Usage

Read the groups of sentences using *forge* and *sanction*. Match the word as used in each sentence with the appropriate meaning. Compare answers with a partner.

1. **forge**

_____ 1. Strong-willed monarchs forged nations out of groups of independent kingdoms.

_____ 2. Workers forged swords out of steel for the conquistadores.

_____ 3. The criminals sold forged letters they claimed had been written by historical figures.

_____ 4. The two countries forged an alliance that has lasted for 50 years.

> **a.** to illegally copy something, for example, a document, a painting, or money, to make people think that it is real
> **b.** to develop a strong relationship with other people, groups, or countries
> **c.** to produce or make something, especially after a long time or a lot of discussion
> **d.** to make something from a piece of metal by heating the metal and shaping it

2. **sanction**

_____ 1. The judge sanctioned the lawyer for disregarding the court's decision.

_____ 2. The president will sanction the use of force if diplomatic efforts fail.

_____ 3. Violence was sanctioned by the Spanish rulers, who wished to conquer the New World.

> **a.** to officially accept or allow something
> **b.** to be made acceptable by something
> **c.** to punish someone for disobeying a rule or law

NOTE-TAKING: Creating a Semantic Map

Use the semantic map below to organize information in the reading that explains why conditions in Scandinavia in the 10th century led to failure, whereas conditions in Europe in the 15th century prepared Europeans for success.

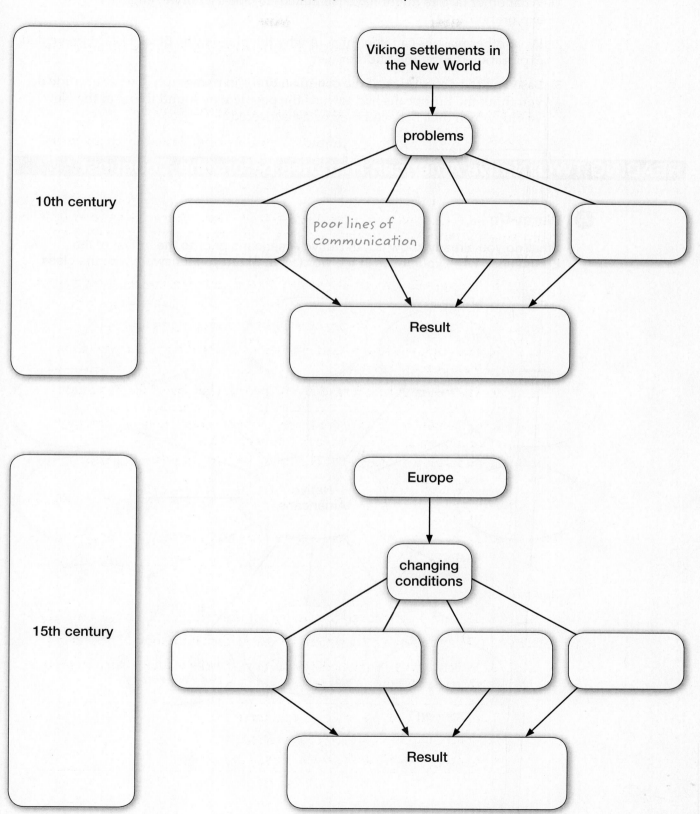

CRITICAL THINKING

Discuss the questions in a small group. Be prepared to share your answers with the class.

1. What other factors might have facilitated Europe's ability to engage in exploration?

2. What other reasons can you think of why the plague (the Black Death) prevented exploration during the Middle Ages?

3. Based on the description of the conquistadores in paragraph 7, what attitude do you think the Europeans had toward the people they found living in the New World, which they believed they had discovered?

READING TWO: Native American Histories before the Conquest

A **Warm-Up**

What do you already know about Native Americans prior to the arrival of the Europeans? Write your ideas in the word web. Share your answers with the class.

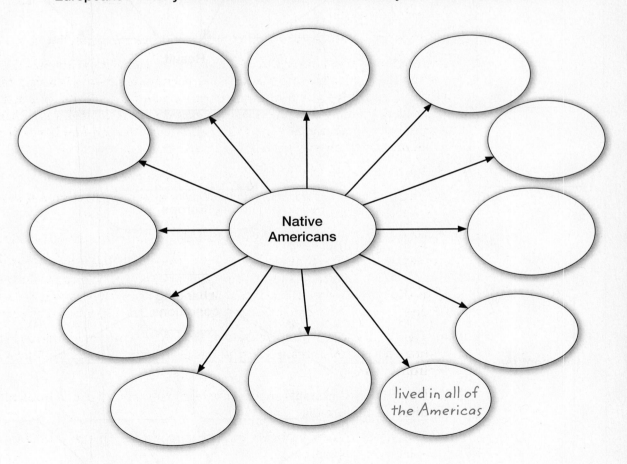

Drawing Inferences

As you learned in an earlier chapter, **drawing inferences** involves understanding what the author **implies** but does not directly state. When we draw inferences, we use the facts at hand, along with our background knowledge, to help us draw accurate inferences.

Read the paragraphs from the reading and decide what you can infer from them. Check (✓) all that may apply. Compare answers with a partner.

1. "As almost any Native American could have informed the first European adventurers, the peopling of America did not begin in 1492. In fact, although European invaders such as Columbus proclaimed the discovery of a 'New World,' the first migrants reached the North American continent some fifteen to twenty thousand years ago. Their social and cultural development over the period was as complex as any encountered in the so-called Old World." *(paragraph 1)*

   ☐ **a.** The Native Americans didn't want to tell the Europeans that they had been living in North America for a long time.

   ☐ **b.** Columbus and other Europeans considered North America basically uninhabited.

   ☐ **c.** The Native Americans did not consider America uninhabited.

2. "Environmental conditions played a major part in the story. Twenty thousand years ago the earth's climate was considerably colder than it is today. Much of the world's moisture was transformed into ice, and the oceans dropped hundreds of feet below their current levels. The receding waters created a land bridge connecting Asia and North America, a region now submerged beneath the Bering Sea that modern archaeologists named Beringia." *(paragraph 2)*

   ☐ **a.** Much of the oceans' water froze 20,000 years ago.

   ☐ **b.** Environmental conditions enabled people to migrate from Asia to North America.

   ☐ **c.** People migrated from Asia to North America because Asia was too cold.

3. "Another theory notes that epidemics have frequently been associated with prolonged contact with domestic animals such as cattle and pigs. Since the Paleo-Indians did not domesticate animals, not even horses, they may have avoided the microbes that caused virulent European and African diseases." *(paragraph 3)*

   ☐ **a.** The Paleo-Indians did not want to domesticate animals such as cattle, horses, and pigs because they wanted to avoid contracting diseases from them.

   ☐ **b.** Domesticated animals such as cattle, horses, and pigs can transmit some diseases to humans.

   ☐ **c.** The Paleo-Indians probably did not contract the diseases that Europeans and Africans contracted.

(continued on next page)

4. "The shift to basic crops—a transformation that is sometimes termed the Agricultural Revolution—profoundly altered Native American societies. The availability of a more reliable store of food helped liberate nomadic groups from the insecurities of hunting and gathering. The vegetable harvest made possible the establishment of permanent villages." *(paragraph 6)*

☐ **a.** Changing from hunting and gathering to agriculture enabled some Native American groups to create settlements.

☐ **b.** The shift from hunting and gathering to agriculture eliminated meat from the Native American diet.

☐ **c.** With the change to raising crops, Native Americans had a food supply they could depend on, so they did not have to be nomadic any longer.

Now read the text and draw inferences. Highlight important information as you read.

NATIVE AMERICAN HISTORIES BEFORE THE CONQUEST

By Robert A. Divine, T. H. H. Breen, George M. Fredrickson, R. Hal Williams, Ariela J. Gross, and H. W. A. Brands

1   As almost any Native American could have informed the first European adventurers, the peopling of America did not begin in 1492. In fact, although European invaders such as Columbus **proclaimed** the discovery of a "New World," the first migrants reached the North American continent some fifteen to twenty thousand years ago. Their social and cultural development over the period was as complex as any encountered in the so-called **Old World**.

The Environment

2   Environmental conditions played a major part in the story. Twenty thousand years ago the earth's climate was considerably colder than it is today. Much of the world's moisture was transformed into ice, and the oceans dropped hundreds of feet below their current levels. The receding waters created a land bridge connecting Asia and North America, a region now submerged beneath the Bering Sea that modern archaeologists named Beringia.

Disease

3   The material culture of the Paleo-Indians differed little from that of other Stone Age[1] peoples found in Asia, Africa, and Europe. In terms of human health, however, something occurred on the Beringian tundra that forever **altered** the history of Native Americans. For reasons that remain obscure, the members of these small **migrating** groups stopped hosting a number of communicable diseases—smallpox and measles being the deadliest—and although Native Americans experienced

---
[1] *Stone Age:* a prehistoric period of time when humans used mainly stones to make tools

illnesses such as tuberculosis, they no longer suffered the major epidemics[2] that under normal conditions would have killed a large percentage of their population every year. The physical **isolation** of the various bands may have protected them from the spread of **contagious** disease. Another theory notes that epidemics have frequently been associated with **prolonged** contact with domestic animals such as cattle and pigs. Since the Paleo-Indians did not domesticate animals, not even horses, they may have avoided the microbes that caused **virulent** European and African diseases.

4   Whatever the explanation for this curious epidemiological[3] record, Native Americans lost inherited **immunities** that later might have protected them from many contagious germs. Thus, when they first came into contact with Europeans and Africans, Native Americans had no defense against the great killers of the Early Modern world.

The Environmental Challenge: Food, Climate, and Culture

5   Some twelve thousand years ago global warming substantially reduced the glaciers, allowing nomadic hunters to pour into the heart of the North American continent. Within just a few thousand years, Native Americans had journeyed from Colorado to the southern tip of South America.

6   The Indian peoples adjusted to the changing environmental conditions. As they **dispersed** across the North American continent, they developed new food sources, at first smaller mammals and fish, nuts and berries, and then about five thousand years ago, they discovered how to cultivate certain plants. The shift to basic crops—a transformation that is sometimes termed the Agricultural Revolution—**profoundly** altered Native American societies. The availability of a more reliable store of food helped liberate nomadic groups from the insecurities of hunting and gathering. The vegetable harvest made possible the establishment of permanent villages that often were governed by clearly defined hierarchies of **elders** and kings, and as the food supply increased, the Native American population greatly expanded, especially around urban centers in the Southwest and in the Mississippi Valley. Although the evidence is patchy, scholars currently estimate that approximately four million Native Americans lived north of Mexico at the time of the initial encounter with Europeans.

Eastern Woodland Cultures

7   In the northeast region along the Atlantic coast, the Indians did not practice intensive agriculture. These peoples, numbering less than a million at the time of conquest, generally supplemented farming with seasonal hunting and gathering. Most belonged to what ethnographers term the Eastern Woodland Cultures. Small bands formed villages during the warm summer months. The women cultivated maize, or corn, and other crops while the men hunted and fished. During the winter, difficulties associated with feeding so many people forced the communities to disperse. Each family lived off the land as best it could.

8   However divided the Indians of eastern North America may have been, they shared many cultural values and assumptions. Most Native Americans, for example, defined their place in society through kinship. Such personal bonds determined the character of economic and political relations. The farming bands living in areas

(continued on next page)

---

[2] *epidemic:* a large number of cases of a particular disease happening at the same time; the disease can be passed from one person to another

[3] *epidemiological:* referring to the causes and control of diseases among people

eventually claimed by England were often **matrilineal**, which meant in effect that the women owned the planting fields and houses, maintained tribal customs, and had a role in tribal government. Among the native communities of Canada and the northern Great Lakes, **patrilineal** forms were much more common. In these groups, the men owned the hunting grounds that the family needed to survive. Eastern woodland communities organized diplomacy, trade, and war around reciprocal relationships that impressed Europeans as being extraordinarily **egalitarian**, even democratic.

A World Transformed

9   The arrival of large numbers of white men and women on the North American continent profoundly altered Native American cultures. Indians discovered that conquest **strained** traditional ways of life, and as daily patterns of experience changed almost beyond recognition, native peoples had to **devise** new answers, new responses, and new ways to survive in physical and social environments that eroded tradition.

Cultural Negotiations

10   Native Americans were not passive victims of geopolitical forces beyond their control. So long as they remained healthy, they held their own in the early exchanges. What Indians desired most was peaceful trade. The earliest French explorers reported that natives waved from shore, urging the Europeans to exchange metal items for beaver skins. In fact, the Indians did not perceive themselves at a disadvantage in these dealings. They could readily see the technological advantage of guns over bows and arrows. Metal knives made daily tasks much easier.

Threats to Survival: Cultural Differences and Disease

11   Over time, cooperative encounters between the Native Americans and Europeans became less frequent. The Europeans found it almost impossible to understand the Indians' relation to the land and other natural resources. English planters cleared the forests and fenced the fields and, in the process, radically altered the ecological systems on which the Indians depended. The European system of land use inevitably reduced the supply of deer and other animals essential to traditional cultures.

12   It was disease, however, that ultimately destroyed the cultural **integrity** of many North American tribes—small social groups of related families. European adventurers exposed the Indians to bacteria and viruses against which they possessed no natural immunity. Smallpox, measles, and influenza decimated[4] the Native American population. Historical demographers[5] now estimate that some tribes suffered a 90 to 95 percent population loss within the first century of European contact. However horrific the crisis may have been, it demonstrated powerfully just how much the environment—a source of opportunity as well as **devastation**—shaped human encounters throughout the New World.

---

[4] *decimate:* destroy or cause deaths in large numbers

[5] *demographer:* a person who studies human populations and how they change

Work with a partner. Discuss the inferences you were able to draw from the reading.

COMPREHENSION

A Main Ideas

Complete the sentences based on information in the reading. Discuss your answers with a partner.

1. Although Columbus claimed that he had discovered a New World,

   _____ .

2. One of the major factors that affected the Native Americans' encounters with Europeans was

   _____ .

3. A significant adjustment that many Native Americans made to changing environmental conditions was

   _____ .

4. Over time, encounters between Native Americans and Europeans

   _____ .

5. The most significant impact on the Native American population was

   _____ .

B Close Reading

Read the quotes from the reading. Circle the statement that best explains each quote. Share your answers with a partner.

1. "For reasons that remain obscure, the members of these small migrating [Native American] groups stopped hosting a number of communicable diseases—smallpox and measles being the deadliest." *(paragraph 3)*

   a. It's not clear why, but small nomadic groups of Native Americans stopped communicating with other people who hosted diseases such as smallpox and measles.

   b. It's not clear why, but small groups of Native Americans suffering from communicable diseases stopped migrating.

   c. It's not clear why, but small nomadic groups of Native Americans no longer contracted various contagious diseases such as smallpox and measles.

   (continued on next page)

2. "The shift to basic crops—a transformation that is sometimes termed the Agricultural Revolution—profoundly altered Native American societies. The availability of a more reliable store of food helped liberate nomadic groups from the insecurities of hunting and gathering." *(paragraph 6)*

   a. An Agricultural Revolution greatly affected Native Americans, causing them to stop hunting and gathering and start growing basic crops so they would be liberated from a nomadic life.

   b. When Native American societies shifted to basic crops, and their sources of food became more stable, they experienced an Agricultural Revolution that greatly changed their societies.

   c. Native Americans preferred growing basic crops rather than hunting and gathering, so they created an Agricultural Revolution to liberate themselves from their nomadic lives.

3. "The arrival of large numbers of white men and women on the North American continent profoundly altered Native American cultures." *(paragraph 9)*

   a. When white men and women arrived in North America, Native American cultures were greatly affected as a consequence.

   b. When white men and women came to North America, they changed Native American cultures to be more like their own.

   c. When white men and women came to North America, Native Americans changed their cultures to be more like those of the newcomers.

4. "English planters cleared the forests and fenced the fields and, in the process, radically altered the ecological systems on which the Indians depended." *(paragraph 11)*

   a. The Indians depended on ecological systems, but the English planters took away their access to these systems by clearing forests and putting fences around fields.

   b. English planters deliberately tried to change the ecological systems that the Indians depended on by clearing forests and fencing the fields.

   c. English planters had different ways of treating the land, and these different ways greatly changed the ecological systems the Indians depended on in their own lives.

5. "However horrific the crisis may have been, it demonstrated powerfully just how much the environment—a source of opportunity as well as devastation—shaped human encounters throughout the New World." *(paragraph 12)*

   a. The crisis demonstrated how powerful environmental factors were in the lives of all Native Americans.

   b. The crisis demonstrated how environmental factors, whether positive or negative, had a significant effect on human encounters in the New World.

   c. The crisis demonstrated how powerless Native Americans were in the face of environmental factors beyond their control.

VOCABULARY

A **Synonyms**

Read the sentences. Match each word in parentheses with its synonym in the box. Compare answers with a partner.

devastation	integrity	profoundly	strained
immunity	proclaimed	prolonged	virulent

1. When the English arrived in the New World, they _____ (announced) that the land belonged to them.

2. The current type of influenza is quite _____. The (harmful) government is encouraging people to get vaccinated.

3. The scene of _____ after the bombing was tragic. Most of (destruction) the city was destroyed.

4. Repeated wars and diseases _____ the people's ability to (weakened) deal with everday life.

5. If a person survives after contracting smallpox, that person develops a(n)

   _____ to the disease and will not get it again.
   (resistance)

6. _____ is valued among Native Americans, and they often (honesty) choose someone with this value as a leader.

7. After their initial experiences, Native Americans became _____ (extremely) distrustful of Europeans.

8. Despite the _____ delay, a peace treaty was eventually (continued) negotiated and signed.

B Understanding Content-Specific Vocabulary

> This reading contains **vocabulary specific to the subject** of the chapter. It is often much easier to learn such vocabulary as a group, within the context of the field itself.

Read the paragraphs and guess the meaning of the words in bold. Then match the words in bold with their meanings below. Compare answers with a partner.

Although European invaders such as Columbus proclaimed the discovery of a "New World," the first migrants reached the North American continent some fifteen to twenty thousand years ago. Their social and cultural development over the period was as complex as any encountered in the so-called **Old World**.

The material culture of the Paleo-Indians differed little from that of other Stone Age peoples found in Asia, Africa, and Europe. In terms of human health, however, something occurred on the Beringian tundra that forever altered the history of Native Americans. For reasons that remain obscure, the members of these small **migrating** groups stopped hosting a number of communicable diseases—smallpox and measles being the deadliest—and although Native Americans experienced illnesses such as tuberculosis, they no longer suffered the major epidemics that under normal conditions would have killed a large percentage of their population every year.

However divided the Indians of eastern North America may have been, they shared many cultural values and assumptions. Most Native Americans, for example, defined their place in society through kinship. Such personal bonds determined the character of economic and political relations. The farming bands living in areas eventually claimed by England were often **matrilineal**, which meant in effect that the women owned the planting fields and houses, maintained tribal customs, and had a role in tribal government. Among the native communities of Canada and the northern Great Lakes, **patrilineal** forms were much more common. In these groups, the men owned the hunting grounds that the family needed to survive. Eastern woodland communities organized diplomacy, trade, and war around reciprocal relationships that impressed Europeans as being extraordinarily **egalitarian**, even democratic.

_b_ 1. **egalitarian**

____ 2. **matrilineal**

____ 3. **migrate**

____ 4. **Old World**

____ 5. **patrilineal**

a. to move as a large group from one place to another

b. believing that everyone is equal and has equal rights

c. refers to a society in which connections between the mothers and daughters in a family are regarded as the most important

d. refers to a society in which connections between the fathers and sons in a family are regarded as the most important

e. the Eastern Hemisphere, especially Europe, Asia, and Africa

C Word Forms

Fill in the chart with the correct word forms. Use a dictionary if necessary. An **X** indicates there is no form in that category.

	NOUN	VERB	ADJECTIVE	ADVERB
1.	devastation			
2.	immunity			X
3.		migrate		X
4.			prolonged	X
5.		strain		X
6.		X	virulent	virulently

Complete the sentences with the correct form of one of the words in the chart. Be sure to use the correct tense of the verbs in the affirmative or negative and the singular or plural form of the nouns. Compare answers with a partner.

1. Every year thousands of children contract diseases such as measles and chicken pox because their doctors _____ them against these illnesses.

2. As bacteria gain immunity to certain antibiotics, the diseases they cause increase in _____.

3. The earthquake last year _____ three villages and killed 2,500 people.

4. The annual _____ of many species of birds from colder climates to warmer climates during the fall are decreasing.

5. Planned exploration for new sources of natural resources _____ the country's budget, but its need for power outweighs this disadvantage.

6. After a _____ war lasting more than ten years, the country's economy was at the point of collapse.

NOTE-TAKING: Creating an Outline

Go back to the reading and read it again. Then use the title, headings, and subheadings to create an outline and fill in details. Use the information you highlighted to help you. Compare your work with a partner.

Native American Histories before the Conquest

I. _The Environment_ _____

_____

II. _____

_____

III. _____

_____

IV. _____

_____

V. _____

_____

   A. _____

_____

   B. _____

_____

CRITICAL THINKING

Discuss the questions in a small group. Be prepared to share your answers with the class.

1. How might the peopling of the New World have differed if there had not been a land bridge between Asia and North America?

2. How might the history of the Native Americans have differed if they had had immunity to the diseases brought by the Europeans?

3. What was the Europeans' attitude toward the Native Americans, and what was the Native Americans' attitude toward the Europeans with regard to land? How did this difference create a potential for conflict?

LINKING READINGS ONE AND TWO

Discuss the questions in a small group. Be prepared to share your answers with the class.

1. Compare the Europeans' encounters with the Native Americans in Reading One with those in Reading Two. How were their encounters similar? In what ways were they different?

2. Compare the societies of 15th-century Europe with those of the Native Americans at the time. How would you describe them from an anthropological point of view? (You might refer back to Chapter Three.)

READING THREE: West Africa at the Time of European Exploration

Ⓐ Warm-Up

Discuss the questions with a partner.

1. What cultural similarities do you think 15th-century century West Africans and Native Americans had?

2. Based on what you have read about the European encounters with native people in the New World, what do you think the reading will describe about their encounters with native Africans?

Ⓑ Reading Strategy

Summarizing

Summarizing involves writing a short, general statement of the main points of a reading, and **not including any details.** A summary is usually **only one paragraph in length.** Remember you do not need to write a sentence for each paragraph of the reading. The main points of more than one paragraph may be combined into one sentence if they discuss the same main point.

For several centuries, Europeans engaged in the slave trade with West Africans.

_____

_____

_____

_____

As you read the text, highlight the main points. You will complete the summary when you finish reading.

WEST AFRICA AT THE TIME OF EUROPEAN EXPLORATION

By Robert A. Divine, T. H. H. Breen, George M. Fredrickson, R. Hal Williams, Ariela J. Gross, and H. W. A. Brands

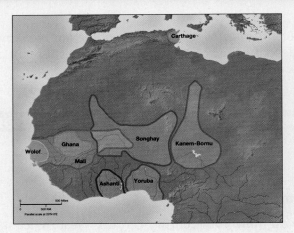

1   During the era of the European slave trade, roughly from the late fifteenth through the mid-nineteenth century, a number of **enduring** myths about sub-Saharan West Africa were **propagated**. Even today, commentators claim that the people who inhabited this region four hundred years ago were **isolated** from the rest of the world and had a simple, self-sufficient economy.

Ancient and Complex Societies

2   The first Portuguese who explored the African coast during the fifteenth century encountered a great variety of political and religious cultures. West Africans spoke many languages and organized themselves into diverse political systems. Several populous states, sometimes termed "empires," exercised loose control over large areas. Ancient African empires such as Ghana were **vulnerable** to external attack as well as internal rebellion, and the oral and written histories of this region record the rise and fall of several large kingdoms. Many other Africans lived in what are known as stateless societies, really largely **autonomous** communities organized around lineage[1] structures. In these respects, African and Native American cultures had much in common.

The Arrival of the Europeans

3   The first Europeans to reach the West African coast by sail were the Portuguese. They journeyed to Africa in search of gold and slaves. Mali and Joloff[2] officials were willing partners in this **commerce** but insisted that Europeans respect trade regulations established by Africans. They required the Europeans to pay tolls and other fees and restricted the foreign traders to conducting their business in small forts or castles located at the mouths of the major rivers. Local merchants acquired some slaves and gold in the interior and transported them to the coast where they were exchanged for European manufactures. **Transactions** were calculated in terms of local African **currencies**: a slave would be offered to a European trader for so many bars of iron or ounces of gold.

4   European slave traders accepted these terms largely because they had no other choice. The African states fielded **formidable** armies, and outsiders soon discovered they could not **impose** their will on the region simply by demonstrations of force. Moreover, local diseases proved so **lethal** for Europeans—six out of ten of whom would die within a single year's stay in Africa—that they were happy to avoid dangerous trips to the interior. The slaves were usually men and women taken captive during wars; others were victims of judicial practices designed specifically to supply the growing American market. By 1650, most West African slaves were **destined** for the New World rather than the Middle East.

---

[1] *lineage:* the way in which members of a family are descended from other members

[2] *Mali and Joloff:* areas in West Africa

Slavery from Africa to the New World

5   Even before Europeans colonized the New World, the Portuguese were purchasing almost a thousand slaves a year on the West African coast. The slaves were frequently forced to work on the sugar plantations[3] of Madeira (Portuguese) and the Canaries (Spanish), Atlantic islands on which Europeans experimented with forms of unfree labor that would later be more fully and more **ruthlessly** established in the American colonies. It is currently estimated that approximately 10.7 million Africans were taken to the New World as slaves. The **figure** for the eighteenth century alone is about 5.5 million, of which more than one-third came from West Central Africa.

6   The peopling of the New World is usually seen as a story of European migrations. But in fact, during every year between 1650 and 1831, more Africans than Europeans came to the Americas. As historian Davis Eltis wrote, "In terms of immigration alone, America was an **extension** of Africa rather than Europe until late in the nineteenth century."

---

[3] *plantation:* a large area of land in a hot climate, where crops such as sugar, tea, and cotton are grown

Go back to page 229 and finish the summary of the reading. You may write one sentence for more than one paragraph. Compare your summary with that of a classmate. If a classmate wrote a different summary, discuss why you think there were differences.

COMPREHENSION

(A) Main Ideas

Answer the questions. Compare your answers with a partner.

1. How did African political systems differ from European political systems of the time?

_____

_____

2. Why did Europeans initiate a slave trade with the West Africans?

_____

_____

(B) Close Reading

Answer the questions based on information in the reading. Discuss your answers with a partner.

1. What cultural characteristic did West African cultures have that was contrary to myth?

_____

(continued on next page)

2. What were some of the trade regulations imposed by the West Africans on the Portuguese?

_____

3. Why did the Europeans accept the West Africans' trade terms?

_____

4. What was one of the reasons that Europeans were unwilling to enter the African interior?

_____

5. Why was the slave trade so extensive in the 15th to early 19th century?

_____

VOCABULARY

(A) Guessing from Context

Read each quote from the reading. Try to guess the meaning of the word in bold from the context. Then match each word with its meaning on page 233. Compare answers with a partner.

1. "During the era of the European slave trade, roughly from the late fifteenth through the mid-nineteenth century, a number of enduring myths about sub-Saharan West Africa were **propagated**. "*(paragraph 1)*

2. "Ancient African empires such as Ghana were **vulnerable** to external attack as well as internal rebellion, and the oral and written histories of this region record the rise and fall of several large kingdoms." *(paragraph 2)*

3. "Mali and Joloff officials were willing partners in this **commerce** [of gold and slaves] but insisted that Europeans respect trade regulations established by Africans." *(paragraph 3)*

4. "Transactions were calculated in terms of local African **currencies**: a slave would be offered to a European trader for so many bars of iron or ounces of gold." *(paragraph 3)*

5. "**Transactions** were calculated in terms of local African currencies: a slave would be offered to a European trader for so many bars of iron or ounces of gold." *(paragraph 3)*

6. "European slave traders accepted these terms largely because they had no other choice. The African states fielded formidable armies, and outsiders soon discovered they could not **impose** their will on the region simply by demonstrations of force." *(paragraph 4)*

7. "By 1650, most West African slaves were **destined** for the New World rather than the Middle East." *(paragraph 4)*

8. "The slaves were frequently forced to work on the sugar plantations of Madeira (Portuguese) and the Canaries (Spanish), Atlantic islands on which Europeans experimented with forms of unfree labor that would later be more fully and more **ruthlessly** established in the American colonies." *(paragraph 5)*

_h_ 1. commerce   a. business deal

_____ 2. currency   b. cruelly

_____ 3. destined   c. easily harmed

_____ 4. impose   d. force

_____ 5. propagate   e. meant; intended

_____ 6. ruthlessly   f. something, such as money, used as a means of exchange

_____ 7. transactions   g. spread an idea or belief to many people

_____ 8. vulnerable   h. trade

B Word Usage

Read the groups of sentences using *figure* and *extension*. Match the word as used in each sentence with the appropriate meaning. Compare answers with a partner.

1. figure

_____ 1. The figure for the eighteenth century alone is about 5.5 million, of which more than one-third came from West Central Africa.

_____ 2. The first president of the United States, George Washington, is an important figure in American history

_____ 3. Albert Einstein is a well-known figure in the field of physics.

_____ 4. The figure for the purchase of Alaska from Russia by the United States was $7,200,000.

> a. someone who is considered to be like a father or mother, or to represent authority, because of their character or behavior
> b. a particular amount of money
> c. someone who is important or famous in a particular way
> d. a number representing an amount, especially an official number

2. extension

_____ 1. "In terms of immigration alone, America was an extension of Africa rather than Europe until late in the nineteenth century."

_____ 2. The student received an extension for completing research on epidemics among Native Americans during the 15th century.

_____ 3. During the 18th and 19th centuries, the government constructed forts as major extensions in order to protect settlers.

_____ 4. The office number for the history department is 555-6000, extension 6530.

> a. an additional period of time that is given to do something
> b. one of many telephone lines having different numbers and connected to a central system
> c. the process of making something bigger or longer
> d. the development of something in order to make it affect more people, situations, areas etc. than before

C Collocations

As you learned in previous chapters, **collocations** refer to **word partners** or **words that are often used together**.

These words appear in various collocations:

enduring: continuing to exist for a long time, especially in spite of difficulties
formidable: very powerful or impressive; difficult to to deal with and needing a lot of effort or skill
lethal: deadly

EXAMPLES:

enduring myth	formidable army	lethal combination
enduring appeal	formidable competitor	lethal dose
enduring practice	formidable challenge	lethal weapon
enduring belief	formidable task	lethal force
	formidable weapon	

Complete each sentence with the appropriate collocation from the box above. Compare answers with a partner.

1. The explorers in the New World introduced guns, a ___*formidable weapon*___ that the native population had never seen, one that gave the explorers a great advantage.

2. The idea of having one's own land to live on and cultivate has had a(n) _____ for Europeans.

3. Hard labor on plantations, harsh treatment, and disease were a(n) _____ that led to the deaths of thousands of slaves in the New World.

4. The legend of a City of Gold was a(n) _____ that drew hundreds of people to the Americas in search of great wealth.

5. Reaching the peak of Mount Everest is a(n) _____. Even people who are in excellent physical condition may not make the difficult climb to the top.

6. The conquistadors often applied _____ against Native Americans in order to defeat and control them.

7. An armed man on horseback represents a(n) _____ to an armed man on foot. The conquistadores had horses; the Native Americans did not.

Uses of the Adverb *Even*

By itself, the adverb ***even*** is used to **emphasize something unexpected or surprising**. For example:

> Ptolemy (a second-century A.D. Roman) and other ancient geographers had mapped the known world and had **even** demonstrated that the world was round.

> Since many Europeans 1,500 years later still believed that the world was flat, it is surprising that someone in the second century had already discovered that the world is round.

Even can also be used with other words to provide emphasis:

> *even today, even before, even if, even so, even though*

Complete each sentence with the appropriate collocation. Compare answers with a partner.

1. _____ the Europeans dreaded the diseases they encountered in Africa, the promise of great wealth motivated them to continue trading.

2. Native Americans gave names to rivers, mountains, and other natural features. _____ these names are used in English. For example, Manhattan is a Native American word that means "island of many hills."

3. The Native Americans eventually realized they could not stop Europeans from taking over their land. _____, they struggled against defeat.

4. _____ Europeans began trading with West Africans for slaves, slavery existed in Africa.

5. Because of the Europeans' superior weapons, the Native Americans would have lost to them _____ they had not been decimated by disease.

CRITICAL THINKING

Discuss the questions in a small group. Be prepared to share your answers with the class.

1. In what major way was the experience of the Europeans in West Africa different from their experience in North America?

2. How might the experiences of the Europeans and Africans have been different if the Europeans' diseases had had the same effect in Africa that they did in North America?

3. What might you conclude about the status of slavery in Africa prior to the arrival of the Europeans?

AFTER YOU READ

BRINGING IT ALL TOGETHER

Discuss the questions in a small group. Then share your group's answers with the class. Use the vocabulary you studied in the chapter (for a complete list, go to page 238).

1. What are some similarities between the Europeans' experiences with Native Americans and their experiences with West Africans?

2. What are some differences between the Europeans' experiences with Native Americans and their experiences with West Africans?

3. What conclusions can you draw from these comparisons?

WRITING ACTIVITY

Write a three-paragraph paper to summarize the readings in the chapter and to give your opinion. Use the vocabulary you studied in the chapter. Follow these instructions.

1. The first paragraph should briefly summarize the Europeans' encounters with Native Americans and West Africans.

2. The second paragraph should describe the consequences of these encounters for those involved.

3. In the third paragraph, give your opinion of these encounters, and describe how you think the Europeans' encounters with Native Americans and West Africans might have been different.

DISCUSSION AND WRITING TOPICS

Discuss these topics in a small group. Choose one of them and write three or four paragraphs about it. Use the vocabulary from the chapter.

1. In Reading One, you read that the Black Death (i.e., bubonic plague) caused the deaths of many people during the Middle Ages. In Reading Two, you read that the Native American population was decimated by diseases brought by the Europeans. In Reading Three, you learned that six out of ten Europeans died of local diseases within a year's stay in Africa. How might history have been different if disease had not been a factor in each of these situations?

2. Would you consider the arrival of slaves in the New World as an example of "immigration"? Why or why not?

3. How does the notion of immigration as it might apply to the arrival of slaves in the New World compare to the immigration to the New World of other groups of people that you have learned about?

Burying victims of the Black Death

VOCABULARY

Nouns	Verbs	Adjectives	Adverbs
autonomy	alter*	centralized	expansively*
commerce	forge	destined	profoundly
consolidation	foster	egalitarian	ruthlessly
currency*	impose*	enduring	
devastation	proclaim	formidable	
exploit*	propagate	lethal	
extension	sanction	matrilineal	
figure	strain	migrating*	
immunity		patrilineal	
incentive*		prolonged	
integrity*		virulent	
Old World		volatile	
prerequisite		vulnerable	
settlement			
transaction			
upheaval			

* = AWL (Academic Word List) item

SELF-ASSESSMENT

In this chapter you learned to:

○ Make connections between sentences

○ Draw inferences

○ Summarize

○ Guess the meaning of words from the context and understand word usage

○ Use dictionary entries to learn different meanings of words

○ Understand and use synonyms, collocations, word forms, and content-specific vocabulary

○ Use the adverb *even*

○ Create a semantic map and an outline

What can you do well? ☑

What do you need to practice more? ☑

CHAPTER 9

BUSINESS: Ethical Issues

BUSINESS: an organized, profit-seeking activity that provides goods and services designed to satisfy customers' needs

OBJECTIVES

To read academic texts, you need to master certain skills.

In this chapter, you will:

- Prepare for a test by anticipating questions and predict answers to questions

- Scan for specific information

- Guess the meaning of words from the context and understand word usage

- Use more advanced vocabulary

- Use dictionary entries to learn different meanings of words

- Understand and use synonyms, idioms, collocations, word forms, and preposition combinations with adjectives

- Write a summary for studying and summarize an argument

- Recognize transitions

Consider These Questions

Discuss the questions in a small group. Share your ideas with the class.

1. Is it more important for a company to make a profit or to satisfy customers' needs? Explain your answer.

2. In business, can an action be legal but still be wrong? Explain your answer.

READING ONE: Promoting Ethics in the Workplace

A Warm-Up

Discuss the questions with a partner.

1. As you read in Chapter 1, as we grow up, we learn values from the people around us. Should the concepts of right and wrong that we learned growing up be the same concepts we should apply in business? Why or why not?

2. Consider the title of the reading. What do you think it means to promote ethics?

B Reading Strategy

Preparing for a Test by Anticipating Questions

Teachers draw on information in the textbook when writing a test. You can prepare for a test **by anticipating what the questions will be**, and **by answering them as a review**. An effective way of doing this is **by writing a question for each paragraph or group of paragraphs** in a reading.

EXAMPLE:
The first paragraph in the reading discusses making ethical decisions. One possible question based on this paragraph is:

How can you make ethical decisions in any given situation?

Read the second paragraph and write a question for it. Compare your answers with a partner.

PARAGRAPH 2: _____

_____

PARAGRAPH 3: _____

_____

PARAGRAPH 4: _____

_____

PARAGRAPH 5: _____

_____

PARAGRAPH 6: _____

_____

PARAGRAPHS 7–11: _____

_____

Now read the text and write questions for the paragraphs as you read.

PROMOTING ETHICS IN THE WORKPLACE

By Courtland L. Bovée, John V. Thill, and Michael H. Mescon

1 How do you make **ethical** decisions? Determining what's ethically right in any given situation can be difficult, as you've no doubt experienced from time to time in your personal life. For instance, is it right to help a friend get a passing grade, even though you know he or she doesn't understand what's going on in the class? One helpful approach is to measure your choices against standards. These standards are usually grounded in universal teachings such as "Do not lie" and "Do not steal" that are aimed at assuring justice—the **resolution** of ethical issues in a way that is consistent with those generally accepted standards of right and wrong. Another place to look for ethical guidance is the law. If saying, writing, or doing something is clearly illegal, you have no decision to make; you obey the law.

(continued on next page)

Ethics in Business

2   The foundation of an ethical business climate is ethical awareness and clear standards of behavior. Organizations that strongly **enforce** company **codes** of conduct and provide ethics training help employees recognize and reason through ethical problems. Similarly, companies with strong ethical practices set a good example for employees to follow. On the other hand, companies that commit unethical acts in the course of doing business open the door for employees to follow suit.

3   To avoid such ethical breaches, many companies proactively develop programs designed to improve their ethical conduct, often under the guidance of a chief ethics officer or other top executive. These programs typically combine training, communication, and a variety of other resources to guide employees. More than 80 percent of large companies have also adopted a written code of ethics, which defines the values and principles that should be used to guide decisions. By itself, however, a code of ethics can't accomplish much. "You can have grand motives, but if your employees don't see them, they aren't going to mean anything," says one ethics manager. To be effective, a code must be supported by employee communications efforts, a formal training program, employee **commitment** to follow it, and a system through which employees can get help with ethically difficult situations.

Managers' Responsibilities

4   A written code of ethics, an ethics hot line, employee training, and other **tactics** are important parts of any effort to ensure strong ethics in your company, but nothing is more crucial than the behavior of the company's owners and managers—and if you're the top executive, you're the most important part of the equation. Your actions say more about the company's virtues than any program or poster.

5   The gap between talk and action has led to a credibility crisis in U.S. companies. In one survey, more than 80 percent of top managers said they consider ethics in their decision making, but 43 percent of employees expressed the belief that managers routinely overlook ethics. When leaders make decisions that show profits winning out over ethics, employees not only lose faith in their leaders but begin to assume that all the glorious talk about ethics is just that—talk. And in an era when many corporate executives can earn staggering sums of money in pay and bonuses that are based on company profits and stock prices, **skeptical** employees might just assume that the unethical behavior is done in pursuit of personal gain.

6   Moreover, questionable behavior at the top creates an environment ripe for ethical **abuse** throughout the organization. If employees see that bending or breaking the rules is not only accepted but the best way to succeed, some will be tempted to start **emulating** their leaders. Then as other employees see those people getting away with it and getting ahead, they'll jump on the bandwagon. The unethical bandwagon doesn't need too many people on it to bring down an entire corporation, either, as Enron, WorldCom, and others have shown. As a leader, you have a moral—and in many cases—legal—responsibility for the actions of your organization.

How to Lead Your Team with Ethical Behavior

7   *Lead by example.* Again, nothing is more important than demonstrating your commitment to ethics than behaving ethically yourself.

8   *Don't **tolerate** unethical behavior.* At the same time, you have to show that poor decisions won't be accepted. Let one go without correction, and you'll probably see another one before long.

9   *Inspire concretely.* Tell employees how they will personally benefit from participating in ethics initiatives. People respond better to personal benefits than to company benefits.

10 *Acknowledge reality.* Admit errors. Discuss what went right, what went wrong, and how the company can learn from the mistakes. **Solicit** employee opinion and act on those opinions. If you only pretend to be interested, you'll make matters worse.

Communicate, Communicate, Communicate.

11 Ethics needs to be a continuous conversation, not a special topic brought up only in training sessions or when a crisis hits. Harold Tinkler, the chief ethics and compliance officer at the accounting firm Deloitte & Touche, says that "Companies need to turn up the volume," when it comes to talking about ethics.

12 *Be honest.* Tell employees what you know as well as what you don't know. Talk openly about ethical concerns and be willing to accept negative feedback.

13 *Hire good people.* Alan Greenspan, a **former** chairman of the Federal Reserve Board, put it nicely: "Rules are no substitute for character." If you hire good people (not people who are good at their jobs, but people who are good, period) and create an ethical environment for them, you'll get ethical behavior. If you hire people who lack good moral character, you're inviting ethical **lapses**, no matter how many rules you write.

Work with a partner. Write answers to the questions you wrote. Compare your questions and answers. How do these questions and answers help you better understand the text?

COMPREHENSION

Ⓐ Main Ideas

Read each statement. Decide if it is *True* or *False* according to the reading. Check (✓) the appropriate box. If it is false, change it to make it true. Discuss your answers with a partner.

	TRUE	FALSE
1. Ethical decisions are usually based on commonly accepted principles of right and wrong.	☑	☐
2. Many businesses provide training to ensure that their employees understand and follow ethical procedures.	☐	☐
3. It is more important for managers to set up codes of ethics than it is to follow the codes themselves.	☐	☐
4. If employees see their executives and managers behaving badly, they are more likely to behave badly, too.	☐	☐
5. Leaders are never legally responsible for the actions of their organizations.	☐	☐
6. One of the most important ways managers can lead is by continually interacting with their employees.	☑	☐

B Close Reading

Answer the questions based on information in the reading. Discuss your answers with a partner.

1. Why is it so important for businesses to establish codes of conduct?

   _____

2. What are some ways that companies can support ethical practices among their employees?

   _____

3. How can unethical behavior on the part of management be detrimental to a business?

   _____

4. What are some of the actions management can take to help ensure ethical behavior within a business?

   _____

VOCABULARY

A Guessing from Context

Read each quote from the reading. Try to guess the meaning of the word in bold from the context. Write the clues that helped you guess and your guess. Then consult a dictionary and write the definition. Compare answers with a partner.

1. "How do you make **ethical** decisions? Determining what's ethically right in any given situation can be difficult, as you've no doubt experienced from time to time in your personal life." *(paragraph 1)*

   Clues: _what's ethically right in any given situation_

   Guess: _morally right_

   Dictionary: _relating to a set of principles that tell people how to behave_

2. "The foundation of an ethical business climate is ethical awareness and clear standards of behavior. Organizations that strongly enforce company **codes** of conduct and provide ethics training help employees recognize and reason through ethical problems." *(paragraph 2)*

   Clues: _____

   Guess: _____

   Dictionary: _____

3. "A written code of ethics, an ethics hot line, employee training, and other **tactics** are important parts of any effort to ensure strong ethics in your company, but nothing is more crucial than the behavior of the company's owners and managers." (*paragraph 4*)

Clues: _____

Guess: _____

Dictionary: _____

4. "If you hire people who lack good moral character, you're inviting ethical **lapses**, no matter how many rules you write." (*paragraph 13*)

Clues: _____

Guess: _____

Dictionary: _____

B **Using More Advanced Vocabulary**

The reading includes many words with specific meanings. You can use simpler words to convey the same meaning, but using **more specific and academic vocabulary** can help you to **vary your style** and **convey what you mean more accurately**.

Read each sentence to determine the meaning of each word or phrase in parentheses. Then select the word from the box that most closely matches its meaning. Compare answers with a partner.

abuse	emulate	former	skeptical	tolerate
commitment	enforce	resolution	solicit	

1. Researchers need to conduct more studies in order to find a(n)

_____resolution_____ to the problem of unethical behavior in business
  (answer)
dealings.

2. The department heads need to _____ the advice of the
                                    (ask for)
general manager.

3. The research team is very _____ about being able to
                                (doubtful)
complete the project by Friday. They only started it this morning.

(*continued on next page*)

4. Junior managers often _____ people in upper
   (act like)

   management. This is one reason it is so important for managers to behave

   ethically.

5. The law does not _____ the manufacture of unsafe
   (put up with)

   products. Businesses that knowingly produce such goods will be prosecuted.

6. The mail room supervisor was fired for verbal _____.
   (misconduct)

   He continually humiliated and harassed the people in his division.

7. The _____ CEO of our company moved to California after
   (previous)

   she retired.

8. Companies often find it difficult to _____ sanctions
   (carry out)

   against employees who engage in unethical behavior.

9. The CEOs all made a _____ to take three weeks of ethics
   (promise)

   training during the coming year.

C Collocations

> As you learned in earlier chapters, **collocation** refers to **word partners** or
> **words that are often used together**. These pairs of words appear in texts
> often and sound natural together.
>
> The words *ethical* and *code* appear in the reading. These words have several
> collocations:
>
> **EXAMPLES:**
>
> | | |
> |---|---|
> | ethical consideration | code of conduct |
> | ethical issue | code of silence |
> | ethical principle | code name |
> | ethical problem | dress code |
> | ethical question | |

Complete each sentence with the appropriate collocation from the box above.
Compare answers with a partner.

1. An investigative journalist recently uncovered a _____ at

   the prison, where prisoners were being abused by several guards. No one would

   talk about it, but the journalist discovered the abuse.

2. Every person who becomes a doctor makes a commitment to the

   _____ "Do no harm."

3. Some companies have a casual _____. Employees do not have to wear suits to work. However, they must be neat, and they cannot wear jeans.

4. An important _____ that many companies face is how to conduct business in a country with conflicting standards of right and wrong behavior in their business operations..

5. The university has a very strict _____ for its athletes. If they violate it by behaving badly, they will be immediately removed from their team.

6. As an employee or manager, whether or not to expose the company one works for when one discovers an abuse is often a difficult _____.

GRAMMAR FOR READING

Recognizing Transition

Transition words or phrases are used to **connect two thoughts in a logical manner.** These words or phrases include *for instance, in addition (to), moreover, on the other hand,* and *similarly.*

EXAMPLE:
I'm traveling to another country next week. I will need a passport and some local currency. **In addition,** I will need an international driver's license.

This sentence means that I need my passport and local currency, and I also need an international driver's license.

- *For instance* is followed by a comma. This phrase serves to introduce an example of something explained in the previous sentence.
- *In addition* is followed by a comma. It introduces an idea that adds information to the preceding idea.
- *Moreover* is followed by a comma. It may come at the beginning of a sentence or in the middle of a complex sentence. It introduces an idea that emphasizes the previous idea.
- *On the other hand* is followed by a comma and comes at the beginning of a sentence, and introduces a second idea that differs from the preceding idea.

Complete each sentence with the appropriate transition word or phrase.

1. Several years ago, a large energy company was charged with destroying or altering its records to hide illegal business practices. _____, the executives were accused of attempting to cheat shareholders and to keep millions of dollars for themselves.

(continued on next page)

2. The recent applicant was offered a position in a new company. She will have a higher salary and a more interesting job. _____, the company may not be successful, and she risks having no work if the company fails.

3. Executives who behave ethically set a positive example for their employees. _____ teachers who act according to principles of right and wrong provide a positive model for their students.

4. An in-depth history of the automobile has just been published. It describes how car designs have changed and how factory employees worked on assembly lines. _____, the author discusses how cars were advertised and how the automotive industry grew.

5. When applicants are on a job interview, they need to pay attention to how they talk. _____, they need to speak clearly, use appropriate vocabulary, and not talk too much.

NOTE-TAKING: Writing a Summary for Studying

Go back to the reading and read it again. Then review the questions you wrote. Write answers using your own words to create a summary of the text.

_____

_____

_____

_____

_____

CRITICAL THINKING

Discuss the questions in a small group. Be prepared to share your answers with the class.

1. Go back to the last section of the reading and consider the seven suggestions for leading by example. Which is the most important? The second most important? Arrange the seven suggestions in order of importance to you.

2. What is one specific action team leaders can take to implement each suggestion? Think of actions that have not been mentioned in the reading.

A **Warm-Up**

Discuss the question with a partner.

Why should businesses be ethical? Make a list.

_____

_____

_____

_____

B **Reading Strategy**

Predicting Answers to Questions

Writers often **begin a reading by posing questions** to the reader. One of the purposes of asking questions is to **get the reader interested** in what comes next. Questions also serve to highlight some of the important points that will be presented in the text. You can use these questions to your advantage by trying to answer them before you read. Doing so involves you in the topic and activates any prior knowledge you may have.

Read the five questions in the first paragraph, and write what you predict the answers will be. Share your predictions with a partner.

1. _____

2. _____

3. _____

4. _____

5. _____

ETHICAL REASONING

By Anne T. Lawrence and James Weber

1   How does a person know what behavior is right or wrong in the business world? What might lead an individual to act unethically? Does the root cause lie in a person's character or in direction given by top management? If so, should people be sent to jail or forced to resign for doing what their bosses told them to do? How can an employee refuse to follow orders, even when their boss is the CEO[1] or CFO[2] of the firm?

Ethics and Ethical Reasoning

2   People who work in business frequently encounter and must deal with on-the-job **ethical** issues. Being ethical is important to the individual, the organization, and the global marketplace. Managers and employees alike must learn how to recognize ethical **dilemmas** and know why they occur. In addition, they need to be **aware of** the role their own ethical character

---

[1] *CEO:* Chief Executive Officer
[2] *CFO:* Chief Financial Officer

plays in their decision-making process, as well as the influence exerted by the ethical character of others. Finally, managers and employees must be able to analyze the ethical problems they encounter at work to determine an ethical **resolution** to these dilemmas.

The Meaning of Ethics

3   *Ethics* is the conception of right and wrong conduct that tells us whether our behavior is moral or immoral, good or bad. Ethics deals with **fundamental** human relationships—how we think and behave toward others and how we want them to think and behave toward us. Ethical *principles* are guides to moral behavior. For example, in most societies lying to, stealing from, deceiving, and harming others are considered unethical and immoral. Being honest, keeping promises, helping others, and respecting the rights of others are considered ethically and morally desirable behavior. Such basic rules of behavior are essential for the preservation and continuation of organized life everywhere.

4   These notions, or concepts, of right and wrong come from many sources. Religious beliefs are a major source of ethical guidance for many. The family institution—whether two parents, a single parent, or a large family with brothers and sisters, grandparents, aunts, uncles, cousins, and other kin—imparts a sense of right and wrong to children as they grow up. Schools and schoolteachers, neighbors and neighborhoods, friends, admired role models, ethnic groups, and the ever-present electronic media and the Internet influence what we believe to be right and wrong in life. The totality of these learning experiences creates in each person a concept of ethics, morality, and socially acceptable

behavior. This core of ethical beliefs then acts as a moral compass that helps to guide a person when ethical puzzles arise.

5   Ethical ideas are present in all societies, organizations, and individual persons, although they may vary greatly from one to another. Your ethics may not be the same as your neighbor's; one particular religion's notion of morality may not be identical to another's; and what is considered ethical in one society may be forbidden in another society. These differences raise the important and controversial issue of ethical *relativism*, which holds that ethical principles should be defined in the context of various periods in history, a society's traditions, the special **circumstances** of the moment, or personal opinion. In this view, the meaning given to ethics would be **relative to** time, place, circumstance, and the person involved. In that case, there would be no universal ethical standards on which people around the globe could agree. However, for companies conducting business in several societies at one time, whether or not (and which) ethics are **relevant** can be vitally important. For the moment, we can say that despite the diverse systems of ethics that exist within our own society and throughout the world, all people everywhere do depend on ethical systems to tell them whether their actions are right or wrong, moral or immoral, approved or disapproved. Ethics, in this sense, is a universal human trait, found everywhere.

6   Business ethics is the application of general ethical ideas to business behavior. Business ethics is not a special set of ethical ideas different from ethics in general and **applicable** only **to** business. If dishonesty is considered to be unethical and immoral, then anyone in business who is **dishonest with** stakeholders— employees, customers, stockholders, or competitors—is acting unethically and immorally. If protecting others from harm is considered to be ethical, then a company that recalls a dangerously defective product is acting in an ethical way. To be considered ethical, business must draw its ideas about what is proper behavior from the same sources as everyone else. Business should not try to make up its own definitions of what is right and wrong. Employees and managers may believe at times that they are permitted or even encouraged to apply special or weaker ethical rules to business situations, but society does not **condone** or permit such an exception.

Why Should Businesses Be Ethical?

7   What prevents a business firm from piling up as much profit as it can, in any way it can, regardless of ethical considerations? There are several reasons why business should be ethical. One reason is to meet the demands of business stakeholders.[3] Organizational stakeholders demand business to exhibit high levels of ethical performance and social responsibility. Some businesses know that meeting stakeholders' expectations is good business. When a company upholds ethical standards, consumers may conduct more business with the firm and the stockholders may benefit as well, as illustrated in the story of the Co-operative Bank, a retail bank based in Manchester, United Kingdom, whose slogan is "Customer led, ethically guided." Some people argue that another reason for business to be ethical is that it enhances the firm's performance, or simply: *ethics pays*. Support for the relationship between being ethical and being profitable was found in a study conducted by the Institute for Business Ethics in the United Kingdom. Three of the four measures used in the study—economic value added, market value added, and price/earnings ratio—were stronger for companies that had a code of ethics than for those that did not.

(continued on next page)

---

[3] *stakeholder:* someone who has invested money in something, such as a business, and who will therefore be affected by its success or failure

8   Still another reason for **promoting** ethics in business is a personal one. Most people want to act in ways that are **consistent with** their own sense of right and wrong. Being pressured to **contradict** their personal values creates emotional stress for people. Knowing that one works in a supportive ethical climate contributes to one's sense of psychological security. An Ethics Resource Center report noted that when employees "perceive that others are held **accountable for** their actions," the overall employee satisfaction at work is 32 percent higher.

Now that you have read the text, review your predictions. Which were correct? Which predictions need to be revised?

COMPREHENSION

(A) Main Ideas

Check (✓) the statements that best express the main ideas in the reading. Discuss your answers with a partner.

- ☑ **1.** Business people rarely deal with ethical issues.
- ☑ **2.** Even in different situations, most people have very similar ethical principles.
- ☐ **3.** People in the same ethical situations will draw on the same ethical principles.
- ☑ **4.** Ethical codes of conduct help facilitate social and business interactions.
- ☑ **5.** Every individual and society has a code of ethics, although the specific principles may vary.
- ☐ **6.** Personal ethics are different from business ethics.
- ☐ **7.** Businesses should be ethical only because if they do not, they will encounter legal problems.
- ☐ **8.** Businesses should be ethical because it is expected.
- ☐ **9.** Businesses should behave ethically because it is good business.
- ☑ **10.** Businesses should follow ethical guidelines because their employees really do want to be ethical.

(B) Close Reading

Answer the five questions that were posed in the first paragraph. Compare them with the answers you wrote before you read the text. Discuss your answers with a partner.

1. "How does a person know what behavior is right or wrong in the business world?"

2. "What might lead an individual to act unethically?"

3. "Does the root cause lie in a person's character or in direction given by top management?"

4. "If so, should people be sent to jail or forced to resign for doing what their bosses told them to do?"

5. "How can an employee refuse to follow orders, even when their boss is the CEO or CFO of the firm?"

VOCABULARY

 **Word Usage**

Read the group of sentences using *promote*. In each sentence, the word *promote* is used with a different meaning. Match the word as used in each sentence with the appropriate meaning. Compare answers with a partner.

promote

_d_ 1. Still another reason for promoting ethics in business is a personal one.

_a_ 2. Governments need to do more to promote the use of clean energy.

_c_ 3. Department stores usually promote the new season's clothing with a sale.

_b_ 4. The sales manager is going to promote her assistant to a higher position in a new department.

---

a. help something to develop and be successful

b. give someone a better and more responsible job in a company

c. make sure people know about a new product, move, and so on, especially by offering it at a reduced price or by advertising it

d. try to persuade people to believe or support an idea or way of doing things

---

B **Preposition Combinations with Adjectives**

Adjectives are sometimes combined with **prepositions**, so you will find it useful to learn them together.

Read each sentence to determine the meaning of each word or phrase in parentheses. Then select the word from the box that most closely matches its meaning. Compare answers with a partner.

accountable to	aware of	dishonest with
applicable to	consistent with	relative to

1. The research findings of this new study are not ____consistent with____ the
   (compatible with)
   findings of two previous studies. Perhaps the statistical analysis is incorrect.

2. Stockholders try to stay ____aware of____ fluctuations in the stock
   (alert to)
   market, especially when it drops quickly.

(continued on next page)

3. CEOs must be held ___accountable to___ for the actions of their
   (responsible for)
   employees as well as for their own actions.

4. The profits of a company need to be considered ___relative to___
   (compared with)
   (compared with) such factors as cost of wages, insurance, and other expenses.

5. People quickly learn to distrust you once they find out you have been
   ___dishonest with___ them.
   (deceitful to)

6. This new building design is ___applicable to___ office buildings,
   (relevant for)
   hospitals, and schools. They all have similar architectural requirements.

C Synonyms

Complete each sentence with a word from the box. Use the synonym or phrase in
parentheses to help you select the correct word. Compare answers with a partner.

circumstances 4	contradict 2	fundamental 1
condone 5	dilemma 6	relevant 3

1. A sound knowledge of business practices is _____ to success.
   (basic)

2. The manager knows that the delivery men are lying because their stories

   _____ each other. One man said his truck was robbed
   (do not match)
   while he was making a delivery, but his partner said that the merchandise fell out

   of the truck while they were driving down the highway.

3. Managers looking to hire people prefer those who have skills

   _____ to the position.
   (applicable)

4. Most supervisors are very critical of employees who come to work late unless

   there are unusual _____ that justify the lateness.
   (conditions)

5. People looking for a job must understand that employers will not

   _____ lying on a resume.
   (tolerate)

6. Sometimes an employee faces a real _____. The employee
   (predicament)
   may want to accept a position with another company but is asked by his or

   her current employer to stay until the end of the year. Whatever decision the

   employee makes, someone will be unhappy.

NOTE-TAKING: Summarizing the Argument

Go back to the reading and read it again. Then fill out the organizer with brief notes in support of each statement. Use your own words.

	STATEMENT	NOTES
1.	Being ethical is important to the individual, the organization, and the global marketplace.	
2.	Ethical principles are guides to moral behavior.	
3.	These notions, or concepts, of right and wrong come from many sources.	
4.	Ethical ideas are present in all societies, organizations, and individual persons, although they may vary greatly from one to the other.	
5.	To be considered ethical, business must draw its ideas about what is proper behavior from the same sources as everyone else.	
6.	There are several reasons why business should be ethical.	

Write a brief summary of the reading. Then write another paragraph expressing your opinion of the points made in the reading.

_____

_____

_____

_____

_____

_____

(continued on next page)

Your Opinion

_____

_____

_____

_____

_____

CRITICAL THINKING

Work in small groups. Consider the information from the text. Agree or disagree and explain your reasons. Be prepared to share your answers with the class.

INFORMATION FROM THE TEXT	AGREE/ DISAGREE	REASONS
In most societies, honesty, keeping promises, helping others, and respecting the rights of others are considered ethically and morally desirable behavior.		
According to the concept of ethical relativism, ethical principles should be defined in the context of various factors such as periods in history, a society's traditions, the special circumstances of the moment, or personal opinion.		
Business ethics is not a special set of ethical ideas different from ethics in general and applicable only to business.		
Ethics pays.		

LINKING READINGS ONE AND TWO

Work with a partner. Fill in the chart with the main ideas from Readings One and Two. Discuss the similarities and differences between the two readings.

	READING ONE: PROMOTING ETHICS IN THE WORKPLACE	READING TWO: ETHICAL REASONING
what ethics are		
sources of our concepts of right and wrong, moral and immoral		
why managers and businesses should be ethical		
promoting ethics in business		

READING THREE: Should Mary Buy Her Bonus?

A Warm-Up

Discuss the questions with a partner.

1. Read the title of the reading. What do you think you will read about?

2. Is it ethical to take one small, questionable action, if it leads to a great gain for yourself?

B **Reading Strategy**

Scanning

Scanning means **looking quickly at a text to find specific information**. Scanning can help provide you with an overview of a reading so that you understand it better when you read the entire text.

Scan the first part of the reading quickly to identify Mary's dilemma. Look for information that will help you see the different sides of her situation. Use the information you learned as you scanned to answer the questions.

1. Who is Mary?

2. Why is Mary's bonus so important to her?

3. What is Mary's dilemma?

Now read the article and highlight important information as you read.

Should Mary Buy Her Bonus?

By Shel Horowitz

1   Mary Kantarian was achingly close to making her million-dollar sales goal—only $1,000 short. If she made the goal by the end of the year, it would mean a fat $60,000 bonus check, and a happy trip to the bank to finance a dream home she'd recently found. Other sales reps[1] also were close, and one had already made the bonus. The books would close in just a few days, but at the end of the year her clients weren't **in a buying mood**.

2   Still, Mary had one hope: inner-city[2] Lincoln High School. Its students, who often had to share textbooks, could really use her company's multimedia educational aids, but Lincoln had no **discretionary** budget for new teaching materials. What if Mary **donated** the money to this needy school for the purchase, and put herself over the magic quota[3]?

3   Or perhaps she could offer partial "donations" to close sales at several

---

[1] *rep:* representative

[2] *inner city:* the part of a city near the middle, where usually the buildings are in a bad condition and the people are poor

[3] *quota:* an amount or number of something that you are expected to produce, sell, achieve, and so on, especially in your job

schools. She would then surpass her quota goal **with room to spare**. The Lincoln school or other needy schools would gain immensely valuable educational programs that would help them serve their students, her company would pick up sales revenue, and she would meet her sales quota. Even better, she would earn a cool $60,000 on an investment of $1,000.

4   At first thought, this seemed like a **win-win** solution. But the idea needled Mary's conscience. The more she thought about it, the more something about it bothered her. Yet if she didn't close this "sale"—one which would help out disadvantaged students—she wouldn't make that bonus, and her dream house would remain **out of reach**. She found herself wondering, What should she do?

Advice on an Ethical Course of Action

5   According to Richard Burch, an adjunct professor at Fairfield University's program in Applied Ethics, Mary should find better ways to help Lincoln H.S. find the funds. Are there other corporate sponsors or community funds available? Could she **pursue** a school fund-raiser, or government grant? As an alternative, Mary could seek out more qualified prospects, or ask current customers to increase an order.

6   Trying to pull off the proposed "donation" **scheme** would be no easy task. Product donations usually have to be **without strings**. Cash gifts will buy what's needed most, like textbooks, not multimedia aids. Also, school systems, like corporations, have formal purchasing procedures, including sign-off points in the purchase-order process that uncover kickbacks[4] and bribes[5] disguised as donations.

7   Each rep knew **where the others stood**. What would be their reactions when they found out Mary made her quota this way? And what if everyone did this? What would be the impact on the company, other sales people, and other schools that would want the same special consideration? And what good is a customer who next time around expects the same deal?

8   Aside from the possible consequences of this deal, Kant would remind us we should do the right thing for the right reason. Mary is under a moral obligation to act loyally and to protect the **legitimate** interests of her employer. She should act in the interests of those who depend on her, even if those interests aren't always the same as her own.

What Actually Happened

9   Mary decided not to pursue offering Lincoln High School a donation. She wasn't comfortable with the idea, and she knew that her sales manager and superiors **all the way up the line** would **object**, on both ethical and practical **grounds**. Mary didn't make her bonus. But her reputation as a hard worker who maintains her **integrity** under pressure led to a promotion and higher pay two years later.

---

[4] *kickback:* money that you pay someone for secretly or dishonestly helping you make money

[5] *bribe:* money or gifts that you give someone to persuade them to do something, especially something dishonest

Use the information you learned as you read to answer the questions.

1. Who provided advice regarding Mary's dilemma?

2. Did he advise Mary to buy her bonus or not?

COMPREHENSION

A **Main Ideas**

Answer the questions. Compare your answers with a partner.

1. What was Mary's dilemma?

   _____

2. What advice did Richard Burch offer Mary?

   _____

3. What was Mary's final decision?

   _____

4. What were the consequences of Mary's decision?

   _____

B **Close Reading**

Read the quotes from the reading. Circle the statement that best explains each quote. Share your answers with a partner.

1. "Mary Kantarian was achingly close to making her million-dollar sales goal." *(paragraph 1)*

   a. Mary Kantarian was far from her one-million-dollar sales goal.

   b. Mary Kantarian was very close to achieving her goal of one million dollars in sales.

   c. Reaching her goal of one million dollars in sales was very painful for Mary Kantarian.

2. "But the idea needled Mary's conscience. The more she thought about it, the more something about it bothered her." *(paragraph 4)*

   a. The idea seemed worse and worse as Mary continued to think about it.

   b. The idea seemed acceptable after Mary had thought about it for a while.

   c. The idea stayed in Mary's conscience so she could think about it some more.

3. "Each rep knew where the others stood." *(paragraph 7)*

   a. Every rep stood where all the other reps were standing.

   b. Every rep knew where the other reps were working.

   c. Every rep was aware of all the other reps' current goal status.

4. "[Mary] wasn't comfortable with the idea." *(paragraph 9)*

    a. Mary felt that offering Lincoln H.S. a donation might not really be ethical.

    b. Mary was not confident that Lincoln H.S. would accept her offer.

    c. Mary's idea of offering Lincoln H.S a donation made people at the school uncomfortable.

VOCABULARY

Ⓐ Using the Dictionary

Read the dictionary entries and the sentences that follow. Then match the number of the definition with the appropriate sentence. Compare answers with a partner.

> **ground** *n.* **1** surface of the Earth   **2** a large area of land or ocean that is used for a particular activity or sport   **3** a particular subject, topic, set of opinions, area of experience, and so on   **4** a reason, especially one that makes you think that something is true or correct

1.

   _4_ **a.** She knew that her sales manager and superiors all the way up the line would object, on both ethical and practical grounds.

   _3_ **b.** At every department meeting, the manager seems to cover the same ground. It would be useful if he could move on to more important business concerns.

   _2_ **c.** The grounds around the new office complex include a parking area, an outdoor lunch area with tables, and a shaded area with benches.

   _1_ **d.** The ground around the building is too hard for planting. The company needs to hire a landscaper to come and prepare it for flowers and bushes.

> **scheme** *n.* **1** an intelligent plan, especially to do something dishonest or illegal   **2** a system that you use to organize information, ideas, and so on   **3 in the scheme of things** in the way things generally happen, or are organized.

2.

   _____ **a.** No one in the accounting department likes the proposed scheme of decoration for the new office.

   _3_ **b.** The budget cuts for next year are unwelcome, but in the greater scheme of things, they won't make too much difference in our operations.

   _____ **c.** Trying to pull off the proposed "donation" scheme would be no easy task. Product donations usually have to be without strings.

B Idioms

Go back to the reading and reread the sentences in which these idioms appear. Be sure that you understand what they mean in context. Then match them with their meanings.

_f_ 1. all the way up the line
_c_ 2. in a buying mood
_d_ 3. out of reach
_e_ 4. with room to spare
_b_ 5. win-win
_g_ 6. where someone stands
_a_ 7. without strings

a. have no special conditions attached
b. situation in which everyone benefits
c. willing to make purchases
d. unobtainable
e. with a little extra
f. to those highest in authority
g. the way someone sees a situation

Complete each sentence with an idiom. Compare answers with a partner.

1. In a business negotiation, a CEO needs to have a clear idea of
where someone stands if she wants to understand that person's actions.

2. If the automobile company puts the tire company's tires on its cars,
and the tire company advertises the cars, both companies will have a
win - win marketing situation.

3. Ethical procedures must be followed by everyone in the company, from file clerks
all the way up the line to the CEO.

4. The new bakery needs a promoter's financial assistance, but the owner won't be
able to do anything in return. The help has to be _without strings_ or
the owner cannot accept it.

5. The art gallery purchased a very large old factory building. The gallery has space
for offices and for exhibiting artwork, _with room to spare._

6. Many consumers were out of work for six months during the recent economic
downturn. Some of them have gotten jobs, but they need to save money, so they
are not _in a buying mood_. Businesses need to be patient.

7. The idea of starting one's own company and becoming a multimillioniare is really
out of reach if a person does not have the ambition to pursue
that dream.

C Word Forms

Fill in the chart with the correct word forms. Use a dictionary if necessary. An *X* indicates there is no form in that category.

	NOUN	VERB	ADJECTIVE	ADVERB
1.	discretion	X	discretionary	X
2.	donation	donate	donated	X
3.	X	legitimize	legitimate	legitimately
4.	objection	object	objectionable	X
5.	scheme	scheme	scheming	X

Complete the sentences with the correct form of one of the words above. Be sure to use the correct tense of the verbs in the affirmative or negative and the singular or plural form of the nouns. Compare answers with a partner.

1. Do you have any __objection__ to the plan? If so, please tell us what they are so we can address them.

2. You need a(n) __legitimate__ reason for spending so much money on your last business trip. Your supervisor will not accept a $2,000 expense for three days in a hotel.

3. Do not trust Mario. He is always getting others involved in his unrealistic business __scheme__, but they never work out.

4. When we are away on business trips, we can be paid back only for business-related costs. __Discretionary__ spending is not covered in our expense account.

5. Every year, Allen, our CEO, __donates__ $10,000 to the office fund, which is used to buy holiday gifts for homeless children.

CRITICAL THINKING

Discuss the questions in a small group. Be prepared to share your answers with the class.

1. Work in a small group. Your automotive company has chosen all of you to form a panel to write a code of ethics for the new company that has just been formed, and of which you are newly hired department managers. Create a code of ethics that will serve as guidelines for all the employees in making ethical decisions.

2. Work in a small group. Your company has chosen all of you to form a panel to decide on the ethics of several situations. Discuss the situations and check (✓) those that are unethical. Decide on what action might be taken by the company in response to each situation you have decided is unethical.

   _____ a. A salesperson arranges to sell merchandise at a special reduced price to a friend.

   _____ b. The company only accepts the return of damaged merchandise if the customer has a sales receipt.

   _____ c. An employee has been accepting gifts from a supplier.

   _____ d. An employee has been taking home promotional items (pens, water bottles, reusable shopping bags) intended for customers.

3. As a class, discuss the code of ethics that the panel(s) decided on in #1. Check them against the decisions about ethics that the panel in #2 made. If the code does not cover one of the actions that the panel determined to be unethical, revise the code to include it.

4. As a class, discuss what other ethical choice Mary might have made to try to get her bonus.

AFTER YOU READ

BRINGING IT ALL TOGETHER

Answer the questions. Use the vocabulary you studied in the chapter. Review the suggestions in Reading One on how to lead a team with ethical behavior. Then consider the concept presented in Reading Two that ethical ideas, while universal, may differ from one society to another. Finally, consider Mary's situation.

1. Which of the seven suggestions presented in Reading One would you consider universal? Why? Which ones might Mary's supervisors have considered important so that Mary had some guidance in making her decision?

2. Which of the suggestions in Reading One are most important to you? If you are from a different culture from Mary's, what principles would guide you in deciding whether to buy a bonus or not if you had been in Mary's situation?

WRITING ACTIVITY

Write a four-paragraph paper to summarize the readings in the chapter and to give your opinion. Use the vocabulary from the chapter (for a complete list, go to page 266). Follow these instructions.

1. The first paragraph should briefly summarize the concept of business ethics.

2. The second paragraph should describe why having a clear code of ethics is important, and what the consequences might be for not having or following ethical practices in business.

3. The third paragraph should briefly outline what Mary's dilemma was, what she did, and what ethical practices she followed in making her decision.

4. In the fourth paragraph, give your overall opinion of business ethics, and whether you feel Mary acted appropriately, given her circumstances.

DISCUSSION AND WRITING TOPICS

Discuss these topics in a small group. Choose one of them and write a short essay about it. Use the vocabulary from the chapter.

1. How do you make ethical decisions?

2. If you saw someone at work doing something you felt was unethical, and which you know the company considers unethical, what would you do? Why?

3. What suggestions would you have for a company that planned to establish a branch in another country where codes of ethical conduct might be different?

4. How might an employee deal with a situation where what is ethical to him/ her differs from what is considered ethical in the organization the employee works for?

VOCABULARY

Nouns	Verbs	Adjectives	Idioms
abuse	condone	discretionary*	all the way up
circumstances*	contradict*	ethical*	the line
code*	donate	former	in a buying
commitment*	emulate	fundamental*	mood
dilemma	enforce*	legitimate	out of reach
grounds	object*	relevant*	where someone
lapse	promote*	skeptical	stands
resolution*	solicit		win-win
scheme*	tolerate	**Adjective/**	without strings
tactic		**Preposition**	with room to
		Combinations	spare
		accountable for	
		applicable to	
		aware of*	
		consistent with	
		dishonest with	
		relative to	

* = AWL (Academic Word List) item

SELF-ASSESSMENT

In this chapter you learned to:

○ Prepare for a test by anticipating questions and predict answers to questions

○ Scan for specific information

○ Guess the meaning of words from the context and understand word usage

○ Use more advanced vocabulary

○ Use dictionary entries to learn different meanings of words

○ Understand and use synonyms, idioms, collocations, word forms, and preposition combinations with adjectives

○ Write a summary for studying and summarize an argument

○ Recognize transitions

What can you do well? ☑

What do you need to practice more? ☑

CHAPTER 10

MIGRATION STUDIES:
In Search of a New Life

OBJECTIVES

To read academic texts, you need to master certain skills.

In this chapter, you will:

- Skim for the main idea

- Draw inferences

- Fill out an organizer and create a timeline

- Use dictionary entries to learn different meanings of words and understand word usage

- Guess the meaning of words from the context

- Understand and use synonyms, suffixes, word forms, and collocations

- Categorize words

- Understand and use phrasal verbs

- Indicate contrast

Immigrants landing at Ellis Island carry entry numbers.

BEFORE YOU READ

Consider These Questions

Discuss the questions in a small group. Share your answers with the class.

1. Consider the title of the chapter, *Migration Studies: In Search of a New Life*. What kind of new life might people be in search of?

2. Look up the definitions of *migration, immigration,* and *emigration*. Discuss examples of each that you know about.

3. Consider the photographs on pages 267 and 269. Human beings have been relocating for thousands of years and continue to do so today. What might be some reasons for this?

READING ONE: Human Migration

A Warm-Up

In a small group, consider the title of the reading: *Human Migration.* Use the questions below to guide your discussion. Share your answers with the class.

1. Read the definition of *migration*. What are some reasons that people move permanently to a new location today? Make a list.

   _____   _____

   _____   _____

   _____   _____

2. What are some positive reasons and some negative reasons for migrating? Use the chart to organize your ideas.

POSITIVE REASONS	NEGATIVE REASONS
chance for a better job	no work

3. Combine all the groups' answers for a single list of positive and negative reasons for migrating. What are the most common reasons for migrating? Are most of them positive or negative?

Skimming for the Main Idea by Reading Topic Sentences

As you learned in an earlier chapter, reading the **topic sentence** of a paragraph will help you understand the main idea of the paragraph. **The topic sentence is often, but not always, the first sentence in a paragraph.** Circling key words in a topic sentence will help you remember the main idea.

Skim the reading and highlight the six topic sentences, circling any key words.

In a small group, discuss what the text will tell you about migration based on the topic sentences of the paragraphs. Take notes on your discussion.

Now read the text to find out more about the main ideas. Highlight important information as you read. You will use your highlighting to fill out an organizer after you read.

HUMAN MIGRATION

By James M. Rubenstein

1   Humans have spread across Earth during the past 7,000 years. This **diffusion** of human **settlement** from a small portion of Earth's land area to most of it resulted from migration. To accomplish the spread across Earth humans have permanently changed their place of residence—where they sleep, store their possessions, and receive legal documents.

2   How many times has your family moved? In the United States, the average family moves once every six years. Was your last move **traumatic** or exciting? The loss of old friends and familiar settings can hurt, but the experiences awaiting you at a new location can be **stimulating**. Think about the multitude of Americans— maybe including yourself—who have migrated from other countries. Imagine the feelings of people migrating from another country when they arrive in a new land without a job, friends, or— for many—the ability to speak the local language.

Reasons for Migrating

3   Why would people make a **perilous** journey across thousands of kilometers of ocean? Why did the pioneers[1] cross the Great Plains, the Rocky Mountains, or the Mojave Desert to reach the American West? Why do people continue to migrate by the millions today? The **hazards** that many migrants have faced are a **measure** of the strong **lure** of new locations and the **desperate** conditions in their former homelands. A permanent move to a new location disrupts traditional cultural ties and economic patterns

(continued on next page)

---

[1] *pioneer:* one of the first people to travel to a new country or area and begin living there, farming, and so on

in one region. At the same time, when people migrate, they take with them to their new home their language, religion, ethnicity, and other cultural **traits**.

Push Factors and Pull Factors

4   People decide to migrate because of push factors and pull factors. A push factor **induces** people to move out of their present location, whereas a pull factor induces people to move into a new location. As migration for most people is a major step not taken lightly, both push and pull factors typically play a role. To migrate, people **view** their current place of residence so negatively that they feel pushed away, and they view another place so attractively that they feel pulled toward it.

Economic Factors

5   Most people migrate for economic reasons. People think about emigrating from places that have few job opportunities, and they immigrate to places where jobs seem to be available. Because of economic **restructuring**, job prospects often vary from one country to another and within regions of the same country. The United States and Canada have been especially **promising** destinations for economic migrants.

Cultural Factors

6   Cultural factors can be especially **compelling** push factors, **forcing** people to emigrate from a country. According to the United Nations, refugees are people who have been **forced** to migrate from their homes and cannot return for fear of **persecution**. Political conditions can also **operate** as pull factors. People may be attracted to democratic countries that encourage individual choice in education, career, and place of residence.

Review the highlighted topic sentences and key words as well as the notes you took during your group discussion. How accurate were your predictions about the information in the text? How well did examining the topic sentences prepare you for what you read?

COMPREHENSION

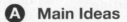 Main Ideas

Answer the questions. Compare your answers with a partner.

1. What have people been doing for thousands of years?

   _____

2. What motivates people to migrate?

   _____

3. When people move to a new location, what do they usually bring with them?

   _____

B **Close Reading**

Answer the questions. Discuss your answers with a partner.

1. What difficulties do people often face when they move to a new country?

   _____

2. What push and pull factors influence people to move to another location?

   _____

3. What cultural factor might influence people to move to another location?

   _____

VOCABULARY

A **Guessing from Context**

Read each quote from the reading. Try to guess the meaning of the words in bold from the context. Write the clues that helped you guess and your guess. Then consult a dictionary and write the definition.

1. "Humans have spread across Earth during the past 7,000 years. This **diffusion** of human settlement from a small portion of Earth's land area to most of it resulted from migration." *(paragraph 1)*

   Clues: *spread across, from a small portion of Earth's land mass to most of it*

   Guess: *movement out from one place to many places*

   Dictionary: *the spreading out of people or things over a large area*

2. "Was your last move **traumatic** or exciting? The loss of old friends and familiar settings can hurt, but the experiences awaiting you at a new location can be stimulating." *(paragraph 2)*

   Clues: _____

   Guess: _____

   Dictionary: _____

(continued on next page)

3. "Why did the pioneers cross the Great Plains, the Rocky Mountains, or the Mojave Desert to reach the American West? Why do people continue to migrate by the millions today? The **hazards** that many migrants have faced are a measure of the strong lure of new locations and the desperate conditions in their former homelands." *(paragraph 3)*

Clues: _____

Guess: _____

Dictionary: _____

4. "The hazards that many migrants have faced are a measure of the strong lure of new locations and the **desperate** conditions in their former homelands." *(paragraph 3)*

Clues: _____

Guess: _____

Dictionary: _____

5. "Because of economic **restructuring**, job prospects often vary from one country to another and within regions of the same country." (paragraph 5)

Clues: _____

Guess: _____

Dictionary: _____

B Word Usage

Read the groups of sentences using *operate* and *view*. Match the word as used in each sentence with the appropriate meaning. Compare answers with a partner.

1. **operate**

_____ **a.** Political conditions can also operate as pull factors.

_____ **b.** The camp surgeon operated on the young boy to repair a part of his eye.

_____ **c.** Commercial drivers know how to operate cars, buses, and trucks.

_____ **d.** The government operates several refugee camps in this area.

> 1. use and control a machine or piece of equipment
> 2. carry out your business or activities in a particular way
> 3. cut open someone's body in order to remove or repair a part that is damaged
> 4. a system or process that works in a particular way and has particular results

2. view

_____ **a.** When they migrate, people often view their current place of residence so negatively that they feel pushed away from it, and view another place so positively that they feel pulled toward it.

_____ **b.** The emigrants viewed their home country for the last time from the ship.

_____ **c.** It is possible to view high-quality documentaries and history-based programs on TV.

_____ **d.** The members of the housing committee viewed several possible new homes for the refugees.

> **1.** look at something, especially because it is beautiful or you are interested in it
> **2.** watch a television show, movie, and so on
> **3.** consider someone or something in a particular way
> **4.** go to see the inside of a house, apartment, and so on that you are interested in buying

C Synonyms

Read the sentences. Match each word or phrase in parentheses with its synonym in the box. Compare answers with a partner.

induce	lure	measure	perilous	promising	stimulating

1. Only the promise of safety, a job, and an education for their children could

_____ Maria and her husband to leave their country.
   (tempt)

2. His willingness to undertake a perilous journey through the mountains in winter

was a(n) _____ of his strong desire to emigrate.
   (clear indication)

3. Attending a new school in a new city was a very _____

   (inspiring)

experience for the children.

4. Even as recently as 100 years ago, traveling across an ocean to a new country

could be an extremely _____ undertaking.
   (hazardous)

5. The response to our plans to move to Canada is very _____.

   (encouraging)

Everyone is very positive about it.

6. Dreams of a better life often _____ people to move to a

   (persuade)

new location.

Indicating Contrast

But, whereas, and *at the same time* indicate **contrast**. Of the three expressions, only *at the same time* can begin a sentence.

EXAMPLES:

John moved to Boston because he wanted to, *whereas* Andrew moved because he had to.

Neil was happy to move to another country, *but* his younger brother wasn't.

Studying abroad can be exciting. *At the same time,* it is very stressful.

Complete each sentence with the correct word or phrase. There may be more than one correct answer. Compare answers with a partner.

1. Some people move many times in their lives, _____ others move only once.

2. When children of school age move to the United States, they often already speak English, _____ their parents do not.

3. Learning a new language can be very difficult. _____, it opens doors to new experiences.

4. When rural people first move to a large city, they are often very curious about it. _____, they feel anxious about living in such an urban environment.

5. Some immigrant families settle into their new life fairly easily, _____ others experience many difficulties.

6. Thousands of newcomers love New York City, _____ many others do not.

NOTE-TAKING: Filling Out an Organizer

Reread the information you highlighted. Work with a partner to fill out the organizer below.

HUMAN MIGRATION	
INTRODUCTION TO THE READING	REASONS FOR MIGRATING
1.	1.
2.	2.
3.	3.

CRITICAL THINKING

Discuss the questions in a small group. Be prepared to share your answers with the class.

1. The average American family moves once every six years. What factors other than the ones mentioned in the reading might account for the frequency of these moves? In what ways can a move within a country be as traumatic as a move to a different country?

2. For the thousands, even millions, of people who have migrated, other thousands and millions remained where they were. What might be the reasons that people do not migrate, even given the push factors and pull factors mentioned in the reading?

A Warm-Up

Discuss the questions with a partner.

1. What do you think travel over land was like during the 19th century in North America? What were roads like? What did people use to carry their possessions and themselves over hundreds of miles?

2. What kinds of difficulties did people encounter when crossing unfamiliar territory? How did they obtain food, for example?

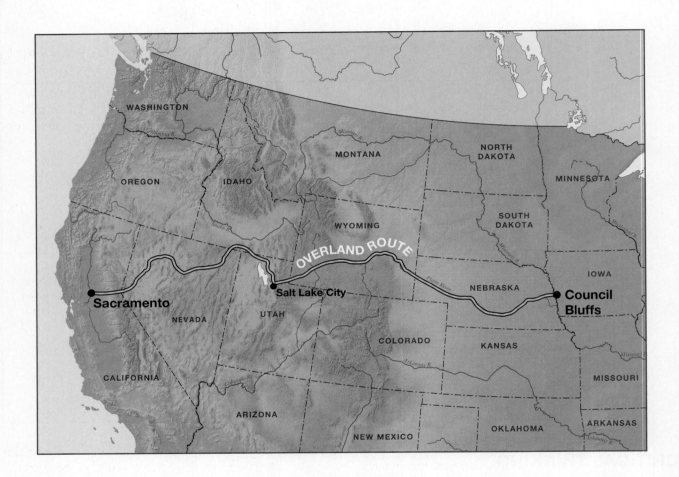

Drawing Inferences

An important component of reading comprehension involves **drawing inferences** as you read. **Information is not always directly stated**, but we can understand and infer information if we **"read between the lines."**

EXAMPLE:
Often there was no one in a wagon train who really knew what the roads would bring, or if there were any roads at all.

We can infer from this sentence that
a. often no one in a wagon train remembered what the roads were like
b. often no one in a wagon train had ever traveled any of the roads
c. often no one in a wagon train knew what to bring on the roads

Read the sentences. Circle the inference you can draw from each. Compare answers with a partner.

1. "For women who were pregnant, the overland crossing could be a nightmare. One never knew for certain where labor might begin: in Indian territory, or in the mountains, or in drenching rain. One might be alone, with no women to help, and only fear at hand." *(paragraph 3)*

   We can infer from these sentences that

   a. pregnant women often had nightmares while they slept

   b. many women became pregnant during the overland crossing

   c. women usually helped other women deliver their babies

2. "It took us four days to organize our company of 70 wagons and 120 persons and say good bye to civilization at Council Bluffs. . . . When we reached Sacramento not more than a dozen of our original train of 120 were with us." *(paragraph 8)*

   We can infer from these sentences that

   a. the trip was so difficult that most people gave up along the way

   b. almost everyone who began the trip finished the trip

   c. most of the people who started the trip were very disorganized

3. "[In Council Bluffs] eggs were 2 ½ cents a dozen—at our journey's end we paid $1 a piece, that is when we had the dollar. Chickens were worth eight and ten cents a piece. When we reached Sacramento $10 was the ruling price and few to be had at that." *(paragraph 10)*

   We can infer from these sentences that

   a. people in Sacramento did not like to sell their eggs and chickens to the wagon train travelers

   b. the price of chickens was high because they were in short supply

   c. wagon train travelers did not know how much eggs and chickens should really cost

Now read the text and draw inferences from it. Highlight important information as you read.

The Westward Journey: A Personal Perspective

By Lillian Schlissel

1   Between 1840 and 1870, more than 250,000 Americans crossed the continental United States,[1] some 2,400 miles of it, in one of the great **migrations** of modern times. They went West to claim free land in the Oregon and California Territories,[2] and they went West to strike it rich by mining gold and silver. The journey started in the towns along the Missouri River between St. Joseph and Council Bluffs. It was an **audacious** journey through territory that was virtually unknown. Often there was no one in a wagon train who really knew what the roads would bring, or if there were any roads at all.

2   On the Overland Trail, as this migration was called, women strove to be equal to the demands of the day. They did the domestic chores: they prepared the meals and washed the clothes and cared for the children. But they also drove the ox teams.

3   For women traveling with small children, the overland experience could be **nerve-wracking**. Children fell out of the wagons. They got lost among the hundreds of families and oxen and sheep. For women who were pregnant, the overland crossing could be a nightmare. One never knew for certain where labor[3] might begin: in Indian territory, or in the mountains, or in drenching rain. One might be alone, with no women to help, and only fear at hand.

4   Hundreds of women wrote of their personal experiences. The women bring us a new vision of the overland experience; they bring it closer to our own lives. In reading their diaries we come closer to understanding how historical drama **translates** into human experience. Through the eyes of the women we begin to see history as the stuff of daily struggle. The excerpt that follows is from the diary of one of these women.

5   *Catherine Haun was a young bride when she and her husband decided to follow the path of the gold rush. Old debts and hopes for a better life in a better climate prompted their move from Iowa.*

---

[1] *the continental United States:* all the states except for Alaska and Hawaii

[2] *Territory:* land that belongs to a country, but is not a state. Oregon and California were territories in 1849, when Catherine Haun journeyed west. California became a state in 1850, and Oregon became a state in 1859. Used as a general term, *territory* refers to an area of land.

[3] *labor:* the process of giving birth

A Woman's Trip across the Plains in 1849

By Catherine Haun

6   Early in January of 1849 we first thought of emigrating to California. It was a period of National hard times and we being financially involved in our business interests near Clinton, Iowa, **longed to** go to the new El Dorado[4] and "pick up" gold enough with which to return and pay off our debts.

7   Full of the energy and enthusiasm of youth, the prospects of so **hazardous** an undertaking had no **terror** for us. Indeed, as we had been married but a few months, it appealed to us as a romantic wedding tour. The territory bordering upon the Mississippi River was, in those days, called "the west."

8   It took us four days to organize our company of 70 wagons and 120 persons and say good bye to civilization at Council Bluffs. There was still snow upon the ground and the roads were bad, but in our **eagerness** to be off we **ventured** forth on April 24th from Clinton, Iowa. This was a mistake as had we delayed for a couple of weeks the weather would have been more settled, the roads better and much of the discouragement and **hardship** of the first days of travel might have been avoided.

9   At the end of a month we reached Council Bluffs, having only travelled across the state of Iowa, a distance of about 350 miles, every mile of which was beautifully green and well watered. We also had the advantage of camping near farm-houses and the generous supply of bread, butter, eggs and poultry greatly facilitated the cooking. Eggs were 2½ cents a dozen—at our journey's end we paid $1 a piece, that is when we had the dollar. Chickens were worth eight and ten cents a piece. When we reached Sacramento $10 was the ruling price and few to be had at that.

10   As Council Bluffs was the last **settlement** on the route we made ready for the final **plunge** into the wilderness by looking over our wagons and disposing of whatever we could spare.

11   Among those who formed the personnel of our train was one family by the name of Lamore, from Canada, consisting of man, wife and two little girls. They had only a large express wagon drawn by four mules and a **meager** but well chosen, supply of food and feed.

12   We saw nothing living but Indians, lizards and snakes. Trying, indeed, to feminine nerves. Surely Inferno can be no more horrible in formation. The pelting sun's rays reflected from the **parched** ground seemed a furnace heat by day and our campfires, as well as those of the Indians cast grotesque glares and terrifying shadows by night.

13   It was the 4th of July[5] when we reached the beautiful Laramie River. Its sparkling, pure waters were full of myriads of fish that could be caught with scarcely an effort.

(continued on next page)

---

[4] El Dorado (Spanish for "the golden one") refers to a mythical lost city of gold that many people looked for in the Americas. The term El Dorado is often used to refer to any search for wealth.

[5] *The 4th of July:* U.S. Independence Day (marking the signing of the Declaration of Independence on July 4, 1776)

After dinner that night it was proposed that we celebrate the day and we all **heartily** join[ed] in.

14   During the frolic when the sport was at its height a strange white woman with a little girl in her sheltering embrace rushed into the corral. She was trembling with terror, tottering with hunger. Her clothing was badly torn and her hair disheveled. The woman could give no account of her forlorn condition but was only able to sob: "Indians," and "I have nobody nor place to go to." After she had partaken of food and was refreshed by a safe night's rest she recovered and the next day told us that her husband and sister had contracted cholera on account of which her family consisting of husband, brother, sister, herself and two children had stayed behind their train. The sick ones died and while burying the sister the survivors were attacked by Indians, who, as she supposed, killed her brother and little son. She was obliged to flee for her life dragging with her the little five year old daughter. Martha, for that was her name, had emigrated from Wisconsin and pleaded with us to send her home; but we had now gone too far on the road to meet returning emigrants so there was no alternative for her but to accept our protection and continue on to California. She made herself useful and loyally cast her lot with us. She assisted me with the cooking for her board; found lodgings with the woman whose husband was a cripple and in return helped the brave woman drive the ox team. Mr. and Mrs. Lamore kept her little girl with their own.

15   It was with considerable **apprehension** that we started to traverse the treeless region of the Great Basin or Sink of the Humboldt. Our wagons were badly worn, the animals much the worse for wear, food and stock feed was getting low with no chance of **replenishing** the supply. It was no unusual sight to see graves, carcasses of animals and abandoned wagons.

16   Our only death on the journey occurred in this desert. Mrs. Lamore, suddenly sickened and died, leaving her two little girls and **grief-stricken** husband. We halted a day to bury her and the infant that had lived but an hour, in this weird, lonely spot.

17   The bodies were wrapped together in a bedcomforter. A passage of the Bible (my own) was read. Every heart was touched and eyes full of tears as we lowered the body, coffinless, into the grave. There was no tombstone—why should there be—the poor husband and orphans could never hope to revisit the grave and to the world it was just one of the many hundreds that marked the trail. Martha and the lamented Canadian wife had formed a fast friendship while on the plains. What more natural than that the dying mother should ask her friend to continue to care for her orphan girls and to make [them] the sisters of her own daughter?

18   We reached Sacramento on November 4, 1849, just six months and ten days after leaving Clinton, Iowa. We were all in pretty good condition. Upon the whole I enjoyed the trip, spite of its hardships and dangers and fear. Although not so **thrilling** as were the experiences of many who suffered in reality what we feared, but escaped, I like every other pioneer, love to revisit, in fancy, the scenes of the journey.

Work with a partner. What inferences can you draw from the reading?

COMPREHENSION

A **Main Ideas**

Answer the questions. Compare your answers with a partner.

1. What is the main idea of this diary?

_____

2. Why did over a quarter of a million Americans journey to the West during the 19th century?

_____

3. What best describes the journey of the Hauns and their wagon train members?

_____

B **Close Reading**

Read each question. Circle the correct answer. Compare answers with a partner.

1. Between 1840 and 1870, where did most people begin the journey westward?

    a. in either Clinton, Iowa, or Council Bluffs, Iowa

    b. along the Missouri River between Council Bluffs and St. Joseph

    c. in towns anywhere along the Missouri River

2. How well did most people know the route from their starting point to their destination?

    a. They hardly knew it at all.

    b. They knew it fairly well.

    c. They knew it very well.

3. What is one of the differences between reading the history of the 1840–1870 westward migrations and reading the diaries of women who made this journey?

    a. The diaries tell us only how the writers felt, not what they really observed.

    b. The historical descriptions describe facts, but the diaries do not.

    c. The diaries give us a firsthand viewpoint that the historical descriptions do not give.

4. What experiences did the Hauns' wagon train have with Indians during their journey?

    a. They had no significant interactions.

    b. They were attacked at least once.

    c. The Indians tried to steal their children.

(continued on next page)

5. Why was it unlikely that Mr. Lamore and his children would ever visit Mrs. Lamore's grave?

   a. because they would not have enough money to travel again

   b. because they would not be able to locate her grave

   c. because they would probably never return east

6. Why was the group so worried about crossing the Great Basin (Sink of the Humboldt)?

   a. because they were in a hurry and the trip was slow

   b. because their circumstances at that point were quite poor

   c. because previous travelers had told them it was a dangerous place

7. Why did Catherine Haun probably enjoy retelling the story of her overland journey?

   a. She wanted to tell others about the dangers she experienced.

   b. She wanted to tell a frightening story to other people.

   c. She liked reliving her experiences of the journey.

VOCABULARY

Ⓐ Categorizing Words

Work with a partner. Put the words and phrases in the box below into two categories.

| apprehension | eagerness | heartily | nerve-wracking | thrilling |
| audacious | grief-stricken | long to | terror | |

POSITIVE OR HAPPY FEELINGS	NEGATIVE OR UNHAPPY FEELINGS

Complete the sentences with the correct word or phrase from the box on page 282. Compare answers with a partner.

1. In his _____ eagerness _____ to emigrate to Canada, Charles studied French and English, learned about the history of the country, and made plans to leave within the year.

2. The members of Catherine Haun's wagon train partied very _____ on July 4th to celebrate Independence Day.

3. The little girl was left behind when the wagon train moved on. It was a time of _____ for her because she was alone. However, her family eventually found her.

4. Crossing the region of the Great Basin was especially _____ because there was no fresh water there, and the supply of water was running low.

5. Many women had strong feelings of _____ when they had to make the journey while pregnant or with small children.

6. Mr. Lamore was _____ after the death of his wife and newborn baby.

7. Whereas Catherine Haun thought the overland trip was _____ and full of adventure, others felt it was dangerous and full of hardship.

8. The plan to travel 2,400 miles across unmapped territory led by people who had never made the trip themselves was a truly _____ idea.

9. Some immigrants _____ visit their home country again, but they are too old to travel so far.

B Suffixes -ness, -ship

As you have learned, **suffixes** are added to the **end of words** and **change or modify their meanings**. They also change the part of speech of words when added to them.

The suffix -*ness* means "the quality of" or "the state of."

eagerness, forgiveness, kindness, sadness

The suffix -*ship* refers to the state of having something

friendship, hardship, partnership, guardianship

Complete each sentence with a word from the box. Compare your answers with a partner.

eagerness	friendship	hardship	partnership
forgiveness	guardianship	kindness	sadness

1. The pioneers were often full of unrealistic dreams in their _____

   to believe that an easier, wealthier life lay ahead of them in California or Oregon.

2. Everyone in the wagon train appreciated the _____,

   thoughtfulness, and patience of others in the group.

3. The westward journey was a severe _____ for anyone who

   was injured or became ill along the way.

4. Many of the children in the wagon train developed a very close

   _____, not only with each other, but also with many of the

   adults.

5. When the parents of small children died, some people took over the

   _____ of these children until a relative could be located.

6. John asked the group for _____ after leading them 100

   miles in the wrong directon, leaving them without water for five days.

7. Although a death along the route caused great _____,

   there was also great joy when a baby was born.

8. When a wagon train reached its destination, some of the people would join

   together in a _____ and set up a new business.

C Word Forms

Fill in the chart with the correct word forms. Use a dictionary if necessary. An **X** indicates there is no form in that category.

	Noun	Verb	Adjective	Adverb
1.	apprehension	X		
2.		replenish		X
3.	terror			X
4.			thrilling	
5.		translate		X
6.		venture	X	X

Complete the sentences with the correct form of one of the words in the chart. Be sure to use the correct tense of the verbs and the singular or plural form of the nouns. Compare your answers with a partner.

1. The people who led a wagon train often had to _____ through territory they were completely unfamiliar with.

2. Catherine Haun reported that her experience was enjoyable, but many others were _____ by the dangers that the trip involved, possibly including death.

3. Historical facts seem very dry and uninteresting until someone _____ events into the personal experience of those who lived at the time.

4. The families who _____ their supplies when they had the chance might face hunger and thirst as the trip continued into the desert.

5. Pioneers often enjoy the _____ of the unknown. It's exciting when every day brings a new adventure.

6. The mother looked around _____ for her lost child, hoping he hadn't been left behind.

NOTE-TAKING: Creating a Timeline

Reread the excerpt from Catherine Haun's diary. Create a timeline with dates and events.

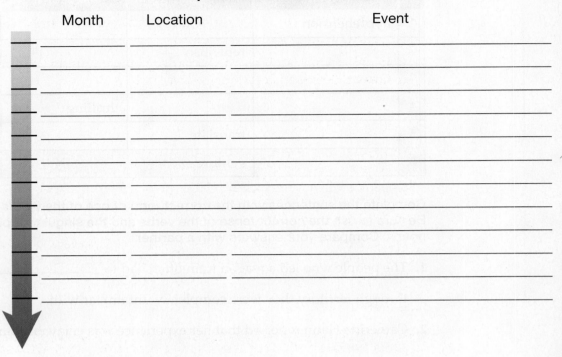

A Trip Across the Plains in 1849

Month	Location	Event

CRITICAL THINKING

Discuss the questions in a small group. Be prepared to share your answers with the class.

1. In the last paragraph, Catherine Haun describes her overall impression of the trip. She claims to have enjoyed it. How might you account for the apparent contradiction between the experiences she writes about and her claim to have enjoyed the trip?

2. Catherine Haun describes how Mrs. Lamore died suddenly. What was really the cause of her death? Why did Catherine only imply this and not state it clearly?

LINKING READINGS ONE AND TWO

Discuss the questions in a small group. Be prepared to share your answers with the class.

1. What was a push factor that motivated the westward migrations in the United States between 1840 and 1870?

2. What were some pull factors that motivated people to immigrate to the western territories of the United States between 1840 and 1870?

A **Warm-Up**

Discuss the questions in a small group. Share your answers with the class.

1. If you had to move to another country, and could take only what would fit into a large box, what would you take? Why?

2. If an object your family owned was very meaningful to your parents, what would make you decide to keep it or get rid of it?

B **Reading Strategy**

Responding to Text

Sometimes when we read, part of the text strikes us as particularly interesting or moving. This is especially true when reading personal accounts because you may be able to **make connections** between the reading and your own life.

To **respond to a text**, divide a sheet of paper into two vertical columns. In the left column, **copy exact sentences or short passages** from the text that you think are important. In the right column, **write your response**.

EXAMPLE:

QUOTES FROM THE TEXT	YOUR RESPONSE
When my parents, my sister, and I finally left the refugee camp in Germany after the war, we were allowed to bring very little, only what would fit into a steamer trunk. The problem was that we couldn't afford to buy one. Not many of the families living in the camps could. You can imagine why that was, so my father did what other people did. He and a friend got together and built a trunk.	The family must have felt very glad to be leaving the refugee camp. At the same time, they must have felt very sad that they could take so little with them. Maybe they had to leave behind things that were important to them. I wonder what I would have wanted to put in the trunk.

After reading the story, copy sentences or short passages from the text into the chart below. Then write your response to each one.

Quotes from the text	Your response

Now read the story. As you read, underline sentences or passages you want to respond to.

Wooden Trunk from Buchenwald[1]

By John Guzlowski

1   When my parents, my sister, and I finally left the refugee camp[2] in Germany after the war,[3] we were allowed to bring very little, only what would fit into a steamer trunk.[4] The problem was that we couldn't afford to buy one. Not many of the families living in the camps could. You can imagine why that was, so my father did what other people did. He and a friend got together and built a trunk.

2   Someplace, somehow, they found a hammer and a saw and nails and some metal stripping and they set to work. Getting the wood wasn't a problem. They got the wood from the walls of the barracks[5] they were living in. It was one of the old German concentration camps[6] that had been **converted** to living space for the **refugees**, the Displaced Persons.[7] If you wanted a board, you could just pull it off of the wall, and that's what my father did. He didn't say a lot about building that wooden trunk, and he probably didn't give it much thought.

3   My parents couldn't get much into the trunk, but they put into it what they thought they would need in America and what they didn't want to leave in Germany: some letters from Poland, four pillows made of goose feathers, a black skillet, some photographs of their time in Germany, a wooden cross, some clothing, of course, and wool sweaters that my mother knitted for us in case it was cold in America.

4   When we finally got to America, my parents didn't **trash** that wooden trunk or break it up, even though there were times when breaking it up and using the wood for a fire would have been a good idea to keep us warm. Instead, they kept it handy for every move they made in the next forty years. They carried it with them when we had to go to the migrant farmers' camp in upstate New York where we **worked off** the cost of our **passage** to America.

(continued on next page)

---

[1] Buchenwald was a German concentration camp where the prisoners worked mainly as forced laborers in nearby armaments factories.

[2] *refugee camp:* a place where people who have been forced to leave their country stay temporarily

[3] World War II, which ended in 1945

[4] *steamer trunk:* a very large type of luggage used for carrying clothing, especially on long trips

[5] *barracks:* a group of buildings where refugees live

[6] *concentration camp:* a prison where prisoners are kept in very bad conditions, especially during a war

[7] *Displaced Persons (DPs):* people who have been forced to leave their country because of war or cruel treatment

And my parents carried it to Chicago, too, when they heard from their friend Wenglaz that Chicago was a good place for DPs, for refugees. And they carried that trunk to all the rooming houses[8] and apartment buildings and houses that we occupied in Chicago. I remember in those early days in Chicago that there were times when the only things we owned were the things my mother and father brought with us in that trunk, and the only furniture we had was that trunk. Sometimes it was a table, and sometimes it was a bench, and sometimes it was even a bed for my sister and me.

5   When my parents retired in 1990 and moved from Chicago to Sun City, Arizona, they carried that trunk with them. That surprised me because they didn't take much with them when they went to Arizona. But they kept that trunk and the things they could put in it.

6   After my father died in 1997, my mother **stayed on** in Arizona. She still had the trunk when she died. She kept it in a small 8 foot × 8 foot utility room off the carport. When my mom died, I was with her. Her dying was long and hard. She had had a stroke and couldn't talk or understand what was said. She couldn't move at all either. When she finally died, I had to make **sense** of her things. I contacted a real estate agent, and he told me how I could get in touch with a company that would **sell off** all of my mother's things in an estate sale.

7   I thought about taking the wooden trunk back home with me to Valdosta, Georgia. I thought about all it meant to my parents and to me, how long it had been with them. How they had carried it with them from the DP camps in Germany to Sun City, Arizona, this desert place so different from anything they had ever known overseas. I knew my sister Donna didn't want the trunk. Donna has spent a lifetime trying to forget the time in the DP camps and what the years in the slave labor camps during the war had cost my parents. But did I want it?

8   I finally decided to leave it there and to let it get sold off at the estate sale. When I'm doing a poetry reading and tell people the story of the trunk and read one of my poems about it, people ask me why I left it. It doesn't make any kind of sense to them. And I'm not sure now that it makes any kind of sense to me either. Why did I leave it?

9   I was pretty much **used up** by my mom's dying. It had been hard. My mother went into the hospital for a gall bladder operation and had had that stroke, and the stroke left her paralyzed,[9] confused, and weak. She couldn't talk or move.

10   When she died, I didn't want to do anything except get back home to my wife Linda in Georgia. Maybe the extra **burden** of **figuring out** how to carry that trunk back to Georgia was more than I could **deal with**. Or maybe I thought that trunk wasn't the same trunk that my parents had brought from the concentration camp in Germany. It had been painted, changed. Or maybe I just wanted that trunk to **slip away** into memory the way my mother had slipped away, become a part of my memory, always there but not there.

---

[8] *rooming house:* a house where you can rent a room to live in
[9] *paralyzed:* unable to move part or all of your body

Copy two more sentences or short passages from the reading into the chart on page 288 and respond to them.

COMPREHENSION

A **Main Ideas**

Answer the questions. Compare your answers with a partner.

1. Why did the author's father use wood from the walls of the barracks to build the trunk?

_____

2. What happened to the trunk over the years?

_____

3. How did the author feel about the trunk after his mother died?

_____

B **Close Reading**

Read the quotes from the reading. Write a paraphrase for each quote. Discuss your answers with a partner.

1. "I knew my sister Donna didn't want the trunk. Donna has spent a lifetime trying to forget the time in the DP camps and what the years in the slave labor camps during the war had cost my parents." *(paragraph 7)*

_____

_____

2. "When I'm doing a poetry reading and tell people the story of the trunk and read one of my poems about it, people ask me why I left it. It doesn't make any kind of sense to them. And I'm not sure now that it makes any kind of sense to me either." *(paragraph 8)*

_____

_____

3. "Or maybe I just wanted that trunk to slip away into memory the way my mother had slipped away, become a part of my memory, always there but not there." *(paragraph 10)*

_____

_____

VOCABULARY

A Using the Dictionary

Read the dictionary entries and the sentences that follow. Then match the number of the definition with the appropriate sentence. Compare answers with a partner.

> **convert** *v.* **1** to change into a different form, or change into something that can be used for a different purpose or in a different way **2** to change your opinions or habits, or to persuade someone else to do this **3** to change from one religion or belief to another, or to persuade someone else to do this

1.

_____ **a.** Buchenwald was a German concentration camp that had been converted to living space for refugees.

_____ **b.** Jennie is going to convert from Methodism to Buddhism.

_____ **c.** The residents were strongly opposed to the plan for constructing a new building on the site of an old house, but they were converted when they learned the building would become a temporary home for political refugees.

> **trash** *v.* **1** to destroy something completely, either deliberately or by using it too much **2** to criticize someone or something severely **3** to throw something away

2.

_____ **a.** When we finally got to America, my parents didn't trash that wooden trunk or break it up.

_____ **b.** Before they left the camp, the refugees trashed the barracks they had been forced to live in.

_____ **c.** The volunteers trashed the idea of leaving the refugees in a location that had no clean water within five miles.

> **passage** *n.* **1** a long narrow area with walls on either side, which connects one room or place to another **2** the process of discussing and accepting a new law, for example in Congress **3** a short part of a book, poem, speech, piece of music, and so on **4** a trip on a ship

3.

_____ **a.** They carried it with them when we had to go to the migrant farmers' camp in upstate New York where we worked off the cost of our passage to America.

_____ **b.** The storage room is in the basement, at the end of a passage.

_____ **c.** The passage of the new bill, or proposal, into law requires a two-thirds majority vote in the legislature.

_____ **d.** The passage describing the group's crossing of the Rocky Mountains was particularly frightening.

sense *n.* **1** a feeling about something   **2** good understanding and judgment, especially about practical things   **3** to have a clear meaning and be easy to understand
4 a natural ability that makes it easy for you to understand or know something

4.

_____ **a.** It doesn't make any kind of sense to them. And I'm not sure now that it makes any kind of sense to me either. Why did I leave it?

_____ **b.** The man from Council Bluffs had absolutely no business sense. Every enterprise he attempted in Sacramento failed.

_____ **c.** When the wagon train arrived at the mountains in November, the travelers did not have the sense to turn back.

_____ **d.** As the member of the group watched the hungry wolves around the camp, he experienced a momentary sense of apprehension.

B **Phrasal Verbs**

As you learned in chapter 6, many **verbs** are **used together with certain prepositions**. These **phrasal verbs take on specific meanings** depending on the preposition. For example, we *take up* a hobby when we become interested in a new activity, we *take off* our coat when we come inside, and we *take out* the trash to be picked up.

Read the sentences containing phrasal verbs. Match the verbs with their meanings in the box on page 294. Compare answers with a partner.

_e_ **1.** Many people who borrowed money to come to the United States spent several years **working off** the cost of their passage.

_____ **2.** Hundreds of thousands of immigrants arrived in the ports of New York, Boston, and Philadelphia. Huge numbers of them continued to other places, but countless numbers of them **stayed on** in these cities.

_____ **3.** Many people who had to leave their countries would often **sell off** their belongings so they would have money to live on until they found jobs.

_____ **4.** When people traveled by ship, they often felt **used up** by the rough trip, which could last several weeks.

_____ **5.** Some of the families from the refugee camps had to **figure out** where to go because they could not return to their homes.

_____ **6.** For people who had lost everything in the war, trying to decide how to build a new life somewhere new was more than they could **deal with**.

_____ **7.** Many people wanted their horrifying experiences of being in a slave labor camp to **slip away** into the back of their minds, and then to forget them altogether.

a. continue to do something
b. discover or determine
c. exhaust of strength
d. gradually disappear
e. pay for something, especially a debt
f. sell something, especially for a low price, because you need the money or want to get rid of it
g. take the necessary action, especially in order to solve a problem

Complete each sentence with the correct phrasal verb. Compare answers with a partner.

1. People sometimes do not know how to _____ the nightmares they have of their experiences in refugee camps.

2. Women and even children become _____ by months of the hard work involved in carrying water every day from rivers back to their refugee camp.

3. How do they plan to _____ the money they borrowed to pay their moving costs and first year's rent?

4. Older men and women are sometimes are so sad about leaving their homeland that they give up and _____.

5. When persecuted people are forced to leave their homes, they often have little time to _____ their property and whatever else they cannot take with them.

6. Throughout the history of the United States, people have wanted to move to where they would have better job opportunities. Today people might try to _____ whether the East Coast or the West Coast would have more advantages for them.

7. After John Guzlowski's parents moved to Chicago, they decided to _____ in that city for many years.

C   Collocations

As you learned in previous chapters, **collocations** refer to **word partners** or **words that are often used together**.

The words *burden* and *refugee* appear in the reading. Each of these words has several collocations.

burden: something that is carried; a duty or responsibility that is difficult to bear
refugee: someone who has been forced to leave their country, especially during a war

EXAMPLES:

added burden	refugee camp
economic burden	refugee issue
heavy burden	refugee resettlement
	refugee status

Complete each sentence with the appropriate collocation from the box. Compare answers with a partner.

1. When people have small children and are caring for elderly parents at the same time, they have a very _____.

2. The government has several criteria it uses to determine an individual's _____. Not everyone who claims to be a refugee is recognized as a refugee.

3. People who are placed in a _____ should be there only a short time. However, some stay for many months.

4. People in charge of refugee camps must provide housing, food, and shelter to the refugees. They must also provide medical care and arrange for relocation. Dealing with the refugees' emotional difficulties is a(n) _____, but one they cannot ignore.

5. Feeding, clothing, and caring for displaced persons is a complicated _____ that has no easy solutions.

6. When a refugee family finally settles in another country, they have many expenses they did not expect. Such a heavy _____ often overwhelms them.

7. The subject of _____ is controversial, especially when relocating thousands of people is involved.

CRITICAL THINKING

Discuss the questions in a small group. Be prepared to share your answers with the class.

1. The author of the reading, John Guzlowski, described how his parents moved from Germany to New York to Chicago to Arizona. What factors do you think influenced these moves?

2. Why did John Guzlowski's parents keep the wooden trunk for the rest of their lives?

3. John Guzlowski offers some possible explanations for why he left his parents' trunk behind. What other reasons might he have had for leaving the trunk behind? Would you have left it? Explain your reasons.

AFTER YOU READ

BRINGING IT ALL TOGETHER

Discuss the questions in a small group. Then share your group's answers with the class. Use some of the vocabulary you studied in the chapter (for a complete list, go to page 298).

1. Think about the experiences of the families who journeyed on the Overland Trail and John Guzlowski's family. What pull factors did they have in common?

2. What push factors did the families who journeyed on the Overland Trail and John Guzlowski's family have in common?

3. What experiences do the families who journeyed on the Overland Trail, John Guzlowski's family, and people migrating today have in common?

WRITING ACTIVITY

Write a four-paragraph essay about migration.

- In the first paragraph, explain the concept of migration: emigration and immigration, and the push and pull factors that influence migration.
- In the second paragraph, give examples of people or groups of people who have migrated and their reasons for migrating.
- In the third paragraph, relate migration to yourself or someone you know.
- In the fourth paragraph, write a conclusion in which you link, or connect, the experiences of all the people and groups you have described, including yourself.

DISCUSSION AND WRITING TOPICS

Discuss these questions in a small group. Choose one of them and write a paragraph or two about it. Use the vocabulary from the chapter.

1. Think about a place or area that interests you, but where you have never been. What images of this location come to mind when you think about it? Why do you have these images of this location? What do you think you might find if you went there? Compare your responses with other classmates. What ideas do you have in common? What would make you consider moving there?

2. What do you think you might do if you migrated to a new destination, but you did not find what you were looking for?

3. Imagine you lived in the United States, somewhere east of the Missouri River, during the middle of the 19th century. What factors would motivate you to remain in your home location? What factors would motivate you to take the difficult journey westward to the Oregon or California Territories? Explain your answer.

VOCABULARY

Nouns	Verbs	Adjectives	Adverb
apprehension	convert*	audacious	heartily
burden	induce*	desperate	
diffusion	operate	grief-stricken	
eagerness	replenish	nerve-wracking	
hardship	translate	perilous	
hazard	trash	promising	
lure	venture	stimulating	
measure	view	thrilling	
passage		traumatic	
refugee	**Phrasal Verbs**		
restructuring*	deal with		
sense	figure out		
terror	long to		
	sell off		
	slip away		
	stay on		
	use up		
	work off		

* = AWL (Academic Word List) item

SELF-ASSESSMENT

In this chapter you learned to:

○ Skim for the main idea

○ Draw inferences

○ Fill out an organizer and create a timeline

○ Use dictionary entries to learn different meanings of words and understand word usage

○ Guess the meaning of words from the context

○ Understand and use synonyms, suffixes, word forms, and collocations

○ Categorize words

○ Understand and use phrasal verbs

○ Indicate contrast

What can you do well? ☑

What do you need to practice more? ☑

VOCABULARY INDEX

Number(s) following each entry indicate the page(s) where the word, phrase, or idiom appears. Words followed by an asterisk (*) are on the Academic Word List (AWL). The AWL is a list of the highest-frequency words found in academic texts.

A

abstract* 48, 63
abundant 70
abuse 242
accelerate 109
accountable for 252
acquainted (with) 21, 49
adjacent to* 151
admiration 41
adornment 70
advocate* 109
agent 170
agony 188
all the way up the line 259
allegorical 179
alter* 212, 220
animosity 178
anthropologist 9
antibiotic 169
appearance 3, 42
appease 179
applicable to 251
apprehension 280
appropriation* 132
around the clock 150
audacious 278
autonomy 212, 230
aware of* 250

B

bacteriologist 161
bear out 150
bearing 100
bring about 151
broad 141
burden 290

C

calculate 100
capital 90
centralized 211
ceremony 63
chance 169
changing nature 20
chaotic 108
characterize 32, 41

circumstances* 251
code* 242
cognitive 63
coincide* 70, 160
collapse* 122
collective 92
commerce 230
commission* 132
commitment* 242
compel 179, 270
compensation* 123
complexities* 49, 64
component* 63
comprehensive* 132
condone 251
confinement* 161
conformity* 21
consistent with 252
consolidation 212
contagious 161, 221
contaminate 151, 169
contemporary* 141
contract* 151
contradict* 252
controversy* 21
convert* 289
correlate 71
correspond* 42
counteract 92
criterion* 132
cultivation 71
currency* 230
curse 188
cycle of life 80

D

daunting 108
deal with 290
demand 141
depict 32
designate 41
desperate 269
destined 230
determine 169
devastation 222
devise 91, 222

diffusion 269
dilemma 250
disable 151
(dis)associated 161
discern 197
discretionary* 258
dishonest with 251
disperse 70, 221
dispossessed 123
distinctive* 3
distribute* 70, 122
donate 258
dramatically* 3
dread 198, 211
drift 198
drive 9
durable 41
dwindle 151
dynamic* 9, 48
dynamics* 108

E

eagerness 279
eclectic 108
edifice 90
efficacy 92
egalitarian 222
eke out 133
elder 80, 221
element* 170
embed 178
embrace 178
emerge* 33
emotional ties 20
emulate 242
enduring 230
enforce* 242
engage in 3
enhance* 170
enlarge 132
entail 92
enterprise 91
equivalent* 108
erratic 99
ethical* 241, 250
ethnicity* 20

evaporate 122
evil 187
evoke 90
evolve* 99
execution 48
expansively* 211
exploit* 211
explosive 48
extension 231
extensive 71
extrapolate 109

F

feat 90
figure 231
figure out 290
fix 197
flair 99
flavor 42
fleeting 33
force 199, 270
forge 212
former 243
formidable 230
foster 211
frame 198
framework* 63
functioning* 20
fundamental* 250

G

gaze 81
generate* 109
ghastly 196
glittering 185
grief-stricken 280
grounds 259

H

hardship 279
harmful 169
harmony 42, 49
hazard 269, 279
heartily 280
hence* 99
herculean 108
hinder 21
his heart sank 151
honor 80

hostility 33, 211
hygienic 161
hypothetical* 108
hysterical 150

I

idealization 33
idle 187
imitation 64
immunity 221
impart 99
impel 49
impose* 230
impression 32
in a buying mood 258
in the neighborhood of 141
incentive* 212
incite 21
indeterminate 3
indispensable 124
induce* 270
infect 160, 170
inhibit* 9
initiate* 20
insist 140
integral* 48
integrate* 41
integrity* 222, 259
intensely* 41
interdependency 71
interference 49
interval* 64
intervention* 123
isolated* 160, 170

K

know the whole story 141

L

lapse 243
launch 132
legend 81
legitimate 259
lethal 230
level off 151
liberate* 33
living on-the-fat 141
long to 279
lure 269

M

magnitude 92
make an extra buck 141
make it 141
malicious 161
manipulate* 71
manipulation* 122
manner 3
matrilineal 222
maturation* 3
meager 90, 279
measure 269
meticulous 33, 151
migrating* 220, 278
minuscule 133
mission 122
mold 169
moral 178
murmur 81

N

navigation 99
neglect 9
nerve-wracking 278
network* 99
non-toxic 170
norms* 3
notoriety 133

O

object 259
obliterate 108
Old World 220
one piece of the puzzle fit 151
operate 270
oral tradition 80
orchestrate 70
original people 80
out of reach 259

P

parched 187, 279
passage 289
patrilineal 222
patron 133, 141
penance 179
perilous 269
periodic* 64
permanence 42

persecute 160, 270
perspective* 63
pioneering 41
pity 188
please 141
plummet 122
plunge 122, 279
potential* 170
precaution 161
precious 81
preconceived 49
predispose 9
predominantly* 9
prerequisite 212
primarily* 64
proceed* 3
proclaim 220
procurement 70
profoundly 221
prolonged 221
promising 270
promote* 252
propagate 230
proper 140
property 99
prosperity 122, 211
pursue* 32, 41

Q
qualified 80

R
radical* 32
rash 178
receptive 20
recovery* 122
redemption 179
refine* 99
refugee 289
relative to 251
relevant* 251
relief 123, 132
relieve 9
replenish 280
representational 32, 141
resolution* 241, 250
resolve* 42
restriction* 141
restructuring* 270
retribution 179
revive 109

revolution* 41
revolutionary* 32
rudimentary 90
ruthlessly 231

S
salvage 169
scale 48
scarce 70
scheme* 259
seclusion 159
sell off 290
sense 290
setting 63
settle on 150
settlement 211, 269, 279
shot holes in 151
shriek 199
skeptical 242
skyrocket 122
slay 186
slip away 290
socialization 3
solicit 243
soul 186
span 90
spell 197
spirit 81
spontaneity 48
spontaneous 33
stabilize* 99
stay on 290
stifle 123
stimulating 269
stir 196
strain 222
stunned 198
subdued 179
subsidy* 133
substance 170
sufficient* 48
supernatural 178
surrogate 9
symbolic* 64, 179

T
tactic 242
technique* 33, 49, 170
temperament 41
terror 279
the clock was ticking 150

thrilling 280
thrive 81
throng 133
tolerate 242
trace* 160
trait 9, 270
transaction 230
transformation* 151,169
transition* 141
translate 278
transmit* 100, 150
trash 289
traumatic 269
trial and error 64
triumphant 108
turbulence 178

U
undertaking* 91
uneasy 197
unintentionally 21, 161
unprecedented 123
unpremeditated 48
upheaval 211
use up 290

V
venture 279
view 270
virtue 132
virulent 221
volatile 212
volume* 42
vulnerable 230

W
weary 187
where someone stands 259
wider range 20
wider society 20
will 185
win-win 259
with room to spare 259
without strings 259
woe 186
woodland 81
work off 289
wound 170
wrench 199
wretch 186

CREDITS

TEXT CREDITS

Pages 3, 9, and 20 Perry, John; Perry, Erna, *Contemporary Society: An Introduction to Social Science*, 11th Ed., © 2006. Reprinted and electronically reproduced by permission of Pearson Education, Inc., Upper Saddle River, New Jersey. **Page 32** Paul Williams, "The Beginning of Impressionist Art," www.impressionist-art-gallery. com. © Paul Williams. Reproduced by permission. **Page 41** Janson, H.W.; Janson, Anthony F., *A History of Art*, Revised-Combines Edition, 5th edition. ©1998. Reprinted and electronically reproduced by permission of Pearson Education, Inc., Upper Saddle River, New Jersey. **Page 42** From Joachim Gasquet's *Cézanne: A Memoir with Conversations* translated by Christopher Pemberton, © 1991 Thames & Hudson Ltd., London. Reprinted by kind permission of Thames & Hudson. **Page 48** Wayne Craven, *American Art*, 1/e © 2003. Copyright © McGraw Hill. All rights reserved. Reproduced by permission. **Page 58** from *How Art Made the World: A Journey to the Origins of Human Creativity* by Nigel Spivey, published by BBC Books. Reprinted by permission of The Random House Group Limited. **Pages 63 and 70** Roberta Edwards Lenkeit, *Introducing Cultural Anthropology*, 3rd Edition. © 2007 by McGraw Hill. Reproduced by permission. **Page 80** Ignatia Broker, "Night Flying Woman: An Ojibway Narrative," 1983. pp. ix, x, xii, 3, 7, 8, 9, 10, 13, 17, 45, 46, 47, 54, 56, 123, 124, 130–131. Copyright © The Minnesota Historical Society. All rights reserved. Reproduced by permission. **Page 90** Robert A. Scott, *The Gothic Enterprise: A Guide to Understanding the Medieval Cathedral*. Copyright © 2003 by The University of California Press. All rights reserved. Reproduced by permission. **Page 99** From *The Mapmakers*, Revised Edition by John Noble Wilford, copyright © 1981, 2000 by John Noble Wilford. Used by permission of Alfred A. Knopf, a division of Random House, Inc. Courtesy of Compass Rose Geocoin. http://compassrosegeocoin.com/crhistory.php. Courtesy of Garmin International. **Page 108** From *The New York Times*, October 17, 2011 © 2011. The New York Times. All rights reserved. Used by permission and protected by the Copyright Laws of the United States. The printing, copying, redistribution, or retransmission of this Content without express written permission is prohibited. **Page 122** Goldfield, David; Abbot, Carl E; Anderson, Virginia DeJohn; Argersinger, Jo Anne E.; Argersinger, Peter H.; Barney, William M.; Weir, Robert M., *American Journey, The: A History of The United States*, Brief Edition, Volume 1 Reprint, 6th Ed., © 2012. Reprinted and Electronically reproduced by permission of Pearson Education, Inc., Upper Saddle River, New Jersey. **Page 132** From *American-Made The Enduring Legacy of the WPA: When FDR Put the Nation to Work* by Nick Taylor, copyright © 2008 by Nick Taylor. Used by permission of Bantam Books, a division of Random House, Inc. **Page 140** Excerpt from *Hard Times: An Oral History of the Great Depression*. Copyright © 2000 by Studs Terkel. Reprinted by permission of The New Press. www.thenewpress.com; **Page 150** "The Puzzle Was a Maddening One," © Fall 2002, in *The Handle*, 609 words. A publication of the University of Alabama of Birmingham School of Public Health. **Page 159** Jennifer Rosenberg, "Typhoid Mary: The Sad Story of a Woman Responsible for Several Typhoid Outbreaks," About.com. Copyright © New York Times Syndicate. All rights reserved. Reproduced by permission. **Page 169** Jennifer Rosenberg, "Alexander Fleming Discovers Penicillin," About.com. Copyright © New York Times Syndicate. All rights reserved. Reproduced by permission. **Page 178** From *Beachiam's Encyclopedia of Popular Fiction*. © 1996 Gale, a part of Cengage Learning, Inc. Reproduced by permission. www.cengage.com/permissions; **Pages 211, 220, and 230** Divine, Robert A.; Breen, T.H.H.; Fredrickson, George M.; Williams, R. Hal; Gross, Ariela J.; Brands, H.W., *America Past and Present*, Volume 1, 9th Ed., © 2011. Reprinted and Electronically reproduced by permission of Pearson Education, Inc., Upper Saddle River, New Jersey. **Page 241** Bovee, Courtland L.; Thill, John V.; Mescon, Michael H., *Excellence in Business*, 3rd Ed., © 2007. Reprinted and Electronically reproduced by permission of Pearson Education, Inc., Upper Saddle River, New Jersey. **Page 250** Anne Lawrence and James Weber, *Business and Society: Stakeholders, Ethics, Public Policy*, 12/e © 2008. Copyright © 2008 by McGraw Hill. All rights reserved. Reproduced by permission. **Page 258** With permission of *Business Ethics* Magazine. **Page 269** Perry, John; Perry, Erna, *Contemporary Society: An Introduction to Social Science*, 11th Ed., © 2006. Reprinted and Electronically reproduced by permission of Pearson Education, Inc., Upper Saddle River, New Jersey. **Pages 278 and 279** From *Women's Diaries of the Westward Journey* by Lillian Schlissel, copyright © 1982 by Schocken Books. Used by permission of Schocken Books, a division of Random House, Inc. **Page 289** Courtesy of John Guzlowski, author of *Lightning and Ashes*. **Dictionary Entries** From *Longman Advanced American Dictionary* 2nd Ed Paper and CD ROM Pack. Copyright © Pearson Education. Reprinted with permission. All rights reserved.

PHOTO CREDITS